BLACK MALE-FEMALE RELATIONSHIPS

A Resource Book of Selected Materials

Edited by

DELORES P. ALDRIDGE

Emory University

KENDALL/HUNT PUBLISHING COMPANY

2460 Kerper Boulevard P.O. Box 539 Dubuque, Iowa 52004-0539

Library of Congress Catalog Card Number: 89–85461

ISBN 0–8403–5553–X

Printed in the United States of America
10 9 8 7 6 5 4 3 2 1

Contents

Preface

The need for a book of writings about Black males and Black females has long been felt by the serious student, the scholar and the general reader. While there has been much sound and fury concerning, first, the Black male, next, the Black female, and finally, Black male-female relationships, the search for serious literature that pulls together a variety of scholarly-generated readings upon the latter subject has simply been difficult to locate.

The present text grows out of the editor's research needs in pulling together materials for a companion text *Focusing: Institutional and Interpersonal Perspectives on Black Male-Female Relationships* which is under contract with Third World Press. Nowhere was there to be discovered a single source that covered the areas necessary to generate a macro-systemic theory by which one could analyze Black male-female relationships. While it cannot be claimed that this work is exhaustive in its coverage of each of the seven topics, the various selections together with their bibliographies enable one to establish a serious starting point in thinking, writing about or researching the topic.

In selecting the seven topic areas for this work, a deliberate choice was made of those areas which seemed to most accurately reflect the results of the situational inequities and sustained oppression that have continued to define the lives of Black people in the United States.

Introduction

There is a growing, but slow, recognition of the need for quality research to be performed by Black scholars on Black male-female relations. While it is true that much research has been reported upon Black males *or* Black females, there has been a curious omission of incisive work focusing upon the dyad. Many reasons could be advanced for this lacunae in the literature.

One of the problems is that much of the research has focused solely upon Black males and, in addition, much of this research has been performed by White males. There appears to be a curious mental and perceptual flaw in many White scholars that enables them to research Black males without adequate considerations of what has elsewhere been termed the institutionalized oppressive ideology that fills every minute of a Black male's life in America. The nature of Blackness is, one might suggest, quite different from the nature of Blackness as it structures the existence of American males.

Another problem lies in the sexiest nature of American society. White males tend to focus their research on Black males, one suspects, in terms of a subconscious kind of male bonding which only interprets male activities as being meaningful material for research. Then, again, there is always the latent threat presented by the Black male to the White male; research can be a way of binding this dangerous creature through conceptual bonds.

The rise of interest in the research oriented minds of scholars towards the Black female follows the national tendency to grant women a grudging sense of importance in the American scene. But even here there has been a series of distortions through which one must work before anything meaningful can be accomplished through research. If one keeps in mind that the Black male and the Black female must continually live out their lives within social and psychological environments structured by an institutionalized oppressive ideology, it will be seen that the failure to include this overriding variable in the basic structuring of one's research simply results in further destructive myths, no matter what the degree of sophistication of one's statistical analyses.

This text represents an attempt to present a selection of the more meaningful work done by a majority of Black scholars in the field of Black males and Black females. By no means can it be said that the contents represent the whole of the best works written in the field. And, while some of the works may contradict each other, they are valuable for a sourcebook. What has been attempted is a selection of representative works that indicate approaches to important issues. As for the divisions presented, their choice has been defined by the critical nature of the issues chosen for inclusion.

We need, for example, to understand demographic aspects of Black existence before choosing to follow a particular line of research on Black males and females. We need to understand the powerful influence of primary groups upon and continuing socialization of Black people. Given these insights, we have a basic preparation for asking meaningful questions concerning Black race and gender. An exploration of psycho-social issues needs, in turn, to be informed by the other sectional issues presented herein. Economic issues are more sharply defined when one has a literacy based upon a critical reading of the total complex of meaningful issues. And, of course, religion needs to be sensitively understood and investigated as one of the basic socialization experiences in the lives of Black people.

Yet, in spite of all that has been said above, there remains an incompleteness to the present volume. For the dyad of Black male *and* Black female presents a different unit of investigation from investigations of Black males *or* Black females. One suspects that Black scholars will begin to give an increasing amount of attention to this vital dyad and move toward the creation of new and more meaningful definitions of Black people in America. The value of the present volume rests in the attempt to make a statement about where we are. The total contents make a strong implication concerning where we need to become.

CHAPTER ONE

Overview of Issues

In her seminal work, Aldridge presents an intellectual *Gestalt* of the issues required to paint the overall canvas of the experiences and the meaning of the experiences of Black males and Black females. Beginning with a structural framework for examining male/female relationships, a number of issues are cited to contextualize the framework and demonstrate how these experiences are shaped. Black male scarcity, differential socialization of males and females, sexism and its relationships to Black women's liberation are some of the issues presented in the article. Modes of connecting, Black women's perceptions and the critical need for quality research to be done with Black people by Black behavioral scientists complete the exposition of Aldridge's presentation.

Approaching the Study of Black Male-Female Relationships

Delores P. Aldridge

There has been growth, albeit recent, in the literature of psychology and sociology concerning the Black male and Black female. The discretion of the literature has been such that there are two streams of writing, one devoted to the Black female and another devoted to the Black male. Representative of the first are such writers as Ladner (1972), Staples (1973), Lerner (1973, and Rodgers-Rose (1980). Wilkinson and Taylor (1977), Liebow (1967), and Gary (1981), among others have written concerning the Black male.

What is curious, however, is a relative lack of social psychological works dealing with Black males and females within the same endeavor. A case can be made, of course, for monadic rather than dyadic focus. The individual organism, stripped from its social ecosystem, is presented for critical analysis. One's vision is not beclouded by the intervening variable of the opposite gender. There remains, of course, the question of the ways in which the opposite gender has affected the overall characteristics of the monad under study. Man is born of woman and so is woman born of woman. Thus it would seem that viewing Black males and females within a social context or, better yet, a social psychological frame of reference enables one to generate a set of questions and insights differing from those drawn from Black monadic studies.

When one begins to draw a border around the global concept of Black males and females, it would appear important to concentrate upon communications that go toward defining Black male/female relationships. A delimitation in terms of Black male/female relationships suggests a series of questions that form topics for the subject:

Why are male/female relationships important?
Why is it significant to isolate as well as focus upon Black male/female relations?

THE WESTERN JOURNAL OF BLACK STUDIES: Toward A Theoretical Perspective for Understanding Black Male-Female Relationships. Vol. 8, No. 4.

What is a useful schematic and structural framework for examining male/female relationships?

What are the manifestations of the schematic and structural framework?

What are the implications of and recommendations for maintaining sound relationships and improving non-existent or weak relationships?

THE IMPORTANCE OF MALE/FEMALE RELATIONSHIPS

Karenga (1981) notes that male/female relationships are of fundamental and enduring concern and importance for several reasons: First, because of their indispensability to the maintenance and development of the species. Second, they are a barometer, i.e., measurement of our distance from the animal world—in other words, our humanity. Third, they are an indicator of the quality of social life; the treatment of women in relationships and, by extension, in society becomes as Toure (1959:72) notes ". . . a mirror that reflects the economic and social conditions, the levels of political, cultural and moral development of a given country." Fourth, they are a measurement and mirror of personal development and identity—a revelation of who persons really are. Fifth, they are a measurement of a people's capacity for struggle and social construction . . . as a fundamental unit of the nation, their strengths and weaknesses determine the nation's capacity to define, defend and develop its interest.

IMPORTANCE OF BLACK MALE/FEMALE RELATIONSHIPS

The issue of indispensability to the maintenance and development of the species within the context of Black male and female relationships may be viewed both in terms of the nuclear family as well as the single parent family. There is a need for an increased amount of sensitive research focused upon the maintenance and development characteristics and outcomes of Black female-headed families. Within a social system frame of reference, one might ask whether the maintenance and development characteristics of Black female-headed families might not represent a type of response by Black people to the overall messages they receive from white America? What is being suggested here is that Black males, as a "subspecies," may need to be socialized by mothers rather than fathers insofar as their role behavior for future functioning in American society is concerned. Note, this is not an issue posed by the differential demography of Black males compared to Black females. Instead, it is a question that arises from demographic givens and becomes proper within the context of a social psychological frame of reference.

The Black female-headed family, differing as it does from the mass media vision of the nuclear family, operates in the eyes of many critics as a deficit model, one whose deviation from the official norm dooms it to internal dysfunctions and external maladaptions to the environment. Such a view is, of course, limited by the analytical focus of those who denigrate the Black female-headed family. From a general system point of view (Berrien, 1968), it can be seen that the Black female-headed family is, once again, an innovative Black adaption to the social-economic and cultural pressures of the dominant society, an adaptation based in and growing from the scarcity of Black males.

It is important to note that the maintenance and development of the species is carried on within the Black female-headed family. But it is also important to note the need for, as noted above, sensible and sensitive research into the structure, dynamics and outcomes of role socialization in the Black female-headed family. One suspects that there are strengths that have not yet entered the official vocabulary of the research literature.

Given the pressures upon Black people in America, the continued maintenance and development of Black children brought about through the love of Black men and women for each other is, indeed, a critical measurement of the strength of Black people. Yet, when one reviews the statement of Toure, cited above that male/female relationships are important—and especially the treatment of women in relationships—one needs to ask what the treatment of Black women reflects in the national political, cultural and moral mirror of American society. One is forced to return, once again, to the image of the Black woman as reflected in the mass media—and even in that latest telecommunications format, musical video.

The standard of beauty that is communicated by television and only partly contradicted by such publications are *Essence* has, one suspects, much to do with setting the criteria of beauty for many Black women and Black men. When it is considered that there are strict limitations on what is acceptable in Black politics, culture and morality on the part of the dominant society, one might be moved to wonderment as to the survival of any Black male/female relationship.

SIGNIFICANCE OF BLACK MALE/FEMALE RELATIONSHIPS

Social scientists, psychologists, novelists, political scientists, and psychiatrists have all discussed and examined the significance of Black male/female relationships. The reader may want to examine the sociological writing (Staples, 1978; Jackson, 1978; Karenga, 1982; Scot, 1976; Hare,1979), the psychological literature (Akbar, 1976; Tucker, 1979; Nobles, 1978), the writings of political scientists (Wilcox, 1979; Gary,1981), the psychiatric literature (Welsing, 1974; Poussaint, 1979; Grier and Cobbs, 1968), and works of fiction (Wallace, 1979; Jordan, 1977). The gamut of perspectives has ranged from an Afrocentric mode (Asente, 1980; Akbar, 1976; Karenga, 1982) to a popularist model (Wallace, 1979).

What unites all the writings cited above is the theme of Black male/female relationships developing and surviving in the face of tremendous odds. At the same time, the presence of quite substantive historical problems whose characteristics have become more acute in the last several decades is also acknowledged. The lack of relationships due to the scarcity of Black males (Jackson, 1971) and the mutually degrading games one plays in order to begin and sustain relationships (Staples, 1978) are but two of the present problems that threaten Black male/female relationships. Even the quality and future of existing Blacks male/female relationships remain open to continuing questions and challenges, given the social stress and strain of living in American society.

Despite what has been said about the problems of Black male/female concerns, the writer is in agreement with Karenga (1982) that the following relevant facts need to form a background for future studies and research:

1. Black male/female relationships are probably no more problem ridden than other male/female relationships.
2. Life, itself, requires problems and the effort to solve those problems.
3. Many Black male/female relationships are healthy, however, enough are in trouble to require a sustained critical view.
4. There are enough Black males and Black females without relationships so that discussion focused upon this fact needs furthering.
5. Any criticism of Black male/female relationships is, at the same time and in equal measure, a criticism of American society—the society that has shaped them to fit and "properly" function in it.

These five facts serve as a point of departure for any serious analysis of Black men, Black women and their relationships. To further underscore the point of view that argues that Black people are products of their social conditions is to use the same argument for the connection between Black relationships and social conditions. In order to properly understand Black men and Black women within the context of their relationships, one must understand the historical characteristics that have shaped them. Superimposed upon these variables is the complexity of mental, emotional and physical factors which have also shaped the behavior of Black men and women.

A STRUCTURAL FRAMEWORK FOR EXAMINING BLACK MALE/FEMALE RELATIONSHIPS

American society is defined by and derived from four major structural and value systems; capitalism, racism, sexism, Judeo-Christianity. Capitalism may be defined as a socio-economic system in which private ownership is the primary means for satisfying human needs. Another characteristic of capitalism is a strong and continuous pursuit of profit. The emphasis upon private ownership of things tends to often shape the view of human relationships, i.e., the conceptual conversion of human beings into things to be owned or similarly the profit motive in which people may subconsciously be viewed as objects for purchase and resale.

Racism may be defined as a system of denial and deformation of a people's history and humanity based primarily on the specious concept of race and hierarchies of races. Racism in America was born from European feelings of racial superiority and bred within the moral contradiction between Christian concepts and economic beliefs. Slavery represented an attempt at dehumiliation of both the proponents as well as those who were enslaved, given the idea of Christianity. On the other hand, slavery represented the extension of private ownership and profit theories into the realm of human relationships. In the contemporary world, neo-colonialism links capitalism and racism, resulting in nations that dominate and nations that are owned by the dominators. In this context it is important to understand that capitalism and racism extend their influence from the intrapersonal system to the world system of human organization.

Sexism is the social system and resultant practice of using gender or sex as an ascriptive and primary determinant in the establishment, maintenance and explanation, i.e., justification, of relationships and exchanges. As a system, sexism is composed of assumptions and acts theories and practices which imply and impose unequal, oppressive and exploitive relationships based upon gender. When capitalism and racism are reviewed for their effects upon human relationships, it may be seen that sexism converts the dominated to a subordinate feminine stereotype, open and waiting to be used.

The Judeo-Christian tradition is a religious system which has its roots in Judaism and Christianity which draw heavily upon the cultural and social experiences of Jews, whites and males. The tradition encourages identification with males as leaders and heros but more importantly it emphasizes the leader-hero tradition as being one with white males and their socio-economic experiences A racist, sexist and Judeo-Christian macrosystem forms the basic framework for understanding Black male/female relationships. From this understanding can be generated a set of questions germane to the topic of this paper:

What are the manifestations of the conceptual framework?
What are the values implied by the conceptual framework?
What are the concrete factors influencing male/female relations emerging out of a racist, sexist, capitalist, and Judeo-Christian society?

In the following discussions, the writer will attempt to respond to these questions.

FACTORS INFLUENCING THE QUALITY OF INTERACTION BETWEEN BLACK MALES AND BLACK FEMALES

Four factors shape the interactive nature of communication between Black males and Black females; the scarcity of Black men, differential socialization of males and females, sexism and women's liberation, and the modes of connecting. Jackson (1971) focuses attention on the shortage of Black males through a novel paradigm that Black males have a higher rate of infant mortality, a shorter life expectancy, a high rate of accidents and homicide, form a disproportionate segment of the prison population, and are a significant segment of the drug addict population. Staples (1978) reports that there is only one acceptable Black male for every five Black females, excluding married, imprisoned and homosexual Black males. Data from the 1977 census indicates that there were 732,000 more Black females than Black males in the 22–24 year old range during 1977. More recent census data show no close of the gap has occurred.

These statistics serve to underline certain grave consequences for Black male/female relationships. The insufficient supply of eligible Black males pit Black women against each other in competition for the attention of this scarce resource. Secondly, many Black men are aware of the imbalance and play a power game with Black women, requiring them to accept the Black male upon his terms. If Black women fail to buy into the power game, interracial courtship is an option increasingly available to those who are so inclined. It comes as not surprise, of course, that the Black woman sees interracial heterosexual relations as a personal rejection of her own desirability.

DIFFERENTIAL SOCIALIZATION OF MALES AND FEMALES

Jourard (1971) explored the deadening aspects of the male role, advancing the notion that the socially-defined male role requires men to appear tough, objective, striving, achieving, unsentimental, and emotionally unexpressive. If behind this social persona a man feels tender, if he cries, he will be viewed as unmanly by others. The contradiction between the ways in which Black men are expected to present themselves in small and large group situations and their real emotional feelings is a key to understanding the nature of being a Black male in America. The learned residency of males to mask their true feelings makes it difficult for Black men to achieve insight into and empathy with Black women.

To the extent that women require expressions of intimate and personal emotions in exchange for their availability as social or sexual partners, the nonexpressive or limited in expressiveness male may find himself in a difficult situation, observed Brathewaite. If he is to execute properly his role as a Black man by associating with women who demonstrate their attraction to him, he must be fairly successful at something for which he has received contradictory signals—that is to express emotions of gentleness, tenderness and verbal affection toward women while at the same time being strong, unexpressive and cool.

According to Braithewaite (1981), the high degree of verbal facility among Black males makes it easier for them to create an initial impression of genuine feelings and, thus, they readily enter into relationships with women. As the relationship continues and the woman becomes familiar with the male's ways, it becomes increasingly difficult for the Black male to camouflage his absence of genuine feelings for his partner. The male must constantly "fake it" and express sentiments he really does not feel. Perhaps this is part of the reason for seemingly unexpected physical attacks upon one's partner followed by loving apologies. Given that the male continuously runs the risk of "blowing his cover" with the outcome of a terminated relationship, the cardinal issue becomes plain. The issue is not one of entering relationships with women. The issue is one of *sustaining* relationships with women.

Tucker (1978) indicates that success with women is important to many men because they are engaged in covert competition with other men. The belief is that success will enable them to avoid ridicule and to be perceived as "hip." Given this process, women become targets and the communication structure by which they become targets assumes the status of an end in itself rather than a means to an end. The process is in many ways dysfunctional to Black men. There is feeling that expression of emotions must not leave the man vulnerable. This rapidly passes over into the self-rejection of those emotions whose display might leave onc vulnerable.

The pattern of initial contact and verbal gaming that is summarized above represents a well-patterned response to the teachings of capitalism and sexism. The woman becomes an object; one gains in profit as one "scores" on an increasing number of women. And, of course, the expression of as well as the possession of emotions that might reveal oneself as well as the women as feeling individual beings is contraproductive to the capitalist mentality. At this point, one is tempted to wonder whether the "new morality" is not, in itself, a logical outgrowth of capitalism and sexism, e.g., the body becomes the object of buying and selling—the inner person is reduced to a dancing (either in public or in the bedroom) object available for the man's pleasure.

Tucker suggests that women can help men by letting the latter know that they measure manhood not in terms of "cool" but in terms of responsiveness, support, care, and honesty. Black women can further help by encouraging Black men to struggle and deal with their emotions rather than to conceal them. Black women need to share with Black men an assurance that a man is found to be more attractive when he shares his feeling with them. And while it is true that Black men may complain about women who force them to deal with issues, but ultimately they respect such women far more than they do meek, compliant women who make no demands (Tucker, 1979).

Given what has been said, one may conclude that self-disclosure is a major force influencing the quality of interaction between Black men Black women.

SEXISM AND WOMEN'S LIBERATION

Many scholars admit that sexism is present among Black males and has the effect of inhibiting and corrupting meaningful relationship. In recent years, the criticism of sexism among Black people has become an issue. It is an issue, however, that threatens the Black community through assault upon the Black male. Staples (1979) argues that female equality involves not only personal relationships, but also political and economic relationships. A substantial number of the inequalities perceived in male and female relationships need to be remedied through re-education of men and women toward changes in their sex-role socialization.

For Black women, involvement in a feminist movement entails a tripartite battle against sexism, racism and capitalism. Racism and capitalism are forces that have subjected Black women to political and economic subordination. Staples (1979) is among those who see feminism as a divisive force in an oppressed community such as Black America. There are other points of view. Lorde (1979) supports feminism, arguing that since Black women bear the brunt of sexism, it is in their interest to abolish it. She contines by suggesting that it is the responsibility of Black women to decide whether or not sexism in the Black community is pathological. According to Lorde, "Creative relationships of which Stales speaks are to the benefit of Black males, considering the sex ratio of males and females." Salaam (1979) contends that the struggle against sexism is not a threat to

Black masculinity. The forces that attack Black women individually, institutionally and ideologically also assault Black men.

On the other side of the question, many Black men and women have spoken out against feminism (Larue; 1970; Duberman, 1975). The argument they advance are:

Black people as a race need to be liberated from racism.
Feminism creates negative competition between the Black male and the Black female for economic security.
White women hoard the benefits of thee struggle from Black women.
Feminism facilitates increased tension in the already strained interpersonal atmosphere in which Black men and Black women interact.

One might argue, in the light of the many views presented above, that women's liberation—as it is presently defined and implemented—impacts negatively on the Black liberation movement and on Black male and female relationships. The essence of the writer's disagreement with women's liberation is the basically conservative mode of its beliefs and functions. Women's liberation operates within the capitalist tradition and accepts the end goals of sexist white males; simply stated, women's liberation strives to place women on an equal par with men without considering whether the male position—the white male position—is basically a humanizing position.

Black women are victims of capitalism and sexism. How, then will the relations between Black males and females be bettered through feminine adherence to a male-defined path? Black liberation involves male and female openly and courageously seeking mutual liberation; Black liberation cannot have the luxury of a liberation movement operating inside the capitalist tradition and seeking goals defined by perpetuators of the sexist tradition. It will be seen, then, that Black liberation, especially within Black male and Black female relations, has a far more complex task than women's liberation. Black liberation seeks the establishment of a lovingly free movement within and between Black males and Black females that re-creates both parties and establishes a tradition that is non-capitalist, non-sexist and draws from the cultural experiences of the Black people.

MODES OF CONNECTING

Black men and women often engage in relationships that are not in their mutual best interest. Karenga (1982) describes four modes through which Black males and Black females come together: 1) The Cash Connection, 2) The Flesh Connection, 3) The Force Connection, and 4) The Dependency Connection. Karenga (1982) defines a connection as "a short-term or tentative association which is utilitarian and alienated and designed primarily for the mutual misuses of each other's body. On the other hand, a quality relationship is a stable association defined by its positive sharing, its mutual investment in each other's psychological well being and development."

The "Cash Connection" is based upon a point of view epitomized by such statements as "everything and everybody has a price," "anything you can't buy ain't worth having," "what you invest assets into is yours," and "money is the measure of solution to everything." The primary motivation in the dyadic relation controlled by the cash connection is the presence of financial resources by at least one of the dyad's members. Women spar with other women over available men with money; men spar with each other over available women with money. In essence, men and women are looking at each other as potential "marks" in a petty confidence game.

The "Flesh Connection" is rooted in the new morality which characterizes much of contemporary society and is based predominantly on the pursuit of sex. This particular linkage focuses on the body and all the things one can do with all selected parts of it. It is not at all extreme to suggest that the flesh connection is basically a *perverse* connection, a corruptive reduction of the members of the dyad to definitions of self and other, primarily, in terms of the physical. A rejection of the body is not at all intended here: instead, what is being said is that Black males and females cannot afford to reduce themselves to an intrapersonal and interpersonal image that define them as slaves. For the slave is seen as a body capable of work, impregnation and reproduction. What one must remember is that the final stage of colonization is the colonial taking over the attitudes of the colonizers and proceeding to maintain a colonial society based upon the colonizer's mentality. The flesh connection is, perhaps, the most damaging of connections for Black males and Black females since it is entirely contradictory to the basic canons of a healthy Black liberation.

The "force connection" is predicated on the violent nature of society, part of the species' inheritance from its earliest ancestors. The force connection is fueled by the "macho" mentality of men who take what they are compelled to take as a result of their illusions of ownership. Lurking behind the macho mentality is a particular self-view that is, once again, delimiting and, ultimately, insecure. It is delimiting in that viewing women as objects to be owned calls for the diminution of any self-view that suggests feeling and thoughts beyond those which enable one to own others. It is insecure since the very idea of a balanced self cannot abide within a self that is limited in its own definition as well as those whom it seeks to own.

The "dependency connection" results from entering into a relationship based upon any of the three preceding connections. The dependency connection is a different level, psychologically and sociologically speaking since it flows from negative connections rather than summarizes an initiating correction. It would be a mistake to call all dependency a negative form of interaction. Positive dependency can be the hallmark of what Karenga (1982) terms a stable association. Positive dependency flows from the growing strength of each member of the Black dyad as they grow within themselves. If love is a process, rather than a "falling in," then it requires the presence of the other within each other as a rewarding stimulus for the individual "I" and the collective "we."

IMPLICATIONS

From the above discussion, one can proceed to recommendations for improving weak relationships, growing out of non-relationship states of being and maintaining sound relationships. Most of the social scientists referenced in this work have advanced theories for improving and maintaining relationships. The consensus being it is important that:

> *Social scientists develop and explore researchable questions examining the nature of the context in which Black male/female relationships are embedded:*
>
> *Demographers focus attention on the scarcity of Black males as a national phenomenon having potentially grave consequences for the race and having deleterious effects on Black women;*
>
> *Black men and women address unsatisfactory interpersonal relationships by participating in personal growth and human relations group sessions:*
>
> *Universities develop and include a course on male and female relationships as a part of their general education curriculum; and*
>
> *Black national organizations place on their program agenda the issue of strategies for strengthening relationships between Black men and Black women.*

If these theoretical constructs are pursued, one suspects that the socially-generated illnesses that define too many Black male and Black female relationships may begin, finally, to diminish and disappear.

The issues explored here should direct one's attention not only to Black male and Black female relationships, but to the foundation of American society. Although this chapter deals with the interpersonal and the intrapersonal, the implications are rooted within the two easily accepted and not too often examined Euro-American roots of this nation. As a nation, America practices upon weaker Third World countries precisely what men and women practice upon each other. Thus, although this paper is intended as a thesis in social psychology, the directional flow of its development is toward philosophy and, in particular, axiology—the study and criticism of values. Values are what shape one's perception of self and other as well as one's internal and external communication, not to mention the definition of social goals.

REFERENCES

Akbar, N. "Rhythmic patterns in African Personality." In L. King et. al. (ed.) *African Philosophy and Paradigms for research on Black Persons.* Los Angeles: Fanon Center, 1976

Asante, M. AfroCentricity: *The Theory of Social Change.* Buffalo, N.Y.: Amulefi, 1980.

Berrien, F. K. *General and Social Systems.* New Brunswick, N.J.: Rutgers University Press, 1968.

Braithewaite, R. L. "Interpersonal Relations Between Black Males and Black Females." In L. E. Gary (Ed.) *Black Men.* Beverly Hills, California: Sage Publications, 1981.

Duberman, L. *Gender and Sex in Society.* New York: Praeger, 1975.

Gary, L. E. (Ed.) *Black Men.* Beverly Hills, Calif.: Sage Publications, 1981.

Grier, W., and Cobbs, P. *Black Rage.* New York: Basic Books, 1968.

Hare, J. "Black Male-Female Relationships." *Sepia* (November 1979).

Jackson, J. "But Where Are the Black Men?" *Black Scholar* (1971) 4; 34–41.

Jordan, J. *Things That I Do in the Dark.* New York: Random House.

Jourard, S. *The Transparent Self.* New York: Jan Nostrand, 1971.

Karenga, M. *Introduction to Black Studies.* Inglewood, California: Kawaida Publications, 1982.

Ladner, J. Tomorrow's Tomorrow: *The Black Woman.* New York: Doubleday, 1972.

LaRue, L. Black Liberation and Women's Lib. *Transaction,* 19709, 8(1), 59–63.

Lerner, G. *Black Women in White America.* New York: Vintage Books, 1973.

Liebow, E. *Talley's Corner.* Boston: Little, Brown and Co., 1967.

Lorde, A. "Feminism and Black Liberation." *The Black Scholar* (1979) 10 (8.9); 17–20.

Noble, J. *Beautiful, also, Are the Souls of my Black Sisters: A History of Black Women in America.* Englewood Cliffs, N.J.: Prentice-Hall, 1978.

Poussant, A. "White Manipulation and Black." *The Black Scholar* (1979) 10(8.9); 52–55.

Rodgers-Rose, L. *The Black Woman.* Beverly Hills, Calif., 1980.

Salaam, K. "Revolutionary Struggle/Revolutionary Love." *The Black Scholar* (1979) 10(8.9); 20–24.

Scott, J. "Polygamy: A Futuristic Family Arrangement for African-Americans." *Black Books Bulletin* (1976); 13–19.

Staples, R. *The Black Woman in America.* Chicago: Nelson-Hall, 1973.

______. "Masculinity and Race: The Dual Dilemma of Black Men." *Journal of Social Issues* (1978) 34(1); 1969–183.

______. "A Rejoiner: Black Feminism and the Cult of Masculinity: The Danger Within." *The Black Scholar* (1979) 10(8.9).

Toure, S. *Toward Full Reafricanization.* Paris: Presence Africane, 1959.

Tucker, R. *Why Do Black Men Hide Their Feelings?* New York: Dial Press, 1979.

Wallace, M. *Black Macho and the Myth of the Superwoman.* New York: Dial Press, 1979.

Welsing, F. "The Cress Theory of Color Confrontation and Racism." *The Black Scholar* (1974) 5; 32–40.

Wilcox, P. Is There Life for Black Leaders after ERA? *Black Male/Female Relationships* (1979) 2(1); 53–55.

Wilkinson, D. and Taylor, R. L. (Eds.) *The Black Male in America.* Chicago: Nelson-Hall, 1977.

CHAPTER TWO

Demographic Issues

Jacquelyne Jackson gives insight into contemporary demographic and sociological influences upon Black males and Black females. Her oft-quoted paper concerning the scarcity of Black males explores social implications for Black male and Black female relationships, especially for the Black family. It also furnishes a guide to regions where Black males outnumber Black females. And, while the male shortage is increasing there are ways to counteract the shortage. Gary is more inclusive in his demographic treatise, choosing to focus upon the Black male from a social and demographic profile of his existence in America. The social profile presented is envisioned as providing a framework for facilitating an understanding of the high psychosocial and economic risk status of Black men that often leads to unhealthy adaptations. Rodgers-Rose completes the dyad through her focus upon demographic statistics of Black females. While the data of the three works may appear to contradict each other at points, they were included because of the extent to which they have been referenced in other sources.

But Where Are the Black Men?

Jacquelyne Jackson

The question, "But where are the males?" refers inevitably to that of the sex ratio (i.e., the number of males per every one hundred females). One highly significant gap in almost all contemporary scientific, pseudo-scientific, and ideological concerns about black women—and especially about black female household heads—is that of the failure to consider the implications of the sex ratio itself. This gap can be attributed directly to the general tendency of social scientists and social policymakers to ignore the realities of the prevailing black sex ratios and concomitant factors, such as the aforenoted tendency of white females to seek black mates.

Such a gap is particularly deplorable in the social sciences, inasmuch as Oliver C. Cox[1] focused specific attention upon sex ratios and their implications at least as early as 1940. For present purposes, it is imperative to note that Cox indicated quite clearly the following:

1. Differences in the marital status of persons in different areas and communities may be due to differences in the ratio of marriageable men to women;[2]
2. The racial sex ratio varies considerably in the different regional divisions of the United States;[3]

1. Oliver C. Cox, "Sex Ratio and Marital Status Among Negroes," *American Sociological Review,* 5:937–947, 1940. Incidentally, no opportunity should be lost in pointing out anew that the significant contributions of Dr. Cox to American sociology, and particularly those valuable in knowing and understanding blacks, have been largely ignored by the white, male-dominated American sociological establishment. At the 1971 annual meeting of the American Sociological Association, however, largely through the efforts of the Caucus of Black Sociologists, and Dr. James E. Conyers especially, the first Du-Bois-Johnson-Frazier Award was conferred upon Dr. Cox in recognition of such contributions. Earlier, the first annual Du-Bois Award established by the Association of Social and Behavioral Scientists (founded in 1935) was given to Dr. Cox in recognition of his distinguished achievements.

2. *Ibid.,* p. 937.

3. *Ibid.*

3. The percentage of Negro families married in cities is particularly sensitive to changes in the sex ratio, while the percentage of males married seems to respond almost not at all.[4]

Thus, as the black sex ratio rose, the percentage of black females who were married rose. As that sex ratio declined, so did the percentage of married black females.

Since 1940, the black sex ratio has actually worsened, if judged at least from the perspective of black females. Yet most contemporary literature is written as if there were one black male for each black female. That literature almost always fails to inquire about male availability levels for black females. Probably the most glaring example is *The Moynihan Report.*[5] Moynihan tended to assume that male unemployment was the critical factor affecting the proportion of female-headed households among blacks, but he failed miserably in dealing with the actual supply of black males for black females.

Census data clearly reveal that females have been excessive in the black population of the United States since at least 1850, or a period of more than 120 years. In 1850, the black sex ratio was 99.1, rising slightly to 99.6 in 1860, but declining to 96.2 in 1870. In 1880, it was 97.8; and in 1920, 99.2. In 1900, 98.6; in 1910, 98.9; and in 1920, 99.2. Since 1920, the black sex ratio has decreased consistently, from 97.0 in 1930, to 95.0 in 1940, to 94.3 in 1950, to 93.3 in 1960, and, in 1970, to 90.8, or approximately 91 black males for every 100 black females. Thus for the past 50 years, black men have becoming scarcer and scarcer. It is not just the case that they are more likely to be missed in the Census counts, but that they are just not there.[6]

If no adjustment is made for age,at least 1,069,694 of the 11,885,595 black females in the population of the United States in 1970 would have been without available,monogamous mates. When age-adjusted and regional-adjusted data are presented, as shown in Table 1, the unadjusted pattern does not undergo any significant change. As can be seen in Table 1, in the United States as a whole, black females are not more numerous than black males only within one age group, that of 5 to 14 years. They are more numerous in all of the remaining age groupings, and especially so during female childbearing ages. The same is true of the geographical divisions, with one exception occurring in the West among the 15 to 24 year-old grouping.

4. *Ibid.*, p. 938.

5. Daniel P. Moynihan, *The Negro Family: A Case for National Action,* U.S. Government Printing Office, Washington, D.C.: 1965.

6. It may be interesting to note that some discussions of this point have brought retorts that the males are there, but simply avoid being counted. The chief argument here is that even if all of the black males throughout the United States were counted, the females would still remain excessive, due to a variety of reasons certainly warranting systematic investigations. Some, of course, are not there due to the unnecessarily high infant and childhood mortality rates especially affecting black males, while some others are dead, victimized by war and wanton killings.

Table 1. Black Sex Ratios by Age and Geographical Location, 1970[1]

	Geographical Location				
Age (years)	**U.S.**	**Northeast[1]**	**North Central[2]**	**South[2]**	**West[2]**
Total, all ages	90.8	87.5	91.3	98.8	97.6
Under 5	99.3	100.7	100.0	90.8	97.6
5–14	100.4	100.7	99.8	100.5	100.3
25–34	93.0	87.1	90.1	94.5	105.6
35–44	84.3	78.6	83.4	85.4	95.7
45–54	86.4	83.4	90.4	84.9	94.0
55–64	85.3	78.3	89.7	85.6	90.3
65 +	76.4	71.7	81.4	76.2	76.3

1. Source of raw data: U.S. Department of Commerce/Bureau of the Census, *1970 Census of Population, Advance Report,* "General Population Characteristics, United States," PC(V2)-1. U.S. Department of Commerce, Washington, D.C., February 1971.

2. Northwestern states include Maine, New Hampshire, Vermont, Massachusetts, Rhode Island, Connecticut, New York, New Jersey, and Pennsylvania; North Central includes Ohio, Indiana, Illinois, Michigan, Wisconsin, Minnesota, Iowa, Missouri, North Dakota, South Dakota, Nebraska, and Kansas; the South includes Delaware, Maryland, District of Columbia, Virginia, West Virginia, North Carolina, South Carolina, Georgia, Florida, Kentucky, Tennessee, Alabama, Mississippi, Arkansas, Louisiana, Oklahoma, and Texas; and the West encompasses Montana, Idaho, Wyoming, Colorado, New Mexico, Arizona, Utah, Nevada, Washington, Oregon, California, Alaska, and Hawaii.

It is relevant now to inquire about alternative familial forms developed in the absence of a sufficient supply of males. Two of those forms, unnecessarily and irrationally viewed as "deviant" by the American white subculture, are those of female-headed households and of illegitimacy. The nomenclature of "illigetimacy" is inappropriately applied to blacks, for any number of reasons, but the common usage of such a concept does not reflect a tendency of many whites to attempt to "desexify" blacks. It is quite important to add that the development of that term occurred at a time when white males exceeded white females in the United States as well. The application of the term was also grossly unfair to blacks who were already in the process of developing alternative familial forms in the absence of a sufficient supply of males, a condition not confronting whites until 1950.

The "problem" of female-headed households can only be perceived as a "problem" by those who act, again, as if there were identical supplies of males and females. When such is not the case, as it is clearly not in the case of blacks, then the phenomenon should be perceived as a rational alternative to an ineffective traditional system. It should be quite obvious that slavery is an insufficient factor to be used in explicating both illegitimacy and female-headed households, for, by the usual measures of family stability, as Frazier has noted, black family stability continued progressively throughout the latter half of the nineteenth century and up until 1910.[7]

7. E. Franklin Frazier, *The Negro Family in the United States,* University of Chicago Press: 1939. Here, perhaps, it should be noted that, contrary to a number of interpretation of Frazier, Frazier did *not* characterize matriarchy as the *dominant* family type among blacks.

In fact, Census data show that in 1900, for persons 15+ years of age, there were no significant differences in marital statuses by race or by sex between black and white females and males. But, since then, as the black sex ratio has decreased, the marital statuses of black females, in particular, have also been affected, as Cox demonstrated.[8] The marital statuses of black females have been far more sensitive to that reducing sex ration than have those of black males, which leads us into an exploration of one of the relationships which may exist between black sex ratios and familial patterns, specifically that of female-headed households.

As that sex ratio has decreased, the proportion of female-headed households among blacks has increased, suggesting thereby that a possible causative factor for the latter may be the former. If we examine available 1970 data on the black sex ratio and the proportion of female-headed households among blacks in each state and the District of Columbia, what will emerge will be a significant inverse relationship between those two variables ($r = -.68$, $df = 49$, and $p > .001$). In other words, as shown in Table 2, there is a tendency for the proportion of female-haded households to increase as the supply of males decreases. Conversely, when the supply of males increases, the proportion of female-headed households decreases. For example, the excess of black males over black females is greatest in Hawaii, where the proportion of black female-headed households ranks quite low. In fact, only two states (North Dakota and South Dakota) rank lower than Hawaii in the proportion of female-headed households among blacks. On the other hand, the sex ratio is lowest in New York (85.9, or approximately 86 males per every 100 females), and 32.1 percent of black families within the state were headed by females in 1970, exceeded only by Massachusetts, where 34.3 percent of black families were female-headed.

Despite the fact that black females are excessive in the black population, that excessive phenomenon is not equitably distributed throughout the United States. In 19 states, black males outnumber females. Those states are Hawaii, Montana, North Dakota, Idaho, South Dakota, Utah, Alaska, Vermont, Maine, New Hampshire, Wyoming, Washington, Colorado, Rhode Island, Minnesota, Arizona, New Mexico, Nevada and Oregon—none are southern states. They are also states containing extremely minute proportions of aged (i.e., 65+ years) blacks, which suggests that they are probably less affected by the considerably shortened life expectancy rates of black males than is true of the remaining states. Thus, the proportion of widowed black females who may find it necessary to assume a status as household head is reduced.

This geographical disproportionment in the distribution of black females and males also has consequences for familial patterns in that, as indicated above and as evident in Table 2, black females are generally least likely to be heads of households where the sex ratio is the highest. Thus, it may be that black male geographical mobility has been significantly different from that of black females, suggesting thereby two different types of policy alternatives for those concerned about the proportion of black female-headed households. One implication may well be that greater geographical mobility could be en-

8. Cox, *op. cit.*

Table 2. Black Sex Ratios and the Percentage of Female-Headed Families and Their Rank Orders in the United States. 1970[1]

State	Sex Ratio	% Female-Headed Families	Sex Ratio Rank[2]	% Female-Headed Families Rank[2]
Hawaii	192.6	7.1	1.0	3.0
Montana	169.2	24.2	2.0	16.0
North Dakota	160.3	2.9	3.0	1.0
Idaho	158.5	9.0	4.0	5.5
South Dakota	157.0	6.2	5.0	2.0
Utah	151.6	21.6	6.0	10.0
Alaska	147.3	7.8	7.0	4.0
Vermont	139.3	13.0	8.0	8.0
Maine	136.9	9.0	9.0	5.5
New Hampshire	130.4	9.9	10.0	7.0
Wyoming	114.2	13.2	11.0	9.0
Washington	113.0	23.1	12.0	12.0
Colorado	105.2	22.1	13.0	11.0
Rhode Island	102.5	31.7	14.0	49.0
Minnesota	102.4	28.5	15.0	36.5
Arizona	102.2	25.5	16.0	21.0
New Mexico	101.1	24.3	17.0	17.5
Nevada	100.8	23.6	18.0	13.0
Oregon	100.5	26.1	19.0	26.0
Kansas	97.9	27.2	20.0	29.0
Iowa	95.9	28.9	21.0	42.0
California	95.2	28.1	22.0	34.5
Virginia	94.7	23.7	23.0	14.0
Wisconsin	94.0	30.8	24.0	46.0
Michigan	93.6	25.7	25.5	22.5
Nebraska	93.6	30.5	25.5	45.0
Kentucky	93.0	27.9	27.0	33.0
Maryland	92.8	27.0	28.0	27.0
Indiana	92.7	24.7	29.5	19.0
Delaware	92.7	28.1	29.5	34.5
Texas	92.4	24.0	31.0	15.0
North Carolina	92.1	25.8	32.0	24.0
Florida	91.7	28.5	33.0	36.5

1 Source of raw data: U.S. Department of Commerce/Bureau of the Census, *1970 Census of Population, Advance Report.* "General Population Characteristics, United States," PC(V2)-1. U.S. Department of Commerce. Washington, D.C., February, 1971.

2 Rank ordering for the sex ratio is from high to low. That is, the state with the highest sex ratio (Hawaii) is ranked 1.0, while that with lowest (New York) is ranked 51.0. Rank ordering for the percentage of female-headed households is from low to high. That is, the state with the lowest proportion (North Dakota) is ranked 1.0, while Massachusetts, with the highest, is ranked 51.0.

Table 2.—*Continued.*

State	Sex Ratio	% Female-Headed Families	Sex Ratio Rank[2]	% Female-Headed Families Rank[2]
South Carolina	91.4	26.0	34.0	25.0
Ohio	90.6	27.1	35.0	28.0
Mississippi	90.1	25.7	36.0	22.5
Louisiana	90.0	27.6	37.0	32.0
Arkansas	89.8	24.3	38.0	17.5
Connecticut	89.7	30.4	39.0	43.5
New Jersey	89.5	30.4	40.0	43.5
Illinois	89.4	28.8	41.0	40.5
Oklahoma	89.3	31.1	42.0	47.0
Missouri	89.1	28.8	43.0	40.5
Massachusetts	88.6	34.3	45.0	51.0
Georgia	88.6	28.6	45.0	38.0
District of Columbia	88.6	28.7	45.0	39.0
Tennessee	88.3	27.9	47.5	30.0
Pennsylvania	88.3	31.3	47.0	48.0
Alabama	88.0	27.4	49.0	31.0
West Virginia	87.6	24.8	50.0	20.0
New York	85.9	32.1	51.0	50.0

couraged among black females, especially those in such states as New York, Massachusetts, Pennsylvania, Oklahoma, New Jersey, and Connecticut, where such encouragement would include the lure of significant opportunities for receipt of higher education, professional occupation, and incomes approximating at least the median income of all individuals in the United States. That might help move the "girls" to "where the boys are."

A second, but different type of implication, might well be the continuing development of alternative familiar forms, including that of polygyny, a system appropriate in the absence of a sufficient supply of males. Polygyny, of course, requires male participants with sufficient resources to maintain adequately several or more families. At the present time, almost no black males are economically equipped within the United States to participate in such a system, which forestalls any present concerns about the acceptability of such a system to black females. Nevertheless, as some keen observers have indicated in various private conversations with at least the writer, the legitimacy of polygyny could well benefit some females who are involved in "playing the polygyny," but who are denied legally any of the benefits to which they may otherwise be entitled.

For example, on a recent visit to Kampala, Uganda, the Vice-Chancellor of Makerere University noted that, in defense of polygyny, the women participating as spouses had a legal status of wife, not that of whore, slut, mistress, et cetera. Thus, not only did such wives not have illegitimate children, but both they and their children had legal protection under the law, which he regarded as a more "civilized" system than that existing in the "civilized" United States. He may have a point worth further investigation. In any case, it is quite clear that there is not one absolute system of marriage and family which must be adhered to at any cost and under any circumstance. Such is even the case among white Americans.

WHITE SEX RATIOS

It has already been established that females have been excessive in the black population since 1850. Table 3, which provides a comparison of the black and white sex ratios, 1850–1970, shows clearly evidence permitting the statement already made that blacks have had a "headstart" on whites in developing alternative familial patterns in the absence of a sufficient number of males. Blacks are at least 100 years ahead of whites in this respect. A cursory examination of such variables as those of marital statuses, illegitimacy rates, and intermarriage rates is invaluable in noting certain trends depicting whites as becoming more like blacks.

Table 3. Black and White Sex Ratios, 1850–1970[1]

	Sex Ratios	
Year	**Black**	**White**
1850	99.1	105.2
1860	99.6	105.3
1870	96.2	102.8
1880	97.8	104.0
1890	99.5	105.4
1900	98.6	104.9
1910	98.9	106.6
1920	99.2	104.4
1930	97.0	102.9
1940	95.0	101.2
1950	94.3	99.1
1960	93.3	97.3
1970	90.8	95.3

1. For whites in 1970, the data include non-blacks. Sex ratios were obtained from *Census* reports for the specified years.

Table 4 provides some limited information on two of the three variables referred to above, namely marital statuses and illegitimacy. If we examine female marital statuses, by race, from 1900 through 1970, we see that in 1900, when the black sex ratio was 98.6 an the white 104.9, there were no significant differences by race in marital statuses. In fact, a slightly higher proportion of the black females were returned as *married*, while a slightly larger proportion of the whites were returned as *divorced*, but slightly fewer as *widowed*.

By 1940, when the black sex ratio had declined to 95.0 while that of the whites remained above 100, it is evident that the divorce rates by race were identical, while the widowhood rate was higher among blacks than whites. In addition, data available for persons married with spouses present (not available in the 1900 Census) showed that the decreasing sex ratio had affected the proportion of black females likely to fall within that category, while the whites remained relatively unaffected.

In 1960, when the sex ratios among both blacks and whites had declined to 93.3 and 97.3 respectively, we actually find that a larger proportion of females in both racial groups were returned as *married, with spouse present.* By that year, their divorce rates were no longer identical, but both were rising., 3.6 among the blacks, and 2.7 among the whites, as compared with the 1940 rate of 1.7.

By 1970, with the sex ratios continuing to decline (90.8 among blacks, 95.3 among whites), it is clear that the proportion of females *married, with spouse present* had declined *both* among black and white females from the percentage given in 1960. In 1970, 9.8 percent fewer black females and 4.9 percent fewer white females were so classified. The major factor contributing to that change may, perhaps, be found in the increased proportion of those single, which is over twice as high among the black females, 1960–1970, than among the white females. In 1970, as it may be recalled, over nine black females out of every 100 would have been theoretically classified as being without monogamous males, true of only about five out of every 100 white females.

Thus, a partial explication of the differences in the marital statuses by race should not be sought, as is quite commonly done, within black family disorganization, but within the effects of sex ratios upon marital statuses. While the divorce rate in 1970 continued to be higher among black than among white females, the rate among the latter also continued to increase from 1960 to 1970.

Data in Table 4 depicting the percent of female-headed families do reveal, as expected, that the proportion of such families is considerably higher among blacks than among whites. However, the proportionate increase among blacks was less from 1960 to 1970 (119.6%) than it was from 1950 to 1960 (127.3%), whereas the proportionate increase among whites was greater in 1960–1970 (104.6%) than between 1950–1960, when it was 102.4 percent. Consequently, although the sex ratios were continuing to decline among both groups, the rate of increase in female-headed families among whites continued to rise between 1950–1970, while it had begun to decrease somewhat among blacks over the same time period.

A similar pattern emerges upon examination of the percentage changes occurring over time in two other variables—the percent of own children living with both parents as the percent of all own children, and the percent change in estimated illegitimacy rates. In the case of the former variable, from 1960–1970, the percent of such children among both races declined, from 75 to 67 percent among blacks, and from 92 to 91 percent among whites, a decrease which may also be related to their decreasing sex ratios and increasing proportions of female-headed families.

Table 4. Selected Statistical Comparisons between Blacks and Whites

Characteristic	Black	White
Female Marital status		
1900, 15+ years of age		
% single	39.8	40.1
% married	55.5	55.4
% divorced	0.2	0.3
% widowed	4.3	4.0
1940, 15+ years of age		
% single	23.9	26.0
% married, spouse present	44.2	56.9
% divorced	1.7	1.7
% widowed	15.8	11.1
1960, 14+ years of age		
% single	22.3	18.7
% married, spouse present	51.8	65.2
% divorced	3.6	2.7
% widowed	14.0	12.0
1970, 14+ years of age		
% single	28.0	21.3
% married, spouse present	42.0	60.3
% divorced	4.3	3.4
% widowed	13.5	12.4
Percent of female-headed families		
1950	17.6	8.5
1955	20.7	9.0
1960	22.4	8.7
1966	23.7	8.9
1970	26.4	9.1
1971	28.9	9.4
Percent of own children living with both parents, as percent of all own children		
1960	75	92
1970	67	91
Percent change in estimated illegitimacy rates		
1940–1944 to 1955–1959	+166	+139
1955–1959 to 1968	–8	+53

Sources of data: U.S. Census Office, *Census Reports,* Vol. 2, Part 2,"Population," U.S. Govt. Printing Office. Washington, D.C. 1902: U.S. Bureau of the Census, *Sixteenth Census of the United States: 1940,* Vol. 1, "Population, Characteristics of the Population," U.S. Govt. Printing Office, Washington, D.C., 1943; U.S. Bureau of the Census, *U.S. Census of Population, 1960.* Vol. 1 "Characteristics of the Population," Part 1, "United States Summary,' U.S. Gov. Printing Office, Washington, D.C., 1964; *The Social and Economic Status of Negroes in the United States, 1970.* BLS Report No. 394, CPR, Series P-23. No. 28, Special Studies, U.S. Department of Commerce/Bureau of the Census, Washington, D.C., July, 1971; and *Social and Economic Characteristics of the Population in Metropolitan and Nonmetropolitan Areas: 1970 and 1960.* Current Population Reports, Series P 23. No. 37. U.S. Govt. Printing Office, Washington, D.C. 1971.

While illegitimacy as usually defined remains higher among blacks than among whites, it is very interesting to note that illegitimacy rates have been declining among blacks, while increasing among whites, as also shown in Table 4. In other words, the rate of illegitimate births is rising among whites while their sex ratio is declining, which is a pattern not at all unlike that which transpired much earlier among blacks. Thus, it appears that as females become more excessive in the white population, the proportion seeking family forms deviating from the traditional is on the increase. In this sense—and a very important sense, to be sure—whites are following trends mapped out earlier by blacks.

Whites, of course, have not yet "caught up" with blacks in developing various alternative patterns for several different reasons, with the most important one probably being that black females are yet more excessive in the black population than are those in the white population, and particularly so during the childbearing years of 15–44, as can be seen by inspecting the data provided in Table 5. For the years 15–44 inclusive, the sex ratios are much lower than among blacks than whites, and especially so for the years 25–44, as of 1970. Interestingly, however, for those 65+ years of age, the black sex ratio is actually higher than that of the whites, a finding readily explicable by the greater longevity of white females as compared with blacks and with white males. In passing, what may also be quite impressive about Table 5 is an inference that the significant differences in the sex ratios between blacks and whites are not reflected to the same extent in the differences in their illegitimacy rates. That is, given the fact again that white females are not as excessive in the white population as are black females within the black population, and considering also that white females have far greater access to black males as marital partners than do black females to white males, one must wonder why the white illegitimacy rate is as high as it is among whites and as low as it is among blacks!

Table 5. Differences in the Black and White Sex Ratios, 15+ Years of Age, 1970[1]

Age Group	Black	White	Difference
15–24 years	93.0	98.8	5.8
25–34 years	84.2	97.8	13.6
35–44 years	82.8	96.2	13.4
45–54 years	86.3	93.8	7.5
55–64 years	85.1	90.2	5.1
65 + years	76.4	71.9	–4.5

1. Source of raw data: U.S. Department of Commerce/Bureau of the Census. *1970 Census of Population, Advance Report,* "General Population Characteristics, United States," PC(V2)-1. U.S. Department of Commerce, Washington, D.C., February, 1971.

SUMMARY AND CONCLUSIONS

By now it may be quite evident that there are at least three major and interrelated concerns running through this discourse about "But where are the men?", with the most important one being that there simply are not enough men available for black women to assure their conformity to traditional patterns of sex, marriage, and family living, as defined for them by the white American subculture. More important, as the white sex ratio becomes more like that of blacks (as measured by excessive females within the population and particularly within the age ranges of 15–44 years), it is quite clear that whites are increasingly utilizing patterns or models already developed by blacks, who have had a "headstart" of at least 100 years.

Ultimately, black women must be concerned with resolution of the issue of an insufficient supply of males, and aid in developing means of increasing that supply (which can take a variety of tactics, not the least of which is improving the life expectancies of black men) or, should that fail, providing viable alternatives to this "supply-and-demand" problem, one of which may be aiding in reducing the supply of black males available to white females, a practice, incidentally, which seems to affect an unduly high number of black coeds on major campuses throughout at least most of the northern and western parts of the United States.

In closing, then, the critical issues confronting many black women are not those of black matriarchy or black female emasculation of the male, but merely that of, *"But where are the men?"*

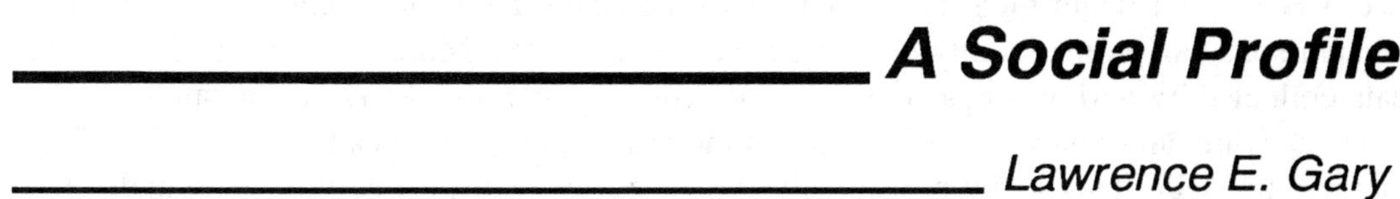

A Social Profile

Lawrence E. Gary

In this chapter, consideration will be given to the social and demographic characteristics of Black men in the United States. As mentioned earlier, there seems to be an impression in the minds of many people that the Black community is composed primarily of Black women and their children. In a provocative essay Jackson (1971) asked, "Where are the Black men?" Although the ratio of Black males to Black females has been declining for many years, there were 12,108,000 Black males in the United States in 1978. This figure represented 47.5 percent of the total Black population (U.S. Bureau of the Census, 1979a).

There is no doubt that Black men are an integral part of Black communities. It is important for us to describe the current social conditions under which these men function in our society. More specifically, in this chapter, we plan to develop a profile on Black men in terms of population growth and distribution, marital and family status, educational attainment, employment and income, and social participation. Health status is discussed in Chapter 2. Moreover, an in-depth analysis of education and training and economics is contained in Chapters 12, 13, and 14.

In developing this profile, it was necessary to exercise considerable judgment in selecting from the enormous body of available data. The primary data sources for this study include the U.S. Bureau of the Census, the U.S. Bureau of Labor Statistics, the U.S. Department of Justice (Federal Bureau of Investigation), and the National Center for Education Statistics. In addition, two government publications, *The Social and Economic Status of the Black Population in the United States 1790–1978* (U.S. Bureau of the Census, 1979b) and *Social Indicators 1976* (U.S. Department of Commerce,1977), have been most useful in developing this chapter. Since the data in this chapter were obtained from a variety of sources, one has to be aware of sampling errors (values from samples compared to those from complete enumeration of particular population groups) and nonsampling errors (refusals of respondents, undercounts of certain groups, poorly designed instruments, falsification of records, incorrect recording of information, and so forth). While appropriate, we shall mention data limitations as different information is presented.

In keeping with the basic theme of this volume, major comparisons will be made between Black and white men, rather than between Black men and women. In some cases, comparisons can be made only between Blacks and whites. Moreover, much of the social data collected by various departments of the federal government have been categorized in terms of white and nonwhite. When this is the case, appropriate acknowledgement of this fact will be made. This social profile will provide a framework for helping us to understand the high psychosocial and economic risk status of Black men in our society. Further, it will document the social frustration of Black men that often leads to unhealthy adaptations. Finally, these social indicators will help us to see the interlocking relationship between Black families and social institutions such as the economy, social services, education, the military, and the penal system.

POPULATION GROWTH AND DISTRIBUTION

As indicated earlier, in 1978, there were over 12 million Black men, compared to 92 million white men. In other words, Black males accounted for about 11.3 percent of the male population in the United States (U.S. Bureau of the Census, 1979a). In 1960,the Black male populations was 9 million, compared to 78 million for white men. These data suggest that since 1960, the Black male population has increased by 33.3 percent, whereas the white male population has increased by only 18 percent.

As indicated in Table 1, the age distribution of the Black male population has shown some changes since 1960, in comparison to little change for the white male population. In 1978, the median age for Black males was 23.2 years, but it was 29.4 years for white males. In other words, the Black male population is younger than is the white male population. The proportion of the Black male population below the age of 21 years was 48 percent, compared to 37 percent for the white male population in 1978. On the other hand, 10 percent of the white male population was 65 years and older, but the corresponding percentage for the Black male population was only 7 percent in 1978. These data suggest that the age dependency ratio (the ratio of persons under 14 years of age and those persons 65 years of age and older—defined as dependents—to those persons between 14 and 65 years of age—defined as economically productive) is much higher for Black males than it is for white males. In 1978, 36 percent of Black males can be defined as being dependent, compared to 31 percent of white males.

Over the past hundred years, the U.S. Bureau of the Census has enumerated more Black females than it has Black males. The sex ratio (the number of males per 100 females) was 96.2 for the Black community in 1870 and 90.6 in 1978 (U.S. Bureau of the Census, 1979a, 1979b). In comparison, the sex ratio was 95.3 for the white community in 1978. As implied in Table 1, the sex ratio is particularly problematic for the Black community during the marriage and childbearing ages. However, this is not the case for the white community. Jackson (1971) has further analyzed sex ratio for the Black community in terms of regions

Table 1. Selected Population Characteristics of the U.S. Male Population by Race

	Black Male	White Male
1. Total population in millions, 1978	12.0	92.0
2. Total population in millions; 1970	10.0	87.0
3. Total population in millions, 1960	9.0	78.0
4. Median age in years, 1978	23.2	29.4
5. Median age in years, 1970	21.0	27.6
6. Median age in years, 1960	22.4	29.4
7. Percentage of population under 22 years of age, 1978	48.0	37.0
8. Percentage of population 65 years of age 1978 and older,	7.0	10.0
9. Percentage of population considered dependents, 1978	36.0	31.0
10. Males per 100 females, 1978	90.6	95.3
11. Males under 14 years of age per 100 females, 1978	101.6	104.8
12. Males 14–24 years of age per 100 females, 1978	96.1	102.4
13. Males 25–44 years of age per 100 females, 1978	84.0	98.8
14. Males 45–64 years of age per 100 females, 1978	86.1	92.8
15. Males 65 years of age and older per 100 females, 1978	71.2	67.9

SOURCE: U.S. Bureau of the Census, *Statistical Abstract of the United States: 1979* (100th ed.). Washington, DC: Government Printing Office, 1979, pp. 28–29.

and states. She has shown that the sex ratio varies according to city, state, and region, and that it has an impact on family stability and behavior. In Chapter 4, Braithwaite discusses the impact of the imbalance in the sex ratio on female and male relationships in Black communities. Some caution must be exercised in accepting the census data with respect to the sex ratio. It has been shown that the U.S. Bureau of the Census undercounted the number of Black people, especially Black males, in the 1970 decennial census (Rodgers-Rose, 1980; Siegal, 1973; U.S. Department of Commerce, 1977). It has been suggested that the corrected sex ratio should be 95, instead of 91 (U.S. Bureau of the Census, 1979b).

MARITAL AND FAMILY STATUS

In 1975, 38 percent of the Black male population 14 years of age and older was single, but only 28 percent of the white male population in this same age group was classified as single. What is interesting to note, as shown in Table 2, is that, in 1940, Black and white men had similar marital statuses. For white men 14 years of age and older, the per-

Table 2. Marital Status of U.S. Males by Race

	Black Male	White Male
1. Percentage of male population 14 years old and older single, 1975	38.0	28.0
2. Percentage of male population 14 years old and older married, 1975	53.0	66.0
3. Percentage of male population 14 years old and older divorced, 1975	4.0	3.0
4. Percentage of male population 14 years and older unattached (single, divorce, widowed, etc.), 1975	46.0	33.0
5. Percentage of male population 14 years old and older single, 1940	33.0	33.0
6. Percentage of male population 14 years old and older married, 1940	61.0	61.0
7. Percentage of male population 14 years old and older divorced, 1940	1.0	1.0
8. Percentage of male population 14 years old and older widowed, 1940	6.0	4.0
9. Divorced males: all ages per 1000 married persons with spouse present, 1975	83.0*	51.0
10. Divorced males 45–64 years of age per 1000 married persons with spouse present, 1975	116.0*	55.0
11. Percentage of male population 14 years old and older widowed, 1975	4.0	2.0

SOURCE: U.S. Bureau of the Census. *The Social and Economic Status of the Black Population in the United States 1790–1978.* Washington, DC: Government Printing Office, 1979, pp. 109–111; and U.S. Department of Commerce. *Social Indicators 1976.* Washington, DC: Government Printing Office, 1977, p.68.

*Data refer to Black and other racial minorities.

centage married increased from 61 in 1940 to 66 in 1975. However, for Black men the trend was the reverse; that is, there was a decrease in the percentage of married Black men. Black men are more likely to be divorced than are white men. In 1978, 6.9 percent of Black males 18 years of age and over were divorced, compared to 2.4 percent in 1960 and 3.6 percent in 1970 (U.S. Bureau of the Census, 1979a). As shown in Table 2, divorce has become more common and widowhood less common for both groups between 1940 and 1975. It should be noted that income, education, region and age will have an impact on the divorce rate for a given population group, but a discussion of these issues is beyond the scope of this chapter (Glick, 1970; Glick and Norton, 1979).

The data tend to suggest that there has been a significant increase in the number and percentage of Black men who are single. When one combines single, divorced, or widowed into a category of unattached or not married, the data in Table 2 show that, in 1975, 46 percent of Black males over 14 years of age are so classified, compared to 33 percent for white

Table 3. Family Status of the U.S. Population by Race

	Black Male	White Male
1. Percentage of own children living with both parents, 1960	75.0	93.0
2. Percent of own children living with both parents, 1970	65.0	91.0
3. Percentage of own children living with both parents, 1978	49.4	85.7
4. Percentage of all families, husband-wife type, 1960	74.1	89.2
5. Percentage of all families, husband-wife type,f 1970	68.1	88.7
6. Percentage of all fami.lies, husband-wife type, 1978	56.1	85.9
7. Percentage of all families, male-headed, no wife present, 1960	4.1	2.7
8. Percentage of all families, male-headed, no wife present, 1978	3.7	2.3
9. Percentage of all families, male-headed, no wife present, 1978	4.6	2.5
10. Percentage of husband-wife families where husband is 14–34 years old, 1960	28.0	27.0
11. Percentage of husband-wife families where husband is 65 years old and older, 1960	11.0	12.0
12. Percentage of husband-wife families where husband is 14–34 years old, 1975	32.0	30.0
13. Percentage of husband-wife families where husband is 65 years old and older, 1975	13.0	14.0

SOURCE: U.S. Bureau of the Census. *The Social and Economic Status of the Black Population in the United States 1790–1978.* Washington, DC: Government Printing Office, 1979, pp. 103, 105, 107, 175, and 178.

males. This larger percentage of unmarried Black males will have an impact on male and female relationships and on the need for social and mental health services for this high-risk group. Further, as is pointed out in Chapters 2 and 8, marital status is correlated with health behavior and other adaptation strategies. Studies (Carter & Glick, 1976; Glick & Norton, 1979; Rosen et al., 1979; Gove, 1972) have consistently shown that unmarried (single, divorced,or widowed) persons are at a greater risk than are married persons for all types of social and health and health disabilities (mental illness, drug and alcohol abuse, arrest, imprisonment, unemployment, homicide, and so forth).

Although the social science literature has tended to focus on the Black male's absence from his family, it should be noted that in 1978 there were 5.8 million Black families in the United States, of which the majority (56.1 percent) were two-parent families; that is, both husband and wife are present (U.S. Bureau of the census, 1979b). Moreover, in the same year, approximately 4.6 percent of all families were headed by men, with no wife present. As indicated in Table 3, Black families are more likely to have no husband present than are white families. between 1960 and 1978, Black husband-wife families declined from 74.1 percent to 56.1 percent of all Black families. By contrast, for whites the decline in husband-wife families has not been as significant. For example, in 1960, 89.2 percent of all white families were of the husband-wife type; in 1978 this family type had declined to 85.9 percent. In 1978, 85.7 percent of white children lived with both parents, compared to 49.4 percent for Black children. In both white and Black communities, there has been a decline in the percentage of children who live with both parents. However, the decline is much more significant for Black families. The data suggest that for both Blacks and whites the proportion of children living with both parents seems to be related to income (U.S. Bureau of the Census, 1979b). For example, in 1975, for Black families with incomes under $4,000, only 17 percent of the children lived with both parents, but for those families with incomes of $15,000 and more, 86 percent lived with their parents. A similar income effect is noted for white families, although at all income levels white children are more likely to live with both of their parents than are Black children.

In general, these data suggest that there has been a significant change in the structure of the traditional family unit in the Black community. First, a large number of Black men are not getting married. In addition, there is an increase in the divorce rate among Black men. While income, age, and regional factors influence marital and family status, it is becoming increasingly clear that family fragmentation is more pronounced in Black communities than it is in white communities. Part II of this volume discusses in some detail the consequences of these changes on family relationships.

EDUCATION AND TRAINING

Education is considered to be a very important value in Black communities (Doddy, 1963; Gary & Favors, 1975; Staples, 1976). To a large extent, many Blacks see education as fundamental to their gaining the necessary economic resources for maintaining a reasonable quality of life. School enrollment rates for Black males are about the same as those for whites, especially since 1960 (See Table 4). Commenting on the school attendance behavior of Black people, the U.S. Bureau of the Census (1979b: 86) concludes:

> *In the past 25 years (1950–1975), substantial increases have been noted in the proportion of Black youth enrolled in school above the compulsory attendance age. . . . The growth in enrollment experienced by the age group 5 to 13 years old is due both to the increased availability of kindergarten classes to Blacks . . . and to increased participation rates at the compulsory school ages 7 to 13.*

The extension of formal schooling to Black men has resulted in a decline in the illiteracy rate from 10 percent in 1959 to 4 percent in 1969, as indicated in Table 4. In 1978, the median years of school completed was 11.6 for Black males, compared to 12.6 for white males. Although Black males' school enrollment rates are very similar to those for white males, Black males continue to lag behind their white counterparts on a variety of educational attainment measures including median years of school completed, percentage of high school graduates, percentage of college graduates, and literacy rates. In an article, "Boys: Endangered Species," Raspberry (1979) reviews some of the behavioral and institutional problems that boys must face as they advance through the public school system.

Table 4. Educational Profile of Males by Race in the United States

	Black Male	White Male
1. Median years of school completed, 1960	7.7	10.7
2. Median years of school completed, 1970	9.6	12.2
3. Median years of school completed, 1978	11.6	12.6
4. Percentage of illiterate in population 14 years old older, 1959	10.0*	2.0
5. Percentage of illiterate in population 14 years old and older, 1969	4.0*	1.0
6. Percentage of persons 5 to 29 years old enrolled in school, 1960	66.0*	69.0
7. Percentage of persons 5 to 29 years old enrolled in school, 1970	69.0*	70.0
8. Percentage of persons 5 to 29 years old enrolled in school, 1975	69.0*	64.0
9. Percentage of high school dropouts among persons 14 to 24 years old, 1970	30.4	14.4
10. Percentage of high school dropouts among persons 14 to 34 years old, 1977	20.0	12.4
11. Percentage of persons 25 years old and older, less than 4 years of high school, 1970	67.5	42.8
12. Percentage of person 25 years old and older, less than 4 years of high school, 1979	50.8	29.7
13. Percentage of persons 25 years old and older with 4 years of high school, 1970	22.2	30.9
14. Percentage of persons 25 years old and older with 4 years of high school, 1979	29.5	33.1
15. Percentage of persons 25 years old and older with 4 years of college or more, 1979	8.3	21.4
16. Percentage of persons 25 years old and older with 4 years of college or more, 1970	4.6	15.0
17. Percentage of total persons 14–34 years of age enrolled in college by race, 1978	44.3	52.9
18. Percentage of total persons 14–34 years old enrolled in college by race, 1970	48.5	60.2

SOURCE: U.S. Bureau of the Census. *Statistical Abstract of the United States 1979* (100th ed.). Washington, DC: Government Printing Office, 1979, pp. 145, 159; U.S. Bureau of the Census. *The Social and Economic Status of the Black Population in the United States 1790–1978.* Washington, DC: Government Printing Office, 1979, pp. 89, 92–93; National Center for Education Statistics. *Digest of Education Statistics 1979.* Washington, DC Government Printing Office, 1979, p. 66; and U.S. Department of Commerce. Population Profile of the United States: 1979. *Current Population Reports, 1980, Series P-20. No. 350, p. 17.*

*Data include Black and other racial minorities.

In Chapter 13, Patton provides additional insight into this problem. Given the negative attitude of the public school system toward Black males, as indicated in Table 4, it should be no surprise that their dropout rate was 20.0 percent, compared to 12.4 for white males in 1977.

As shown in Table 4, the data indicate that Black men have been making gains in higher education, but they still lag behind their white counterparts. For example, in 1979, 8.3 percent of Black men 25 years of age and older had four years or more of college, compared to 21.4 percent for white men in that age group. Although there has been an increase in the number of Black men enrolled in college, they are quite a distance from reaching parity with white men. In 1978, 1.0 million Black adults were enrolled in college; of this number, 452,000 were Black men (U.S. Bureau of the Census, 1979a). In other words, Black males represented 44.3 percent of the Black adults enrolled in college. For the white community, males accounted for 52.9 percent of the adult college enrollment. While Black men and women are near parity in regard to college enrollment, Black men still lag behind white men. Once enrolled in college, Black men experience a variety of problems. In Chapter 14, Fleming examines the impact of higher education on Black males.

EMPLOYMENT AND INCOME

How educational attainment benefits Black men is a continuing question that is asked by many in the Black community. Yankelovich (1979:31) in an essay entitled "Who Gets Ahead in America," answered the question in the following manner:

> *If you are "finishing" and have been persuaded to stay in school because "finishing high school will help you find a better job later on," forget what you have been told. Even for whites the economic advantages of finishing high school without going on to college are marginal at best; for Blacks, they count for almost nothing.*

These conclusions are based on findings from a study conducted by Jencks and his colleagues. Apparently, the Black men who drop out of high school are making rational decisions based on these research observations. Nevertheless, the predictions for success in employment and income seem to be better for Black males who go to college. Commenting on this issue, Yankelovich (1979:31) concludes:

> *If you are Black and in college and suspect that finishing college is not going to help you economically, you are wrong. Buckle down, hang in there and finish at all costs. If it's money and a good job you are after, stay in college, no matter how you do it. . . . Economically it does not matter what you study, how you learn or where you go to college—as long as you finish.*

Although data seem to support these assertions, some caution should be exercised in accepting them at face value. Nonetheless, data do show that education, especially at the college level, influences the direction of a number of economic status variables, such as unemployment rates, labor force participation rates, earnings and so forth. Although college education has a positive impact on economic success for Black males, it should be noted that only 8.3 percent of them were college graduates in 1979 (see Table 4).

Given this reality, one should expect a high level of economic frustration for the vast majority of Black men. The data in Table 5 show that the labor force participation rate for civilian Black males has decreased from 83.4 percent in 1959 to 71.9 percent in 1979. For white males, the labor force participation rate was 78.6 percent in 1979. Commenting on the Black male participation rate in the labor market, Stewart and Scott (1978:84) wrote:

> *One source of frustration of employed Black males is the crowding of these workers into low-status occupations of which the associated wage rates are inadequate to provide for a standard of living significantly above the poverty level.*

An examination of the occupational distribution of employed Black males indicates that the majority are blue-collar and service workers. In Table 5, one can observe that in 1977 over one-half (58 percent) of the employed Black males were blue-collar workers, for example, craft, operatives and non-farm laborers—while 17 percent were service workers. It should be noted that 3 percent of Black males were employed as farm workers and 23 percent were employed as white-collar workers (U.S. Bureau of the Census, 1979b). In contrast, during the same year, there were nearly twice as many (42 percent) white males employed in white-collar jobs, while less than half (45 percent) were blue-collar workers and 8 and 4 percent, respectively, were service or farm workers.

Not only have the majority of Black males occupied lower-status jobs than have white males, but they have also experienced high rates of unemployment over the last several decades. During the period of 1954–1974, the unemployment rate for Black males 20 years of age and older was either more than double or slightly less than double that of the white males (U.S. Bureau of the Census, 1979b). As depicted in Table 5, the unemployment rate for Black males 20 years of age and older was 9.1 percent in 1979, but it was only 3.6 percent for white males in this age category. The data in this table also indicate that young Black males have had a much higher unemployment rate than has the Black male population as a whole. In 1979, the unemployment rate for Black males between the ages of 16 and 17 years old was 34.4 percent, but it was only 16.1 percent for white males in the same age category. Furthermore, young Black male veterans also experienced a high level of unemployment. In all cases, the unemployment rate for Black men is substantially higher than that for white men.

When Black men are able to find work, their earnings lag behind those of white men. In 1979, Black males had a median income that was $4,962 less than that of white males; the median incomes of Black and white males, respectively, were $13,068 and $18,030 (U.S. Department of Commerce, 1980a). The gap in median incomes between Black and white men was only $3,830 in 1978. The median income of Black male-headed families was $13,443, compared to $17,848 for their white counterparts in 1977. Further, in the same year, when wives were also in the paid labor force, the median Black family income was $17,078, compared to $20,518 for white families. Studies (Datcher, 1980; Duncan,

Table 5. Economic Profile of Male Population in the United States by Race

	Black Male	White Male
1. Civilian Labor Force Participation rates for persons 16 years and older, 1979*	71.9	78.6
2. Civilian Labor Force Participation rates for persons 16 years and older, 1969*	76.9	80.2
3. Civilian Labor Force Participation rates for persons 16 years and older, 1959*	83.4	83.8
4. Unemployment rates for civilians 20 years and older, 1979	9.1	3.6
5. Unemployment rates of male Vietnam-era nonveterans 20–24 years of age,1979*	20.5	9.8
6. Unemployment rates of male Vietnam-era nonveterans 20–24 years of age, 1979*	15.6	6.9
7. Unemployment rates of persons 18 and 19 years old, 1979*	29.6	12.3
8. Unemployment rates of persons 16 and 17 years old, 1979*34.4 16.1		
9. Median family income, male-headed, 1977	13,443	17,848
10. Percentage of employed men who are white-collar workers, 1977	23.0	42.0
11. Percentage of employed men who are blue-collar workers, 1977	58.0	45.0
12. Percentage of employed men who are service workers, 1977	17.0	8.0
13. Percentage of employed men who are farm workers, 1977	3.0	4.0
14. Victimization of rates for persons 12 and older, crimes of violence, 1977	57.4	45.3
15. Victimization rates for persons 12 and older, robbery, 1977	19.8	7.5

SOURCE: U.S. Department of Labor, *Employment and Training Report of the President.* Washington, DC: Government Printing Office, 1980, pp. 225–226, 230–231, 233–234, 254–255; U.S. Bureau of the Census, *The Social and Economic Status of the Black Population in the United States 1790–1978.* Washington, DC: Government Printing Office, 1979, p. 190, 218; and U.S. Department of Justice. *Criminal Victimization in the United States.* Washington, DC: Government Printing Office,1979, p. 13.

These data include Black and other racial minorities. Blacks represent about 90 percent of those classified as Black and others.

199; Miller, 1966; Siegel, 1965) have shown consistently that black men earn lower wages than do white men working in the same occupation. Commenting on wage differences between Black and white men, Stolzenberg (1975:300) concluded:

> *It has been found repeatedly that Black men are less successful than their white counterparts in "converting" years of schooling into dollars or earnings, even when*

racial differences in schooling, family background, occupation and other factors are taken into consideration. Numerous analyses have also carried the argument that these racial differences in wage returns to schooling are not merely artifacts of hiring discrimination which keep educationally qualified Black men out of the more remunerative occupations; a number of studies have found racial differences in wage returns to schooling within occupational categories.

The economic system generates widespread frustration for many Black males. Due to their high level of unemployment, concentration in low-level occupations and low earnings in comparison to white men, other family members—including wives and children—are forced to enter the labor market or to seek public assistance in order to augment the earnings of the Black male. Even when the wife works, the median income of Black families still lags behind that of white families. For example, in 1978 the family income of Black male-headed households where the wife worked was about the same as that of white male-headed households where the wife did not work (U.S. Bureau of the Census, 1979b). In fact, regardless of the number of wage earners in the family, Blacks earned less than did their white counterparts. Moreover, some data suggest that affirmative action programs in employment have had a negative impact on the economic status of Black males. In their analysis of statistics collected by the Equal Employment Opportunity Commission (EEOC), Brimmer and Company (1980:96) observed:

White women are winning out over Blacks in competing for occupational upgrading. . . . In 1973, white women held 30 percent of the EEOC-reported jobs. By 1978, their participation was up to 31.7 percent. . . . The overall position of Black men actually deteriorated in the same period. They filled 6.4 percent of the jobs in 1973 and 2.6 percent of those in 1978.

It is believed that the Black male's frustration with the economic system leads to his disproportionate involvement with America's criminal justice system. It is assumed that there is a relationship between economic conditions and crime against property. Arrest data suggest that Blacks are arrested disproportionately for offenses that have a functional relationship to economic frustrations. In 1979, for example, 505,754 Blacks were arrested for property crimes. This figure represents 29.4 percent of those arrested for these offenses. In addition, Blacks accounted for 56.9 percent of those arrested for robbery, 52.6 percent of those arrested for prostitution and commercialized vice and 67.9 percent of those arrested for gambling in 1979. Similar statistics hold for offenses such as forgery and counterfeiting, fraud, stolen property (burglary, receiving and processing), and weapons and drug abuse violations (U.S. Department of Justice, 1980).

The data in Table 5 summarize the extent to which Black males are victimized by the economic system as reflected in the high incidence of crime in Black communities. For example, in 1977, the victimization rate for persons aged 12 years and older for crimes of violence was 57.4 percent for Black males, but it was 45.3 percent for white males. The

Table 6. Persons in the U.S. Armed Forces, 1971–1980

Year	Total	White Males	Black Males	White Females	Black Females
1980	2,036,672	1,507,569	358,865	129,374	40,864
1979	1,013,233	1,514,641	348,655	116,994	32,943
1978	2,047,880	1,586,622	327,966	107,775	25,517
1977	2,063,074	1,643,726	301,626	97,555	20,167
1976	2,070,424	1,672,763	288,623	91,165	17,873
1975	2,116,281	1,732,229	287,302	81,681	15,069
1974	2,150,618	1,789,166	286,955	63,562	10,895
1973	2,241,230	1,915,545	270,615	47,995	7,075
1972	2,311,300	2,014,774	252,028	39,279	5,219
1971	2,701,208	2,388,586	270,299	37,656	4,667

SOURCE: U.S. Department of Defense, Equal Opportunity, unpublished data, 1981.

victimization rate for robbery was 7.5 percent for white males aged 12 years old and over, and 19.8 percent for Black males in that age group in 1977. Moreover, Blacks in general have a much higher rate of incarceration than whites have. Further discussion of the impact of the criminal justice system on Black males is contained in Chapter 17. Nonetheless, these data suggest that economic pressures and frustration push a large number of Black males into the criminal justice system, which temporarily separates them from the Black community and their families.

Many Black men who have difficulties dealing with the economic system often join the armed forces. In discussing the involvement of Black men in the military, Stewart and Scott (1978:87) commented, "The pressures which push Blacks into the penal correction system also push them into the enlisted ranks of the military. . . . Blacks that are nonfunctional in the civilian labor market may still be functional in the military establishment." Table 6 indicates that in 1980 there were 358,865 Black males in the military. This figure represents 17.6 percent of the total persons in the military. It is interesting to note that, while the number of white males in the armed forces is on the decline, it has increased for Black males. According to Carl Rowan (1980), Black volunteers for the armed forces have more formal schooling than do white volunteers.

The military experiences of Blacks have both positive and negative components (Moskos, 1973; Moskos & Janowtiz, 1974; Stewart & Scott, 1978). On the positive side, the military provides steady income, good benefits, and opportunity for travel and advancement. On the other hand, Black men are overrepresented in the combat and service units. They have a higher expulsion rate than do their white counterparts. As pointed out in Chapter 18, many Black men are incarcerated in the military. According to Stewart and Scott (1978:88), "channeling Black males into the military, then, complements operations of the public-assistance system in mitigating violent protests against the economic frustrations associated with civilian Blacks. Once Blacks leave the military, however, they are recaptured by civilian institutional decimation.'' The implication is that a large number of Black men have negative interactions in the armed forces. Once they return to civilian life, they continue to experience economic frustrations as reflected in the high unemployment rate for veterans, especially those who served during the Vietnam period (see Table 5). Of course, economic frustration will have consequences for the family life of Black men as well as for their adaptation strategies.

SOCIAL PARTICIPATION

In developing a social profile of Black men, it is important to examine the extent to which they are actively involved in different forms of personal and community associations and activities. Unfortunately, there are not many data on the social participation of Black men. The government and other institutions and individuals have collected a great deal of information on family status, income and employment, health status, crime, education, and so forth. More consideration needs to be given to developing a data base on social participation on the part of Black men and women, for these data will provide us with the necessary information for developing more functional coping strategies for dealing with the negative institutional outcomes from the majority community.

One type of participation where some data have been collected is in the area of politics. In 1980, 68.3 percent of white men reported that they were registered to vote, compared to only 57.2 percent for Black men (see Table 7). In the same year, the majority (60.9 percent) of white men reported that they voted in the 1980 election, but less than half (47.5 percent) of Black men reported that they voted. In other words, in 1980, there were 7.3 million black men of voting age, but only 3.5 million indicated that they voted. Furthermore, 3.1 million black men were not registered to vote in 1980. While one can argue that Black men have some involvement in political activities, the data suggest that the majority of Black men of voting age are not very active in the political process in this country. As shown in Table 7, age has an impact on political behavior of both Black and white men. Younger men are less active in politics than are older men for both racial groups. It is also assumed that income, education, and family background influence political activities for both white and Black men. It is clear, however, that Black men are less likely to be involved in political participation than are white men.

One important outcome of the political process is the election of officials. Table 1.8 shows the number of persons elected at the federal government level. In 1979, white men represented 93.1 percent of the persons in the House of Representatives and 99 percent of the persons in the senate. There were no Black men in the senate, and they represented only 3.2 percent of the persons in the House of Representatives. The picture is about the same for the 97th Congress (1981); that is, both houses of Congress are basically composed of white males. Given their population size, Black people are distressingly underrepresented in the Congress. A similar pattern exists for high-level appointments in all branches of the federal government.

Table 7. Reported Voting and Registration of the Male Population of Voting age by Race, 1980

Age	Percentage Reported Registered		Percentage Reported Voted	
	White Male	Black Male	White Male	Black Male
18–20	45.4	35.6	36.2	25.9
21–24	53.1	42.8	43.5	30.9
25–34	62.4	53.4	55.0	43.8
35–44	70.5	63.4	64.3	54.1
45–54	75.5	62.8	69.3	54.2
55–64	80.4	68.7	74.1	60.1
65–74	81.1	72.2	73.9	63.2
75 and older	77.5	69.6	67.2	54.6
All ages above 18	68.3	57.2	60.9	47.5

Source: U.S. Department of Commerce, Voting and Registration in the Election of November 1980, Current Population Reports (Population Characterstics, Series P. 20, No. 359, advance copy). Washington, DC: Bureau of the Census, January 1981, pp. 4–5.

At the state and local levels of government, Black people are also underrepresented. In 1979, there were 4,607 Black Americans who held popularly elected offices in the United States; of this number, 80 percent were newly elected (Joint Center for Political Studies, 1979). There has been a significant increase in the number of Black elected officials at all levels. For example, in 1969 there were 1,124 Black elected officials, but by 1975 there were 3,503. In 1980 there were over 4,912 Black elected officials in 44 states, the District of Columbia, and the Virgin Islands (''Number of Black Elected Officials up by 6.6 Percent,'' 1980). It should be noted that for federal, state, and local government levels, Black elected women held a larger share of Black elected offices that white women held. Related to this fact is that the proportion of Black men holding elected offices has declined from 88 percent in 1969 to 80 percent in 1980. It is estimated that there are over 490,265 elected state and local government officials (U.S. Bureau of the Census, 1979a). Given this fact, one can observe that Black people are grossly underrepresented at these levels of government. In evaluating the functions of Black elected officials, the Joint Center for Political Studies (1979) concluded:

> *Black elected officials tend to have fewer resources to deal with the problems and needs of their constituents than do white elected officials. At the top levels of government, where elected officials wield considerable power and are routinely provided a variety of professional support services with which to administer their power, there are relatively few Black elected officials.*

Table 8. Members of Congress by Race and Sex, 1979

	Male			Female			Total
	Black	White	Total	Black	White	Total	
Congress							
Representatives	14	404*	418	2	14	16	434
Senators	0	99*	99	0	1	1	100
Representatives	14	503	517	2	15	17	534

SOURCE: Joint Center for Political Studies. *National Roster of Black Elected Officials,* Vol. 9. Washington, DC: Joint Center for Political Studies, 1979; and U.S. Bureau of the Census. *Statistical Abstract of the United States 1979* (100th ed.). Washington, DC: Government Printing Office, 1979, p. 509.

NOTE: Figures exclude vacancies and representatives from the Virgin Islands.

*These figures include other racial groups (1 senators and 3 representatives).

Historically, in the Black community, great emphasis has been placed on the importance of participating in voluntary associations (Laying, 1978; Orum, 1966; Ross and Wheeler, 1971; Yearwood, 1980). According to Tomech (1973:99),

> *studies . . . show higher participation rates for Blacks at all social levels, especially lower class. For whatever reasons, Blacks have indeed become joiners. The rise of a wide range of Black associations in recent years indicates that voluntary associations are not the preserve of the white middle-class. . . . Whatever the case may be, the response of Blacks to segregation appears to be quite the opposite of indifference and apathy.*

Often, Black people including Black men, have used voluntary organizations to solve personal and community problems. In addition, these organizations serve as service centers, information exchanges, forums for job and business-related issues, and support mechanisms in personal development. Hard comparative data on the participation rates of Black and white men in voluntary associations are not available. Nevertheless, we are aware of a variety of organizations that have a high level of involvement on the part of Black men (see the list of some of these organizations in Table 9).

Black men have not held as many executive positions and offices in traditional professional associations and organizations, such as the American Medical Association, American Bar Association, American Economic Association, American Legion, American Dental Association, Chamber of Commerce of the United States, and the National Rifle Association of America, as have white men. It was estimated that in 1978, there were more than 13,589 national associations covering a range of areas such as health, social welfare, commerce and business, public affairs, recreation, labor unions, veterans, and education (U.S. Bureau of the Census, 1979a). For the most part, Black people do not play important roles in these organizations.

In many cases, Blacks have developed their own organizations and associations. The church and fraternal organizations have provided many opportunities for Black men to ex-

Table 9. List of Selected Organizations with High Levels of Black Male Involvement

Business and Commerce
American Association of Blacks in Energy
Interracial Council for Business Opportunity
National Alliance of Postal and Federal Employees
National Association of Black Accountants
National Association of Black Manufacturers
National Association of Broadcasters
National Association of Market Developers
National Association of Minority Contractors
National Association of Real Estate Brokers
National Bankers Association
National Business League
National Funeral Directors and Morticians Association
National Insurance Association
National Newspaper Publishers Association
Opportunities Industrialization Centers of America
United Mortgage Bankers of America
Civic and Civil Rights
Affirmative Action Association of America
Congress of Racial Equality
Congressional Black Caucus
Frontiers International
National Association for the Advancement of Colored People
National Black Veterans Organization
National Conference of Black Lawyers
National Conference of Black Mayors
National Urban League
One Hundred Black Men, Inc.
People United to Save Humanity
Southern Christian Leadership Conference
United Black Fund
Veterans Association, Inc.
Fraternal Organizations
Alpha Phi Alpha Fraternity, Inc.
Ancient and Accepted Rite Masons

writers (Franklin, 1974; Hill, 1972; Staples, 1976) have pointed out the significant role played by Black churches in helping Black people, including men, to cope with societal pressures and stresses. In Chapter 16, Tinney provides us with specific insight into the role of the church in the life of Black men.

Fraternal organizations have been one formal mechanism Black men have used to operationalize the value of mutual aid. According to McPherson et al. (1971:158), "next to the church, the fraternal and mutual benefit societies were the most [important] social institutions in the Black community." In his book, *The Negro in America*, Frazier (1957:378) reached a similar conclusion:

> *The fraternal organizations offered economic relief in time of sickness and provided decent burials. . . . The organization and growth of mutual aid associations and secret fraternal societies among Negroes have been in response to social and economic forces within Negro life as well as the result of the relations of the races.*

In any social profile of Black men, consideration must be given to sports. As with other areas of social participation, there are very little hard data on the participation of the Black male in sports except in professional, collegiate, and secondary school areas. But if one drives through any Black community and observes, there will be some Black males involved in a variety of sports. In the 1975 Health Interview Survey (HIS), there were several questions concerning the participation in sports by adults 20 years old and over (National Center for Health Statistics, 1978). It was discovered that 43.2 percent of white males were involved in at least one type of sport, compared to 29.2 percent for nonwhites. As one would expect, age and income influence the degree to which a person was active in organized sports. Higher-income persons were more likely to be involved in sports than were lower-income parents. As age increases, the level of involvement in sports decreases. Further analysis of data is not possible since the data were not broken down by racial and sex groups. But the data did suggest that Black men are more likely to be involved in basketball than they were to be involved in swimming, tennis, or golf. Bowling, softball, and baseball are also favorite sports of Black men.

Several studies (Anderson, 1976; Liebow, 1967) suggest that Black men spend a great deal of their leisure time in unorganized activities, such as playing checkers and chess, shooting pool, and gambling. These recreational activities take place in pool rooms, bars, and barbershops. Moreover, many Black men spend time in informal settings with their friends, talking and playing around on "the corner" or on "the block." One has to appreciate the fact that these informal networks provide cognitive and affective services to those men who are in need of help. According to Gary (1978:39),

> *Many Black people with personal problems customarily turn t informal organizations. . . . These informal groups . . . such as barbershops, peer groups, gangs, and storefront churches make up the social network of the Black community. . . . These informal organizations . . . have enabled many Blacks to develop the necessary talent for functioning in a hostile racist environment.*

While these informal networks include recreational activities, many Black males are very much involved in professional and semiprofessional sports.

In their book, *Jock: Sports and Male Identity,* Sabo and Runfola (1980) discuss some of the negative consequences of placing so much emphasis on sports in the American society. They examine the interrelationships among sexism, racism, violence, and sports. In most Black communities, one can find young Black males preparing themselves for the professional world of sports. Many Black parents and their male children believe that sports are the most democratic area of our society (Sabo & Runfola, 1980). These parents believe that athletics constitute the main mechanism by which their sons will achieve manhood. The media, especially television, have promoted cultural stereotypes of Black males as athletic and sexual supermen. Although professional sports have helped many Black males to achieve recognition and to earn good salaries, there is ample evidence that Black athletes are victims of racial oppression (Edwards, 1969; Johnson & Marple, 1973; Pascal & Radding, 1972). Commenting on racism in sports, Eitzen and Yetman (1977:13) conclude:

> *Despite some indication of change, discrimination against Black athletes continues in American team sports; sports are not a meritocratic realm where trace is ignored. . . . if discrimination occurs in a public area, one so generally acknowledged to be discrimination free and one where a premium is placed on individual achievement rather than race, how much more subtly pervasive must discrimination be in other areas of American life, where personal interaction is crucial and where the actions of power wielders are not subject to public scrutiny.*

CONCLUDING COMMENTS

The data in this chapter show that there have been notable changes in the demographic and social characteristics of Black men over the past twenty years in comparison to white men. Contrary to myths projected by the media and social science literature, Black men are an integral part of Black communities. As of 1978, there were 12 million Black males, of which 7.3 million were adults, that is,18 years or older. Although there is a growth in the male population, the sex ratio, that is, the number of males per 100 females, has been declining during this century. The imbalance in the sex ratio is particularly problematic for the Black community during the marriage and childbearing ages. Moreover, there has been a significant increase in the number of Black men who are single compared to white men who are single. Given the employment and income conditions of Black men, one can understand why the Black family seems to breaking down.

Many Black men do not earn adequate incomes to provide for their families. Black men have made some gains in higher education and in employment, but data suggest that affirmative action programs directed at white women have eroded some of their advancements. There is much evidence to suggest that the economic frustration of Black men has led some of them to engage in criminal activities in order to support themselves and their families. In addition, many Black men who have difficulties dealing with the economic system join the armed forces, but once enlisted they continue to experience rapid oppression. They learn some skills in the armed forces, but often those skills are not transferable to the civilian world of work. The data show that the unemployment rate is higher for Black than for white veterans. The data also suggest that the basic institutions of our society have developed techniques for systematically making a large percentage of Black males useless for fulfilling their obligations.

Although the government has not collected many data on the social participation of Black males, we were able to identify some areas where they have had a more positive experience. Black men have developed their own voluntary associations and organizations, especially in the areas of fraternities and benefit societies, civic and professional organizations, and the church. In the political area, Black men are grossly underrepresented at all levels of the government. Also, Black men experience considerable discrimination in the area of professional sports. One can conclude that the data indicate that Black men, in comparison to white men, have had a difficult time protecting themselves from the pressures of the major institutions in our society, and these institutional outcomes have had negative consequences for family relationships in Black communities.

REFERENCES

Anderson, E. *A place on the corner.* Chicago: University of Chicago Press, 1976.

Brimer and Company. Facts and figures: A statistical profile of Black economic development. *Black Enterprise,* 1980, *11, 96.*

Carter, H., & Glick, P. *Marriage and divorce: A social and economic study* (Revised edition). Cambridge, MA: Harvard University Press, 1976.

Datcher, L. Effects of community, family and education in earnings of Black and white men. *Review of Black Political Economy,* 1980, *10,* 291–394.

Doddy, II. The progress of the Negro in higher education. *Journal of Negro Education.* 1963, *32*(4), 485.

Duncan, O. Inheritance of poverty or inheritance of race? In D. P. Moynihan (Ed.). *Understanding poverty.* New York: Basic Books, 1969, 85–110.

Edwards, II. *The revolt of the Black athlete.* New York: Macmillan, 1969.

Eitzen, D., & Yetman, N. Immune from racism? Blacks still suffer from discrimination in sports. *Civil Rights Digest, 1977,* 2–13.

Franklin, J. *From slavery to freedom: A history of Negro Americans* (4th edition). New York: Knopf, 1974.

Frazier, E. *The Negro in America* (Rev. ed.). New York: Macmillan, 1957.

Gary, L. (Ed.) *Mental health: A challenge to the Black community.* Philadelphia: Dorrance, 1978.

Gary, L, & Favors, A. (Eds.). Restructuring the educational process: A Black perspective. Washington, DC: Institute for Urban Affairs and Research, 1975.

Glick, P. Marriage and marriage stability among Blacks. *Milbank Memorial Fund Quarterly,* 1970, *63,* 100–103.

Glick, P., & Norton, A. Marrying, divorcing and living together in the U.S. today. *Population Bulletin,* 1979, *32,* 4–38. (Updated reprint)

Gove, W. The relationship between sex roles, marital roles, and mental illness. *Social Forces,* 1972, *51,* 34–44.

Hill, R. *The strengths of Black families.* New York: Emerson Hall, 1972.

Jackson, J. Where are the men? *The Black Scholar,* 1971, *3,* 30–41.

Johnson, N., & Marple, D. Racial discrimination in professional basketball: An empirical test. *Sociological Focus,* 1973, *6,* 6–18.

Joint Center for Political Studies. *National roster of Black elected officials* (Vol. 9). Washington, DC: Author, 1979.

Jones, D., & Matthews, W. (Eds.). *The Black church: A community resource.* Washington, DC: Institute for Urban Affairs and Research, 1977.

Layng, A. Voluntary associations and Black ethnic identity. *Phylon,* 1978, *39,* 171–179.

Liebow, E. *Tally's Corner.* Boston: Little, Brown, 1967.

McPherson, J., Holland, L., Banner, J., Weiss, N., & Bell, M. *Blacks in America: Bibliographic essays.* Garden City, NY: Doubleday, 1971.

Miller, H. *Income distribution in the United States,* Washington, DC: Government Printing Office, 1966.

Moskos, C. The American dilemma in uniform: Race in the armed forces. *Annals of the American Academy of Political and Social Science,* 1973, *406,* 94–106.

Moskos, C., & Janowtiz, M. Racial composition in the all volunteer force. *Armed Forces and Society,* 1974, *I,* 109–123.

National Center for Education Statistics. *Digest of education statistics 1979.* Washington, DC: Government Printing Office, 1979.

National Center for Health Statistics. Exercise and participation in sports among persons 20 years of age and over: United States. *Advance Data,* 1978, *19.*

Number of Black elected officials up by 6.6 percent. *Focus,* 1980, *8* (12), 6.

Orum, A. A reappraisal of the social and political participation of Negroes. *American Journal of Sociology,* 1966, *76,* 32–46.

Pascal, A., & Radding, Z. The economics of racial discrimination in organized baseball. In A. Pascal (Ed.), *Racial discrimination in economic life.* Lexington, MA: D. C. Heath, 1972.

Ploski, H., & Kaiser, E. *The Negro almanac.* New York: Bellwether, 1971.

Raspberry, W. Boys: Endangered species? *The Washington Post,* March 1979, p. A23.

Rodgers-Rose, L. *The Black woman.* Beverly Hills, CA: Sage Publications, 1980.

Rosen, B., Goldsmith, H., & Redick, R. Demographic and social indicators: Uses in mental health planning in small areas. *World Health Statistics,* 1979, *32*(1), 11–102.

Ross, J., & Wheeler, R. *Black belonging: A study of social correlates of work relations among Negroes.* Westport, CT: Greenwood, 1971.

Rowan, C. Moshe Dayan insults Black GIs. *New York Amsterdam News,* December 1980, p. 17.

Sabo, D., & Runfola, R. *Jock: Sports and male identity.* Englewood Cliffs, NJ: Prentice-Hall, 1980.

Siegal, J. *Estimates of coverage of the population by sex, race and age in the 1970 census.* Paper presented at the annual meeting of the Population Association of America, New Orleans, Louisiana, April 26, 1973.

Siegal, P. On the cost of becoming a Negro. *Sociological Inquiry,* 1965, *35,* 41–57.

Staples, R. *Introduction to Black sociology.* New York: McGraw-Hill, 1976.

Stewart, J., & Scott, J. The institutional decimation of Black American males. *Western Journal of Black Studies,* 1978, *2,* 82–92.

Stolzenberg, R. Education, occupation and wage differences between white and Black men. *American Journal of Sociology,* 1975, *81,* 299–323.

Tomeh, A. Formal voluntary organizations: Participation, correlates and interrelationships. *Sociological Inquiry,* 1973, *43*(3), 89–110.

U.S. Bureau of the Census. *Statistical abstract of the United States: 1979* (100th ed.). Washington, DC: Government Printing Office, 1979. (a).

U.S. Bureau of the Census. *The social and economic status of the Black population in the United States 1790–1978* (Special Studies Series P-23), No. 80). Washington, DC: Government Printing Office, 1979. (b)

U.S. Department of Commerce. *Social indicators 1976.* Washington, DC: Government Printing Office, 1977.

U.S. Department of Commerce. Money, income and poverty status of families and persons in the United States: 1979. *Current Population Reports* 1980, Series P-60. No. 125, advance report. (a)

U.S. Department of Commerce. Populations profile of the United States: 1979. *Current Population Reports,* 1980, Series P-20, No. 350, p. 17. (b)

U.S. Department of Commerce. Voting and registration in the election of November 1980. *Current Population Reports, Population Characteristics,* 1981, Series P-20, No. 359, advance copy.

U.S. Department of Defense. Washington, DC: Department of Defense, Equal Opportunity, 1981. (Unpublished data)

U.S. Department of Justice. *Criminal victimization in the United States.* Washington, DC: Government Printing Office, 1979.

U.S. Department of Justice. *Crime in the United States.* Washington, DC: Government Printing Office, 1980.

U.S. Department of Labor. *Employment and training report of the president.* Washington, DC: Government Printing Office, 1980.

Yankelovich, D. Who gets ahead in America. *Psychology Today,* July 1979, pp. 28–34;40–44.

Yearwood, L. (Ed.) *Black organizations: Issues and survival techniques.* Lanham, MD: University Press of America, 1980.

Some Demographic Characteristics of the Black Woman: 1940 to 1975

La Frances Rodgers-Rose

Many myths exist about the overall status of the Black woman in American society. Some scholars would suggest that the Black woman has reaped benefits from society while the Black male fell further behind her socially and economically. One way we can begin to piece together the recent history and conditions of the Black woman is to analyze her status through the use of government statistics, recognizing that statistics are imperfect. One can see the imperfection of government statistics by analyzing the sex ratio of the Black population. For example, the Census Bureau recognized as early as 1861 that there was an undercount of the Black population in the 1860 census. They also admit that the undercount existed in the 1870 and 1880 census, but no corrections were ever made of these statistics. It is the male population that is undercounted more often than the female population. In viewing the data from Table 2, the reader must keep in mind the general undercount of the Black population.

Taking the last official census, 1970, we find that 1.88 million Blacks were not counted in that census. This accounted for 7.7 percent of the total Black population. For whites, 1.9 percent of the population was missed. It is suggested that one out of every eight Black males 20 years and older was missed in both 1970 and 1960. This means that the sex ratio is not as drastic as it might at first appear. Jacob Siegel of the Bureau of the Census, writing in 1973, suggested 627,000 Black men between the ages of 20 and 44 were missed by the census in comparison to only 214,000 Black women (Siegel, 1973). It is in this age group that the greatest discrepancy exists in the male-female ratio. It was data from the 1970 census that led Jacquelyne Jackson to ask the question, "But Where Are the Men?"

Table 1. Undercount of the Black Population, 1970, Ages 20–40 (in thousands)

Age Group	Census Count		Midrange Correction	
	Male	Female	Male	Female
20–24	1,045	1,160	116	54
25–34	1,423	1,673	278	105
35–44	1,106	1,226	233	55
Totals	3,574	4,169	627	214

Our answer to that question is that many men were never counted. Table 1 shows Siegel's midrange corrections of the 20- to 44-year age group.

In that age group, rather than a count of 3,574, the midadjusted count based on the birth and death specific rates for each subgroup, the count would be 4,201 for males. For the female population the adjustments are not as great, showing that Black males are missed nearly three times as often as Black women. The 1970 census showed 4,169 females in the above age group, and the adjusted count is 4,383.

Table 2. Black Population by Sex and Sex Ratio, 1820–1974*

Year	Male	Female	Sex Ratio
1820	900,796	870,860	1,034
1840	1,432,988	1,440,660	995
1860	2,216,744	2,225,086	996
1890	3,735,603	3,753,073	995
1910	4,885,881	4,941,882	989
1930	5,855,669	6,035,474	970
1940	6,269,038	6,596,480	950
1950	7,269,170	7,757,505	937
1960	9,097,704	9,750,915	933
1970	10,748,316	11,831,973	908
1974	11,452,000	12,592,000	909

*All statistical tables are from the U.S. Department of Commerce, Bureau of the Census, *Historical Statistics of the United States: Colonial Times to 1970,* House Document No. 93-78; and Current Population Reports, Special Studies Series P-23, No. 54, *The Social and Economic Status of the Black Population in the United States, 1970, 1973, and 1974.*

Therefore, instead of the sex ratio of 857 for this age group, which says that for every 1,000 Black women in the age group of 20–44, there are only 857 males in the same age group. The adjusted rate, based on Siegel's data is 958. This sex ratio is significantly different from the official 1970 census count.

Analyzing the male-female sex ratio is very important to the survival of Black people in general, and the Black female specifically. For some people would have us believe that there is a drastic shortage of Black males. It is indeed true that there is a difference in the sex ratio, but the difference is not as great as we have been led to believe. Siegel's data also suggest that the sex ratio has not changed significantly since 1940. One should note in Table 2 the significant drop in the sex ratio between 1910 and 1930 and again between 1930 and 1940. Part of the undercount for these censuses must be explained by the changing distribution of the Black population. As men and women began the mass migration from the south to the north, many were "lost" in the great exodus north. However, there has been no systematic attempt on the part of the Bureau of the Census to correct these past statistics. Given the data in Table 2, we must be very cautious in accepting census data without careful analysis.

One of the things we can see from the census count of the population is that Black females live longer than Black males. In part, the differences in life expectancy account for the uneven sex ratio. That is, although more males are born, women live longer than men. The differences in the life expectancy of Black men and women can be seen in Table 3. This table also shows the progress Blacks have made in the past 70 years in increasing their life expectancy. Specifically, we can see that the Black female has gone from a life expectancy of 33.5 years in 1900 to 69.4 years in 1970. On the average, Black women are living eight years longer than the white man.The lowest life expectancy rate is for the Black man, who is expected to live a little over 61 years. His life expectancy is seven years less than that of the white male.

Most of the increase in the life expectancy of Blacks can be accounted for by the tremendous drop in the infant mortality rate that whites reached more than 25 years ago (see Table 4). In 1973, the infant mortality rate was 26.2 for Blacks. Whites had a rate of 15.8, and in 1950 the rate was 26.8 for whites. Blacks still fall behind whites in these vital statistics. The poor economic conditions of Blacks account for these differences. Without economic resources, Blacks cannot afford the doctors needed to maintain health, nor can they buy the kinds of food that would ensure their physical health.

Education is a key factor in determining the economic resources of Black people, and whites continue to outdistance Blacks in education. Rather than the question of whether Black women receive more education than Black men, the crucial question is to what extent Blacks have been able to close the educational gap between Blacks and whites. In viewing Table 5, we find that in 1850, more than half of the white population was enrolled in school, compared with less than two percent of the Black population. By 1970, an equal number of Blacks and whites were enrolled in school. However, this does not mean that an equal number of Blacks and whites finish high school, or that the average number of years of schools completed is the same. As late as 1940, the Black female had completed an average of 6.1 years of school, and the Black male had completed 5.4 years. By 1970, the white male and female had graduated from high school, averaging over twelve years of schooling. We can further see that the educational attainment of Black women did not nor does it differ from Black males significantly. That is, what difference does it make, economically or socially, if the Black male finished 9.6 years?

Table 3. Expectation of Life at Birth by Race and Sex, 1900–1970

Year	Male		Female	
	White	Black	White	Black
1970	68.0	61.3	75.6	69.4
1960	67.4	61.1	74.1	66.3
1950	66.5	59.1	72.2	62.9
1940	62.1	51.5	66.6	54.9
1930	59.7	47.3	63.5	49.2
1920	54.4	45.5	55.6	45.2
1910	48.6	33.8	52.0	37.5
1900	46.6	32.5	48.7	33.5

Table 4. Infant Mortality Rates by Race, 1940–1973 (per 1,000)

Year	Black	White
1973	26.2	15.8
1970	30.9	17.8
1965	40.3	21.5
1960	43.2	22.9
1950	44.5	26.8
1940	73.8	43.2

Table 5. School Enrollment Rates Per 100 Population by Sex and Race, 1850–1970

Year	Male		Female	
	White	Black	White	Black
1970	91.9	89.6	89.7	89.1
1960	90.6	86.6	87.3	85.7
1950	79.7	74.7	78.9	74.9
1940	75.9	67.5	75.4	69.2
1930	71.4	59.7	70.9	60.8
1920	65.6	52.5	65.8	54.5
1910	61.4	43.1	61.3	46.6
1900	53.4	29.4	53.9	32.8
1890	58.5	31.8	57.2	33.9
1880	63.5	34.1	60.5	33.5
1870	56.0	9.6	52.7	10.0
1860	62.0	1.9	57.2	1.8
1850	59.0	2.0	53.3	1.8

Table 6. Median Years of School Completed by Sex and Race, 1940–1970

Year	Male		Female	
	White	Black	White	Black
1970	12.2	9.6	12.2	10.2
1960	10.6	7.9	11.0	8.5
1950	9.3	6.4	10.0	7.2
1940	8.7	5.4	8.8	6.1

Table 7. Percentage of the Black Population Over 25 with At Least Some High School by Sex, 1940–1970

Year	1–3 Years High School		Graduated High School		1–3 Years College		4 + Years College	
	Male	Female	Male	Female	Male	Female	Male	Female
1970	20.6	23.5	22.4	24.6	6.2	6.4	6.8	5.6
1966	20.1	24.0	17.4	21.2	5.3	5.4	5.0	4.4
1959	14.7	19.6	11.5	14.7	3.7	3.5	3.6	2.9
1950	11.6	14.4	7.2	8.9	2.8	3.1	2.0	2.3
1940	7.3	9.8	3.8	5.0	1.6	2.1	1.4	1.2

Table 8. Percentage of the Population Over 25 Who Completed Four or More Years of College by Race and Sex, 1940–1974

Year	Black		White	
	Male	Female	Male	Female
1974	8.8	7.6	24.9	17.2
1970	6.8	5.6	15.0	8.6
1966	5.0	4.4	13.3	7.7
1960	3.5	3.6	10.3	6.0
1947	2.0	2.6	6.5	4.8
1940	1.4	1.2	5.8	4.0

If one looks at those persons over 25 years of age who graduated from college (Table 7), there is very little difference between males and females. In none of these figures do we see such drastic differences that would call for the kind of theorizing that exists about why Black women are more "educated" than Black males. Nor do we see the kind of data that suggest that Black daughters have been preferred over Black sons in terms of education. The fact is that both Black men and women have very similar educational levels compared with white men and women. For example, in 1940, 4.0 percent of the white females and 5.8

percent of the white males had graduated from college. This was true for only 1.2 percent of the Black females and 1.4 percent of the Black males. By 1970, the number of Black women graduating from college had increased, but so had the number of whites, and the differences by race were still larger than the differences by sex; 5.6 percent Black females and 6.8 percent Black males had completed four years of college. This was true for 8.6 percent of the white females and 15.0 percent of the white males. What we note in these statistics is the great difference between the white male and female. There has been a tendency for white social scientists to look at near parity in the college education of Blacks and see that as a disadvantage for Black males, since white females do not graduate from college nearly as often as white males. Whatever disagreements might exist between Black males and females cannot be blamed on the excessive educational advantage of Black women.

One must ask what the educational advancement of Black women has meant to them. In looking at Table 9, we can see the significant changes that have taken place in the occupational structure of Black women. In 1964, more than half of all employed Black women were service workers, and 33 percent of them were in private household work. By 1974, the number of service workers had decreased to 37 percent and 11 percent of all Black women were in private household work. Over the 10-year period there has been little change in the number of white women in service work—19 percent—or the number in private household service—from 5 to 3 percent. The number of Black women in professional or technical fields rose from 8 percent in 1964 to 12 percent in 1974. For white women, the percentage has remained the same; 15. Very few women, Black or white, are found in managerial jobs—2 percent for Blacks and 5 percent for whites. There has been an increase of over 100 percent in the number of Black women in clerical jobs: The percentage has gone from 11 in 1964 to 25 in 1974; whereas, again,the percentage for white women over the 10-year period has remained about the same, a little over one-third of all employed white women. What we see from Table 9 is that the Black woman has seen significant changes in her employment pattern over the past 10 years: She has left the field of service workers in significant numbers and gone into the clerical field. However, the largest number of Black women is still found in service work. From Table 9, we also note that more Black women than men are in professional and technical fields. What one must remember is that of the 12 percent of Black women who are professional, 42 percent of these were teachers (excluding college). This was true for only 22 percent of the Black males.

Although the employment pattern of the Black woman has changed, she is still more often unemployed than the Black male, white female, or white male. Table 10 shows the unemployment rates from 1948 to 1970 by race and sex. First, one can see that the unemployment rate of Blacks is much higher than the rate for whites. Further, Black women, on the whole, have a higher unemployment rate than Black men. Whereas the unemployment rat for whites is about 4.5 percent, it is almost 8.0 percent for Blacks. This rate does not reflect the underemployment of Black men and women. We know that gains have been made in the occupational and educational fields, but Blacks are more often hired in jobs for which they are overqualified.

Table 9. Occupation of Employed Men and Women by Race, 1964, 1970, and 1974 (in percentages)*

	1964		1970		1974	
	Black	White	Black	White	Black	White
WOMEN						
White-collar workers	23	61	38	64	42	63
Professional & tech.	8	14	11	15	12	15
Teachers, except college	5	6	5	6	5	6
Mgrs. & admin.	2	5	3	5	2	5
Sales workers	2	8	3	8	3	7
Clerical workers	11	34	21	36	25	36
Blue-collar workers	15	17	19	16	20	15
Service workers	56	19	43	19	37	19
Private household	33	5	18	3	11	3
Farm workers	6	3	2	2	1	2
Total	100	100	100	100	100	100
MEN						
White-collar workers	16	41	22	43	24	42
Professional & tech.	6	13	8	15	9	15
Teachers, except college	1	1	1	2	2	2
Mgrs. & admin.	3	15	5	15	5	15
Sales workers	2	6	2	6	2	6
Clerical workers	5	7	7	7	7	6
Blue-collar workers	58	46	60	46	57	46
Service workers	16	6	13	6	15	7
Farm workers	10	7	6	5	4	5
Total	100	100	100	100	100	100

*Percentages may not equal 100 due to rounding.

Table 10. Unemployment Rates by Race and Sex, 1948–1974

Year	Male		Female	
	Black	White	Black	White
1974	8.4	4.3	10.1	5.9
1970	7.3	4.0	9.3	5.4
1965	7.4	3.6	9.2	5.0
1960	10.7	4.8	9.4	5.3
1955	8.8	3.7	8.4	4.3
1950	9.4	4.7	8.4	5.3
1948	5.8	3.4	6.1	5.9

Table 11. Median Money Wage or Salary Income of Year-Round Full-Time Workers, by Sex and Race, 1939–1975

Year	Male		Female	
	Black	White	Black	White
1975	$10,000	$12,961	$7,486	$7,617
1973	7,953	11,800	5,595	6,598
1970	6,598	9,373	4,674	5,490
1965	4,367	6,814	2,713	3,960
1960	3,789	5,662	2,372	3,410
1955	2,831	4,458	1,637	2,870
1939	639	1,419	327	863

The underemployment of Black women and men can be seen in the median income of year-round full-time workers. What one notes in Table 11 is that Black women have consistently earned less than white men, Black men, and white women. Therefore, it is unfair to suggest that Black women have somehow managed to outdistance Black men in earnings; this has never been the case. Not only does the Black woman earn less than any other group, but, as noted above, she is more often unemployed. For example, in 1975, the white male earned an average of $12,961 per year; the Black male earned $10,000. The Black female was earning only $7,486 while the white female earned $7,167. Although the earning power of Black and white females is near equal, one must keep in mind that Black women stay in the economic marketplace longer. Unlike white women, they tend to remain in the job market until their children start school. They must work for low wages, even if they do not want to. The economic institution has greater impact on Black people in general and the Black woman specifically.

Another area of interest to Blacks is political participation (see Table 12). Again, the impression might be that Black women are more active in politics than are Black men. However, the data collected by the Joint Center for Political Studies show this is far from the truth. In 1975, only 13.1 of all Blacks elected officially were female, and the majority of them were in the field of education. Of the 530 Black females elected officials, 214 of them were in education. There is a tendency to pay undue attention to Black females who hold high elected positions and to assume they represent what Black women are doing nationally. For example, we fail to see that of the 18 U.S. Representatives only four are female. Black women are participating in the political process, but not at the same rate as men. Blacks in general make up less than five percent of all U.S. Senators and Representatives. Therefore, we can begin to see that Blacks are severely underrepresented given their population size, and Black women are the minority in the elected group that does exist.

What kind of impact has the above data had on the Black family? We find that for the most part, the impact has been negative. Table 13 shows that, since 1950, the number of husband-wife families has dropped from 77.7 percent to 60.9 percent in 1975—a per-

Table 12. Black Elected Officials by Sex and Type of Office,May 1975*

Total 4,033	Male 3,503(84.9%)	Female 530(13.1%)
U.S. Senators and Representatives	18(81.8%)	4(18.2%)
State legislators and executives	281	35(11.1%)
Mayors	135	9(6.2%)
Others	3,069	482(13.6%)
County	305	31(9.2%)
Municipal	1,438	203(12.4%)
Law enforcement	387	34(8.1%)
Education	939	214(18.6%)

*SOURCE: Joint Center for Political Studies

Table 13. Percentage Distribution of Black and White Families by Type, 1950–1975

Year	Husband-Wife		Female Headed		Other Male	
	Black	White	Black	White	Black	White
1950	77.7	88.0	17.6	8.5	4.7	3.5
1955	75.3	87.9	20.7	9.0	4.0	3.0
1960	73.6	88.7	22.4	8.7	4.0	2.6
1965	73.1	88.6	23.7	9.0	3.2	2.4
1970	68.1	88.7	28.3	9.1	3.7	2.3
1971	65.6	88.3	30.6	9.4	3.8	2.3
1972	63.8	88.2	31.8	9.4	4.4	2.3
1973	61.4	87.8	34.6	9.6	4.0	2.5
1974	61.8	87.7	34.0	9.9	4.2	2.4
1975	60.9	86.9	35.3	10.5	3.9	2.6

centage change of nearly 17 points in 25 years. Conversely,the number of Black women heading households has increased from 17.6 percent in 1950 to 35.3 percent in 1975. For whites, the change has been only two percentage points—from 8.5 percent in 1950 to 10.5 percent in 1975. When one views the increase in the number of female-headed households the assumption is, quite often, that the increase is due to the break-up of already existing relationships. Table 14 reveals that the greatest change has come about in the single, never-married category, where percentage has gone from 12 in 1960 to 20 in 1973. Over this 13-year period there was a change of 66 percent. The category of separated or divorced accounted for a 25-percent change, going from 40 percent in 1960 to 49 percent in 1973. That is, marital discord does not account for 50 percent of the female-headed households. We can see other changes taking place in Black families by looking at Table 14, which shows

Table 14. Marital Status of Black Female Heads of Families, 1960, 1967, 1970, and 1973 (in percentages)

Marital Status	1960	1967	1970	1973
Single (never married)	12	12	16	20
Separated or divorced	40	47	48	49
Separated	29	33	34	33
Divorced	11	13	14	16
Husband temporarily absent	6	7	7	4
Armed forces	—	2	2	1
Other reasons	6	5	4	3
Widowed	42	35	30	28
Percentage	100	100	100	100

Table 15. Percentage of Ever-Married Women Not Living with Spouse Because of Marital Discord,1950–1973

Year	Separated		Divorced	
	Black	White	Black	White
1950	11	2	3	3
1951	9	2	3	3
1952	10	1	3	3
1953	8	2	4	3
1954	14	1	4	3
1955	12	2	3	3
1956	11	2	4	3
1957	10	1	4	4
1958	12	2	3	3
1959	14	2	4	3
1960	11	2	5	3
1961	11	2	5	3
1962	11	2	5	3
1963	11	2	6	3
1964	12	2	5	4
1965	12	2	5	4
1966	11	2	5	4
1967	11	2	5	4
1968	12	2	6	4
1969	12	2	6	5
1970	13	2	6	4
1973	15	2	8	5

the percentage of ever-married women not living with husbands because of marital discord. In 1950, 14 percent of ever-married Black women were not living with husbands because of marital discord. By 1960, the percentage has risen to 16 and by 1970 it was 19 percent. It took 20 years to show a percentage point difference of four in this category. However, it took only three years to go from 19 percent in 1970 to 23 percent in 1973.

It is obvious from these data that something is happening in the society which accounts for the drastic ahnges in the number of married Black women not living with their husbands because of marital discord. Likewise, we need to study the causes for the large increase in single, never-married Black women. We know that a large nubmer of single female-headed households include children: In 1974, 70 percent of all such households included children, and these households accounted for 39 percent of all black children under 18 years of age. Further, in 1960, 75 percent of all Black children lived with both parents; by 1970, the percentage was down to 64; and for the first time in 1976, less than half of all Black children lived with both parents. Whites have also seen a change in the nujmber of children living with both parents. In 1960, 92 percent of all white children under 18 lived both parents; in 1970 it was 90 percent, and by 1977 it was down to 79 percent—a percentage drop of 11 points in seven years. Some authorities suggest that the changes in the white family are due to the changes in women's status brought on by the women's liberation movement. The same line of reasoning has not been suggested to explain the changes in Black families and the lives of Black children. Rather, the changes have been viewed as indications of family disorganization without looking for the cuases other than the acting individuals. However, we know that the one factor which accounts for the greatest variance in the number of Black children living with both parents is income. In Table 16, we can readily see the difference income makes in the number of Black children living with both parents, For families with incomes over $15,000, 90 percent of all Black children live with both parents. Since slightly more than half of all Black children live with one parent, we can be sure that the vast majority of these children are in households below the poverty level. For example, the median family income for a Black male-headed household was $7,766 in 1974, while a Black female-headed household had an income level of $3,576. In 1974, 52.8 percent of all Black female-headed households were below the poverty level. This was true for only 24.9 percent of all white female-headed households and 14.2 percent for all Black male-headed households. What these data show is that Black women who are heading households are living in or near poverty and raising children who do not have the basic necessities of life. Rather than malign these women, we need to systematically study their needs and their coping strategies, and help develop ways to give them the income they need to live decent lives.

The data in this chapter show that significant changes have taken place in the lives of Black women on a national demographic level. Most of these changes can be tied to the urbanization process. Although poor and living in an oppressive economic system, it would seem that Black women and their families were able to maintain certain stabilities within the family. More wives and husbands stayed together and worked to maintain a family. The urban move has meant that Black women are still poor, but, unlike their forebears they no

Table 16. Own Children Under 18 by Presence of Parents and Family Income, 1974

Income	Black		White	
	Both Parents	One Parent	Both Parents	One Parent
Under $4,000	18	82	39	61
4,000–5,999	35	65	66	34
6,000–7,999	53	47	77	23
8,000–9,999	78	22	88	12
10,000–14,999	86	14	94	6
15,000 and over	90	10	97	3

longer have the land on which to raise their food. The urban environment has imposed a structure which tends to separate wives from their husbands. The welfare state will not "support" struggling families; aid is only given to dependent children. Therefore, from 1940 to 1975, we have witnessed a drastic increase in the number of children living with both parents. In 1976, less than 50 percent of all Black children lived with both parents. We know that in the vast majority of case these are po or Black children, living with poor Black mothers. For example, we see that only 18 percent of all Black children living in families with less than $4,000 per year were with both parents, whereas 90 percent of all Black children who were in families with incomes over $15,000 were living with both parents in 1974. The economic system is destroying the poor Black family.

We have also seen that the life experience of Black women has changed significantly over the past 40 years. She can expect to live on an average of 70 years. If the Black female can survive the first year of life, her life expectancy does not differ significantly from the white female. Also, we noted that there is a difference in the Black male-female sex ratio, with more women than men present. However, we say that in every census the Black male population is undercounted more often than the female population. When we correct for the undercount, the sex ratio is not as drastic as it might first appear.

Finally, it was noted that significant changes can be seen in the educational levels of Black women. From 1940 to 1970, the average number of years of school completed increased by four. However, the Black had still only completed 10.2 years of school in 1970.

Additionally, changes occurred in the kinds of jobs held by Black women. They are no longer exclusively in service occupations. In fact, from 1964 to 1974, the number of women in private household jobs declined to 11 percent in 1974. A larger number of Black women are now in the clerical field. Only 12 percent of all Black female workers are in professional and technical occupations, and nearly 50 percent of them are teachers below the college level. Black women continue to earn less money than Black or white men and, although they work more frequently and remain in the labor force longer, they still earn less than white females.

It is very difficult to justify the concept of the positive-negative force of being Black and female from these data. One cannot see the positive advantages. The data show that Black women still comprise the most destitute group—educationally, economically, and politically. These institutions are affecting Black women in such a way that the very survival of the Black family is being threatened, and the survival of Black children is becoming more and more doubtful. Unless our children can survive both physically and mentally, we as a people can no longer survive.

REFERENCES

Farley, R. (1970) Growth of the Black Population: A Study of Demographic Trends. Chicago: Markham.

U.S. Dept. of Commerce, Bureau of the Census (1976) Historical Statistics of the United States: Colonial Times to 1970. House Document No. 93-78. Washington, DC: US. Government Printing Office.

________(1979) Current Population Reports, Special Studies Series P-23, No. 54, The Social and Economic Status of the Black Population in the United States. Washington, DC: U.S. Government Printing Office.

Siegal, J. S. (1973) "Estimates of coverage of the population by sex, race, and age in the 1970 Census." Presented at the annual meeting of the Population Association of America, New Orleans, Louisiana, April 26.

CHAPTER THREE

Sex and Gender Issues

Algea Harrison sees growing up as a Black and as a female to be a dilemma shaped by the political-economic subsystem that lead to the development of feminine and masculine role traits. She discusses how the Black female attempts to resolve the dilemma of femininity and how achievement goals. A review is made of the Black female's aspirations and accomplishments, and an analysis is made of differences between Black and white females.

Betty Collier-Watson, Louis Williams and Willy Smith investigate sexism and its effects upon gender differences. Gender differences are viewed as both favorable and unfavorable to women. In a systematic sense, women lose because of the inequalities that characterize the operation of social institutions. Conversely, in a vitalistic manner, men lose because their morbidity and morality rates are higher than those of women. It is demonstrated that when men lose, Black men lose the most. Thus, sexism is seen as a two-edged sword. Women gain in some areas and lose in others. It is concluded that Black men and women gain the least and lose the most of the sex-race groups.

Bogart Leashore notes the ways in which racism and ideologies affect the development of racist social policies. This work illustrates how social policies operate to maintain racial inequality, especially with respect to Black males. It is shown how domestic policies related to taxes and budget cuts have differentially affected Black families and how racism and ideologies have influenced the development of social policies in the United States. Health care, employment and income support, and crime and justice are three areas delineated for alternative social policies.

An Alternative Analysis of Sexism: Implications for the Black Family

Betty Collier-Watson • Louis N. Williams
Willy Smith

INTRODUCTION

Over the past two decades since the mid-sixties, it has become quite popular for Black writers to engage in debunking of myths concerning the Black family. The reasons are obvious. The ideational content of knowledge is always socially determined and human thought has historically served as a critical instrument in the institutionalization of inequality. Thus, it has been incumbent on Black social Scientists to inquire, explicate, and reiterate thoughts, ideas, and analyses towards a more accurate understanding of the Black family.

Such a task is, however, a difficult one. On societies characterized by inequalities, an epistemological catch-22 exists. On the one hand, various groups within the society may seek to be involved in the advocacy of measures to ameliorate social dysfunction to the degree that such a state is socially produced. Yet, in order to intermediate, a body of knowledge must exist that accurately reflects the magnitude and nature of the dysfunction so that programs and policies can be teleologically related to causes. However, when inequality exists within a society, the inequalities are so far-reaching that the disadvantaged groups are also underrepresented in the production and distribution of knowledge about their own condition. Furthermore, their disadvantaged status is often so psychosocially entrenched that they often fall victim to the same epistemological myopia that tailors the knowledge produced and distributed by the dominant group. The thesis herein is that over the last two decades the stability of the Black family and of Black male/female relationships has been reduced because Black social scientists have failed in promoting accurate discourse about the interactive relationship of race, gender, and class. Indeed, not only white but also Black social scientists have promoted the axiomatic view that race and sex have operated and continue to operate as parallel systems of oppression. Such a view has not leapt into Black consciousness. Rather, Black scholarship regarding sexism and sex role modeling has tended to play the role of passive beneficiary to the models and paradigms of sexism that have been promoted by white scholarship.

Accordingly, the tasks herein are several. At the first level, the objective of this discussion is that of examining the functioning of sexism between Black males and females. To accomplish this task, however, it is necessary too reanalyze and reconceptualize the functioning of sex role asymmetry in U.S. society.

SEX ROLE ASYMMETRY: A CONTEMPORARY PROFILE

For the most part, Black social scientists have adopted what can be called a unilateral model of sexism. A unilateral conception of the operation of sexism postulates that U.S. society is characterized by sex role asymmetry (inequality). Implicit within this conception is the view that this asymmetrical arrangement is one in which females lose and males gain. Indeed, inequalities of sex are viewed as constituting a system of male dominance. United States society is also characterized by forms of asymmetry based on race and class. These phenomena are similarly viewed as operating n such a fashion that inequalities emerge with gains accruing to the dominant race and/or class. For the purposes of the analysis herein, inequalities emerging as a consequence of the operation of sex, class, and/or race within a society will be separated into two separate but related categories. Those inequalities that characterize the operation of social institutions can be denoted as systemic inequalities. In contrast, those inequalities that characterize the chances of survival among the members of a given society will be called vitalistic.

Societies exist to enhance the chances of survival of its members. *Thus, the ultimate test of the impact of asymmetry on a given group in a society cannot be completely measured by an examination of the asymmetrical functioning of social institutions. Rather, the ultimate impact of asymmetry in that society reveals itself through the impact on the length and quality of survival.* Such a statement implies that systemic and vitalistic inequalities are *directly* related. That is, systemic gains ar reflected in vitalistic gains. Conversely, systemic losses are reflected in vitalistic losses.

Empirical data support this assumption when asymmetries based on social class are examined. In U.S. society individuals of the lower classes experience systemic inequalities. Indeed, they receive unequal benefits from the major pivotal institutions. Such groups receive less income and wealth (Krauss, 1976; Miller and Roby, 1977). Additionally, members of the lower classes have less political power and influence (Turner and Starnes, 1976). Such a pattern extends itself into the educational institutions. Children of lower-class families graduate from high school 250% less often, attend college 400% less often, graduate from college 600% less often; and receive postgraduate training 900% less often (Sewell, 1971). Also, the lower classes have more children and more divorces (Krauss, 1976). Such systemic inequalities are directly correlated with a similar vitalistic trend.

Lower classes in the United States have lower life expectancies and higher death rates (Tumin, 1967; U.S. Department of Health, Education, and Welfare, 1976). Similarly, individuals within these classes experience a higher incidence of psychosis (Faris and Durham, 1939; Hollingshead and Redlich, 1958). Surveys reveal that lower-class individuals report less happiness (Bradburn and Caplovitz, 1965) and more job boredom and dissatisfaction (Chinoy, 1955; Wooten, 1974). Lastly, lower-class individuals experience higher rates of crime as victim and victimizer and higher death rates from all major diseases (Collier and Smith, 1981). Indeed, when class asymmetry is examined, the direct relationship between systemic and vitalistic inequalities is most apparent.

Without detailing the data, it can be said that a similar direct relationship between systemic and vitalistic variables exists by race. Not only do minority groups have lower median family incomes, higher levels of unemployment, and disproportionate rates of poverty, but they also have: (1) lower life expectancies, (2) higher rates of crimes as victims and victimizers, (3) higher rates of criminal conviction, (4) higher divorce rates, (5) higher death rates from all major diseases, and so on, than do nonminority groups (Collier and Smith, 1981).

When sex role asymmetry is examined from such a perspective, however,, and systemic as well as vitalistic variables are considered, a dual system of asymmetry becomes apparent. Systemically, females, for the most part, lose and males gain. Vitalistically, females gain and males lose. When these dual areas are interlocked, there emerges a unique type of asymmetry. More specifically, a bilateral relationship is revealed. Again, a detailed review of data supports these assertions.

The U.S. economy epitomizes an area in which systemic inequalities based on sex prevail. In 1983, for example, median weekly earnings for all families was $470. When the data are stratified by sex, however, significant differences emerge. Married couple families had median family incomes of $27,286. While single householders of both sexes had median weekly earnings less than those of married couple families, families maintained by women had median family incomes of only $11,789.[1] Similarly, in 1984 34% of female-headed families existed below the poverty level and 44.2% below 125% of poverty, in contrast to 13.1% and 19.8% of all families respectively.[2]

When employment by sex and occupational category is examined, a slightly different form of asymmetry emerges—females in contemporary U.S. society are disproportionately white-collar workers and males are disproportionately blue-collar workers. Whereas the overall earnings of males in these various occupational categories exceed those of females, it is not often pointed out that vitalistic losses are incurred by males. In one year, for example, males experienced 92.6 work-related accidents and injuries per 1,000 persons in contrast to 12.8 per 1,000 persons for females.[3] A similar pattern exists when occupational category is further disaggregated by sex. Females constitute only 13.4% of physicians, dentists, and related practitioners, for example.[4] Whereas such occupations are overwhelmingly male, such statuses carry with them one of the highest rates of suicide of all occupational categories as well as average life expectancies below those of males in general.

A brief glance at other pivotal institutions reveals a clear pattern of systemic inequalities from which males gain. Before the 1980 national elections, for example, 417 representatives were male and only 16 were female, and 99 senators were male and only 1 was female. State and local public offices followed a similar pattern. Some 3% of state executive and judiciary officials, 9.2% of state legislators 3.1% of county commissioners, and 7.8% of mayors and city councilpersons were female.[5] This asymmetrical holding of statuses and roles by males extended itself into the religious institution, in which 89% of all religious workers were male.

The educational institution, however, displayed an asymmetrical pattern that was less clear in terms of gains and losses. Some 70% of all non-university and college teachers were female. Again, a disaggregation of the data reveals that 96.8% of prekindergarten and kindergarten, 85.1% of elementary, 49.6% of secondary, and 36.6% of college and university teachers were female.[6] Yet males were disproportionately represented in higher statuses within the educational institution; over 72% of college professors were male.

When this systemic data is conjoined with vitalistic data, the existence of a bilateral pattern of sex role asymmetry becomes most apparent. During the same time period, the life expectancy of females was 78.3 years in contrast to 71.1 years for males.[7] In addition, males died from diseases of the heart 129% more often, from pneumonia 123% more often, from cirrhosis of the liver 200% more often, and from suicide 295% more often than females did (percentages calculated by authors). Indeed, males suffered from all major diseases except cardiovascular diseases, diabetes mellitus, and arteriosclerosis at a greater rate than that for females.[8]

The asymmetry extends itself into other areas. In this same period males were victims of all crimes except rape at a greater rate than that of females. Males were victims of robbery with injury 300% more often, robbery without injury 350% more often, aggravated assault 300% more often, simple assault 172% more often, and personal larceny 128% more often than females.[9] Lastly, males were victims of homicide 300% more often than females. Not only does asymmetry exist in victimization rates, it also exists in rates of arrest and convictions. Males were arrested for crimes 594% more often than females. Finally, since 1979 males have been sentenced to death 8000% more often than females.[10]

Parallel patterns exist in other areas. In 1980, 129% more males than females were in mental hospitals and residential treatment centers. As the disproportionate victims of lung diseases, 240% more males were in tuberculosis hospitals. Similarly, 129% more males were in homes and schools for the mentally handicapped, 266% more males were in homes and schools for the physically handicapped, 147% more males were in homes for dependent and neglected children, and 378% more males were in detention homes. Additionally, as would be expected, 5020% more males were in military barracks.[11] The only institutions with disproportionately higher female populations were homes for the aged and dependent and homes for unwed mothers.

Other data could be introduced. However, the data discussed is sufficient to lend validity to the hypothesis that U.S. society is characterized by an asymmetry from which males benefit systemically while losing vitalistically. In contrast, females lose systemically while gaining vitalistically. It is this aspect of sexism that is often underdeveloped in existing literature in the area. Additionally, it is this aspect of sexism that supports as assertion that unlike social asymmetries based on class and race, the phenomenon of sexism operates as a bilateral process. Before an analysis of the relations among sex, race, and class can be presented, it is necessary to address another thematic thread that emerges from the use of the explicit and implicit assumptions of models of sexism that focus on systemic asymmetries. Specifically, the existence of systemic asymmetries is viewed as implying the operation of system of male dominance. Indeed, many social scientists have exonerated white females from responsibility for racial oppression by arguing that white females were merely victims of male dominance.

The notion that the history of women is a history of male dominance is so widely accepted that it too has become an axiom. Examples from literature and religion are used to demonstrate the existence of cultures imbued with sexist ideology (Campbell, 1959; Diner, 1973; Janeway, 1971). Male dominance is also viewed as not only reflecting itself in male control of the major pivotal institutions but also in the generally disproportionate accrual of prestige, power, and privilege to males. Indeed, male dominance is viewed by many as being so thorough and so indisputedly present in all relationships between males and females that sex, like race and class, has come to be viewed as another form of social stratification characterized by the oppression of females by males. This view is well summarized by Sheila Rowbotham (1974:35–46):

> *The social situations of women and the way in which we learn to be feminine is peculiar to us. Men do not share it, consequently we cannot be simply included under the heading of "mankind." The only claim that this word has to be general comes from the dominance of men in society. As the rulers they presume to define others by their own criteria.*

Accordingly, the implications or our bilateral conceptions of sexism for the male dominance thesis must be explored before the relationships between sex, race, and class can be examined. Although the primary focus of the analysis herein is upon the operation of sexism among Blacks , the concepts of sex role asymmetry and male dominance have become central themes in Black male/female relationships.

SEX ROLE ASYMMETRY: MALE DOMINANCE WITHIN A BILATERAL CONCEPTION OF SEXISM

The existence of systemic sex role asymmetry is widespread in human societies. Similarly, the view that such societies are characterized by male dominance is widespread. The anthropologist W. M. Stephens (1963), in a study of forty-one societies, concluded that males were dominant in 65% of the societies studied, males and females shared power in 26%, and females were dominant in only 7%. Such findings have been confirmed in other studies (Gough, 1971; Hunt, 1973; Romney, 1965). Indeed, the analyses of George Murdock's world ethnographic sample by D'Androde (1966) indicated that 66% of a sample of 565 societies throughout the world were patrilocal, whereas only 14% were matrilocal. Some 80% of the cultures sampled were patrilineal and 99% permitted polygyny but not polyandry. The substantial body of literature on the phenomenon of male dominance from a cross-cultural perspective has been adequately reviewed elsewhere (Parker and Parker, 1979).

An additional glance at the literature reveals that social scientists have also sought to locate the causes of systemic asymmetry and male dominance. A relatively widespread view is that male dominance is a consequence of biological factors (Goldberg, 1973; Tiger and Shepher, 1975). A less well accepted explanation of the alleged existence of male supremacy is the idea that prestate warfare is the causal factor (Divale and Harris, 1974; Hirschfeld, Howe, and Levin, 1978; Lancaster and Lancaster, 1978). The most prevalent explanations, however, view biological factors that emerged into a division of labor by sex as having led to male dominance (Brown 1970; Murdock and Provost, 1973). This view can be examined in greater detail.

For both Blacks and whites, sex role asymmetry fulfills several systemic functions. On the one hand, sex roles provide the basis for a division of labor and economic specialization. Additionally, critical social functions are fulfilled by the existence of sex roles. Importantly, sex role differentiation functions as the foundation of marriage and the family. This function is implicit in the definition of a family, which has been described as "a social arrangement based on marriage and the marriage contract, including recognition of the rights and duties of parenthood, common residence for husband, wife, and children and reciprocal economic obligations between husband and wife" (Stephens, 1963:8). The systemic functions of sex role asymmetry via its relationship to the family cannot be overemphasized because such functions relate directly to the themes of sex and class. These points can be examined more closely.

Not only is the family traditionally the basic unit of a society, it and the educational institution are the central mechanisms for preserving the value system of that society (Bell and Vogel, 1968). The division of labor by sex traditionally assigned to females the responsibilities of the socialization of children while assigning to males primary responsibility for the satisfaction of physical and biological needs of the family (e.g., food, shelter, and protection). These functions of males and females within the family interact in support of the family's role in another critical aspect of the society. Specifically, males and females within a family act out roles that cause the family to act as a major agent for creating and maintaining the existing systems of social stratification. Males are assigned the responsibilities for acquiring the artifacts of production and artifacts of power for placement within stratified hierarchy. Similarly, females are assigned the task of socializing the young into those beliefs, values, and practices that correlate to the family's position within the social hierarchy. Thus, both males and females are coparticipants in class and race-based oppression. Such statements do not imply the application of a structural functionalist (Parsons, 1955) approach to sex role asymmetry and the concept of male dominance. The oversimplification implicit in such a position has been adequately discussed elsewhere (Aronoff and Crano, 1975).

Indeed, a rejection of the view that sex role asymmetry emerged as a functional adaptation of the species as a whole has led to the adoption of other overly simple analyses. Some theorists have suggested that systemic asymmetry and male dominance emerged as a correlate of the development of economic surplus (Gough, 1971). Still others have viewed systemic inequality and male dominance as emerging from a fear of rape (Brownmiller, 1975). Independent of the causes of the emergence of sex role asymmetry, the accepted position is that sex role asymmetry cross-culturally has led to the emergence of a system of social stratification characterized by male dominance. This system of social stratification is viewed as (1) operating in the interest of males and (2) maintained and supported by males. Additionally, this system of male dominance is viewed, like social stratification based upon race and class, as being supported by sanctions, myths, and other social psychological mechanisms that reinforce existing inequalities. Accordingly, the issue of whether systemic inequalities constitute a system of male dominance is actually subsumed by the issue of whether sex role asymmetry constitutes a system of social stratification. More importantly, it is critical to understand how sex role asymmetry is linked with race and class asymmetries.

Systems of social stratification have been recognized as consisting of inequality in three major components: (1) rights over property, (2) differential power or control, and (3) differential prestige or esteem (Weber, 1958). Such inequalities we have characterized as *systemic* inequalities. In addition, we have demonstrated that systemic inequalities in a system of social stratification exists, systemic and vitalistic inequalities together delineate a set of *class interests* for the dominant and subordinate groups.

Our analysis of U.S. society, however, demonstrated clearly an inverse relationship between systemic and vitalistic asymmetries for males and females. Although data is not available for measuring and correlating vitalistic asymmetry with systemic asymmetry in traditional societies, *existing data support the conclusion* that even in traditional societies, females and males do *not* have separate class interests. Males and females do not separately compete for either property and/or power. Whereas it is true that greater prestige accrues to males, it is critical to our analysis to note that the benefits of property, power,and prestige accrue differentially to family units. *Although intrafamilial relationships may be characterized by various inequalities, these are not so intense as to create a separate set of class interests for males and females.*

As other systems of social stratification emerge, such as racism, such systems become sex and gender linked. First, the physical attributes of the sex role model for that society are determined by the physical attributes of the dominant race and/or class. Second, gender role expectations and behaviors are dictated by standards derived from the dominant race and/or class. Thus, an *interactive* relationship exists between sex role asymmetry and other forms of social stratification. Importantly, neither males nor females as a *class* are the beneficiaries of sex-based system of social stratification. *Rather, the family unit becomes the intervening variable through which sex-based roles provide benefits.* The family continues to function as the basic unit of social organization based on division of labor and specialization. Each family defends its position in the hierarchy in the struggle for property, power, and privilege. Males and females *share* class interests. Between males and females, males are allotted legitimate power while females share in other forms of power. An asymmetry does exist. This asymmetry produces benefits and losses for males and females within the family unit and thus must be more appropriately viewed as a system of exchange based on common goals and common interests. Thus, male/female interaction can be more appropriately characterized as cooperative and accommodative. *In contrast, males and females within families jointly cooperate in a competitive and conflicting interaction with families from other strata (e.g., Black versus white families).*

Thus, the position herein is that the prevalent view of sex role asymmetry as a system of social stratification characterized by male oppression of females represents tremendous oversimplification. Rather, the positions taken herein can be summarized as follows: (1) Different forms of sex role asymmetry exist for both males and females. (2) Under conditions of stable family units, such asymmetry constitutes a division of labor and specialization that is functional to the survival of the family members. (3) Similarly, when stability of the family exists, male/female asymmetry does not constitute a system of stratification based upon sex, but rather the male/female units act to preserve, in unity, their own race/class interests.

In contemporary U.S. society, however, sex and gender roles are being detached from their function as the foundation of the family unit. Indeed, the numerous factors leading to an increase in single family households has undermined the functioning of sex role asymmetry as a bilateral system of exchange. Within this context, the existence of sex roles achieves an additional importance beyond their impact on the self-actualization of males and females.

The increasing shift away from the family as the basic unit of social organization creates a basis for the emergence of class interests by sex. Males and females who choose to exist without attachment to a family unit become responsible for the total need satisfaction of self. Each individual, then, regardless of sex, must be expressive and instrumental in the tasks performed. Each individual must compete for limited social statuses and scarce economic resources. Because family units benefit from increasing returns to scale, the emergence of one-person social units, as well as single male or female-headed households, places an additional burden on limited economic resources (e.g., housing, energy, and transportation). Accordingly, it is accurate to conclude that sex-based class interests may be emerging in U.S. society. How such a social phenomenon relates to existing forms of stratification has important implications for social change movements in the United States.

CLASS, RACE, AND SEX

If sex role asymmetry is beginning to emerge as a struggle for resources between males and females, the U.S. system of social stratification, already based on class ad race, becomes even more complex. For the most part, unilateral models of sexism view the oppression of females by males as a separate phenomenon that operates across class and across race lines (Beal, 1975). In addition, unilateral models of sexism promote the viewpoint that women experience an oppression that parallels racial and class oppression. Such concepts have led many writers to conclude that in U.S. society, black females, for example, often suffer a triple oppression (Beal, 1975:2–3).

> *Since her arrival on these alien shores, the black woman has been subjected to the worst kinds f exploitation and oppression. As a black, she has had to endure all the horrors of slavery . . . ; as a worker, she has been the object of continual exploitation. . . . In addition, besides suffering the common fate of all oppressed and exploited people, the Afro-American woman continues to experience the age old oppression of woman by man.*

Although the assertion is often made in the literature that both sexism an racism are products of capitalism (Lewis, 1977; Rowbotham, 1974; Staples, 1979) and some efforts have been made to point out essential differences in the functioning of class, race, and sexism (Rowbotham, 1974), few systematic efforts have been made to identify the precise relations that exist between asymmetrical relations based on sex and those based on race and class. Thus, the task within this section is that of using our bilateral conceptualization of sexism to examines the interrelations among all three systems of social stratification.

As mentioned earlier, the ideals embodied in sex and gender role models are neither class nor race neutral. Sex and gender-based role models prescribe ideal physical and behavioral attitudes for each sex. It has been asserted that losses and gains differentially accrue to individuals on the basis of how closely their physical and behavioral attributes fit the model for their sex. Also, a type of stratification occurs as males and females who more closely fit the model choose each other as mates (Collier and Williams, 1981). If sex role models are intrinsically race and class based, it follows that the interactive relationship between these three factors function so as to promote and sustain existing patterns of inequality. Studies on similarity attraction not only document that dating and/or marriage occurs disproportionately between those of similar class and race, but also between similar males and females as measured by other criteria. For example, Maslow (1963) pointed out that self-actualizing males tend to marry self-actualizing females. This tendency has since been confirmed by other investigators (King, 1974). Similarly, attraction has also been demonstrated by still other investigations. Males and females of parallel abilities are attracted to each other (Zander and Havelin, 1960). Of course, males and females of comparable socio-economic classes more often marry (Byrne, Cleve, and Worchel, 1966). In addition, physically beautiful females marry economically successful mates (Elder, 1969).

Again, such data assume particular importance since inequalities by class and race are built into the sex role models that operate within U.S. society. Additionally, such data imply that beyond their socialization function, marriage and the family are mechanisms through which class and racial inequalities are perpetuated.Racial and class exploitation, then, serve the interests of both males and females of the dominant race and class. *If such a thesis is correct, it would then follow that sexism reinforces patterns of inequality based on class and race.* That is, using the assumptions of our bilateral model, we can conclude that sex, race, and class would function in such a way that if the three are interactive, in those areas where males gain, males of the minority race and subordinate class will gain less. conversely, in those areas in which males lose, the greatest losses would accrue to the victims of social stratification. Similarly, in those areas in which females gain, females of the minority race and subordinate class would gain less and in those areas in which females of the minority race and subordinate class would gain less and in those areas in which females lose, the converse would occur. Similarly, in those physical and behavioral standards defining sex role models, males and females of the minority race and subordinate class would fall the greatest distance from the norm. Thus, it can be said that sex, race, and class form a comprehensive and interactive system of social stratification within U.S. society. This thesis can also be tested by a brief review of the empirical data. Because the data are unavailable by sex, race, and class, only the interactive effects of sex and race will be examined.

It was mentioned earlier that while men as a class gain systematically from sex role asymmetry, males as a class lose vitalistically. If there exists an interactive relation between stratification by sex and race, this pattern should be evident in vitalistic data by race ad sex. And the data are quite clear. When life expectancy data are stratified by sex and race, a telling statistical portrait emerges. White females have a life expectancy 106% greater than that of minority females, 111% higher than that of white males, and 120% higher than that of minority males. Similarly, the age-adjusted mortality rate for minority males is 13.4% greater than that of white males, 169% greater than that of minority females, and 244% greater than that of white females.[12]

When other vitalistic data are included, the interactive effects of race and sex are even more apparent. Minority males dies from diseases of the heart 100% more often than white males, 157% more often than minority females, and 217% more often than white females. Minority males die from malignant neoplasms 128% more often than white males, 168% more often than minority females, and 190% more often than white females.[13] When social causes of death such as homicide are included, the pattern continues. Minority males are victims of homicide 682% more often than white males, 480% more often than minority females, and 2072% more often than white females.[14]

When data on crime and crime victimization are examined in greater detail by sex and race, the interactive effects of these two forms of social stratification are equally distinct. Minority males in 1978 were robbed without injury 200% more often than white males, 200% more often than minority females, and 200% more often than white females. Similarly, minority males were robbed with injury 200% more often than white males, 250% more often than minority females, and 600% more often than white females.[15] While males in general are victims of all crimes except rape at greater than the rate for females, the data indicate that minority males in general are more often the victims of serious crime. For example, white males suffer from simple assault 105% more often than minority males, but minority males suffer from aggravated assault 106% as often as the males. In the area of criminal justice administration, this trend is also apparent. Over the period from 1930 to 1979, 3,862 persons were executed. Within this group, 54% of those executed were black, 45% were white, and 1% were members of other races. Less than one-tenth of 1% of those executed were females of either race.[16] Indeed, the data quite clearly support our thesis that in those vitalistic areas in which males lose, the interactive effects of race and sex create additional losses for Black males.

As mentioned earlier, sexual asymmetry affects females negatively from a systemic perspective. Again, the data support the assertion that sex and race are interactive social forces. The median income of minority males more nearly approximates that of white males than does the median income of white females. In contrast, the differential between minority females and white males is greatest of all. Similarly, minority male-headed, white female-headed, and minority female-headed families exist in poverty more often than Black male-headed families. If the analysis is extended to the political institution, a parallel trend is seen.

Even when systemic asymmetries are examined in combination with vitalistic asymmetries to demonstrate that sex and race are interactive forces, the portrait of the impact of this interaction is incomplete. Sex role models negatively affect the lives of males and females by (1) constraining self-actualization, (2) skewing the distribution of systemic and vitalistic losses and gains, (3) creating a system of rewards and punishments that differentially accrue to individuals on the basis of their physical and behavioral closeness to the ideal. When race and sex are operative forces, individuals are confronted with constraints to self-actualization as a consequence of race and sex. As has been demonstrated, systemic and vitalistic losses are compounded. Finally, however, the psychosocial impact of sex role models creates additional trauma for Black individuals. Such persons are permanently constrained from being able to achieve the physical and sometimes behavioral attributes of the ideal standard. Thus, additional trauma is created as such persons aspire to the unobtainable while their worth is measured by an implicitly biased model.

CONCLUSIONS AND IMPLICATIONS

Several different yet related reconceptualizations in the area of sexism have been highlighted herein. These can be summarized as follows. The first task was that of statistically demonstrating that sex role asymmetry functions in such a manner that females lose systematically while males gain. Simultaneously, data were introduced in support of the thesis that females gain vitalistically from sex role asymmetry while males lose. Second, this bilateral system of gains and losses does not tautologically cause a system of social stratification. Rather, in order for a system of social stratification to emerge, males and/or females as a group must have separate *class interests*. Third, the point was made that the changing patterns regarding organization of the family have caused a breakdown in the division of labor function of sex roles and have led to a struggle for resources between males and females. Fourth, it was concluded that this struggle for resources does not define sexism as a *separate* form of social stratification from race and class but rather as an *interactive* one based on race and class. Fifth, the thesis was introduced that race and class variables condition those attributes incorporated into sex role models. Thus, sexist standards are implicitly racist and class biased. Sixth, it was empirically demonstrated that in those areas in which females lose, Black females lose most and that in those areas in which males lose. Black males lose most. Finally, it was pointed out that the existence of sex role models creates special psychosocial problems for those who are Black.

In other words, both Black males and females are victims of a triple and interactive system of oppression. This interactive system poses psychological, sociological, and economic barriers to Black family development and growth.

FOOTNOTES

1. U.S. Department of Commerce, Bureau of the Census, *Statistical Abstract of the United States, 1986.* ''Median Family Money Income by Number of Earners and Race of Householders, 1983,'' No. 757 (Washington, D.C.: Government Printing Office), 453.
2. U.S. Department of Commerce Bureau of the Census, *Statistical Abstract of the United States, 1986.* ''Persons below Poverty Level and below 128 Percent of Poverty Level by Race of Householders and Family Status: 1959–1984,'' No. 767 (Washington, D.C.: Government Printing Office). 458.
3. U.S. Bureau of the Census, *Statistical Abstract of the United States,* ''Occupations of Work-Experienced Civilian Labor Force, by Sex: 1970 and 1980,'' No. 697 (Washington, D.C.: Government Printing Office), 600.
4. Center for the American Woman and Politics. *Women in Public Office: A Biographic Directory and Statistical Analysis, 1980* (New Brunswick, N.J.)
5. Bureau of the Census, 1980 Census of Population.
6. Op. cit.
7. U.S. Department of Commerce, Bureau of the Census, *Statistical Abstract of the United States, 1986,* ''Expectation of Life at Birth: 1920–1984,'' No. 106 (Washington, D.C.: Government Printing Office), 68.
8. Percentages calculated from data in U.S. Bureau of the Census, *Statistical Abstract of the United States, 1986,* ''Death Rates by Selected Cases and Selected Characteristics: 1960–1982,'' No. 115 (Washington, D.C.: Government Printing Office), 74.
9. Percentages calculated by author from data found in U.S. Bureau of the Census, *Statistical Abstract of the United States,* ''Victimization Rates for Crimes against Persons: 1973–1983,'' No. 284 (Washington, D.C.; Government Printing Office), 169.
10. Percentages calculated from data taken from the U.S. Department of Justice, Bureau of Justice Statistics, Capital Punishment, 1982.
11. U.S. Bureau of the Census, *Statistical Abstract of the United States,* ''Population in Institutions and Other Group Quarters, by Sex, Race, and Type of Quarters: 1960–1980,'' No. 73 (Washington, D.C.: Government Printing Office), 48.
12. Percentages calculated by the author from data in the U.S. Department of Commerce. *Statistical Abstract of the United States, 1986,* ''Expectation of Life at Birth: 1920–1984,'' No. 106 (Washington, D.C.: Government Printing Office), 68.

13. Percentages calculated by the author from U.S. Bureau of the Census, *Statistical Abstract of the United States,* "Death Rates by Selected Cases and Selected Characteristics," No. 115 (Washington, D.C.: Government Printing Office), 74.
14. Percentages calculated from U.S. Bureau of the Census, "Victimization Rates for Crimes against Persons: 1973–1983," *Statistical Abstract of the United States,* No. 284 (Washington, D.C.: Government Printing Office), 169.
15. Ibid.
16. Percentages calculated from data taken from the U.S. Department of Justice, Bureau of Justice Statistics, Capital Punishment, 1982.

REFERENCES

Alberle, David, 1966. *The Peyote Religion among the Navaho.* Chicago: Aldine.

Aronoff, Joel, and William D. Crano, 1975. "A Re-examination of the Cross-Cultural Principles of Task Segregation and Sex Role Differentiation in the Family." *American Sociological Review* 40 (February):12–20.

Beal, Frances, M. 1975."Slave of a Slave No More: Black Women in Struggle." *The Black Scholar* 6(6, March):2–10.

Bell, Norman W., and Ezra F. Vogel, 1968. "Towards a Framework for Functional Analysis of Family Behavior." In *A Modern Introduction to the Family,* pp. 1–34. New York: Free Press.

Bradburn, Norman M., and David Caplovitz, 1965. *Reports on Happiness: A Pilot Study of Behavior Related to Mental Health.* Chicago: Aldine.

Brown, J. K. 1970. "A note on the Division of Labor by Sex" *American Anthropologist 72:1073–1078.*

Brown, Radcliffe, and Alfred Reginald, 1948. *The Andamon Islanders.* Glencoe, Ill,: Free Press.

Byrne, D. 1971. *The Attraction Paradigm.* New York: Academic Press.

Byrne, D., G. Cleve, and P. Worchel, 1966. "Effects of Economic Similarity—Dissimilarity on INterpersonal Attraction." *Journal of Personality and Social Psychology* 19:155–161.

Campbell, J. 1959. *The Masks of God: Primitive Mythology. New York. Viking.*

Center for the American Woman and Politics, 1980. *Women in Public Office: A Biographic Directory and Statistical Analysis.* New Brunswick, N.J.: Author.

Chinoy, Ely, 1955. *Automobile Workers and the American Dream.* Garden City, New York: Doubleday.

Collier, Betty J., and Louis N. Williams, 1981. "Towards a Bilateral Model of Sexism." *Human Relations* 34(2):127–139.

Collier, Betty J., and Willy Smith, 1981. "Racism, Sexism and the Criminal Justice System." *National Urban League Review* 6 (1,Fall):46–54.

D'Androde, Roy G. 1966. "Sex Differences and Cultural Institutions." In *The Development of Sex Differences,* Eleanor D. Maccoby, ed., pp. 174–204. Stanford: Stanford University Press.

Diner, H. 1973. *Mothers and Amazons? The First Feminine History of Culture.* Garden City, New York: Anchor.

Divale, W. and M. Harris, 1974. "Population, Warfare, and the Male Supremist Complex." *American Anthropologist* 78:521–538.

Duberman, Lucille. 1976. *Social Inequality: Class and Caste in America.* Philadelphia: Lippincott.

Elder, G. H. 1969. "Education in Marriage Mobility." *American Sociological Review* 34:519–533.

Faris, Robert, and Warren Hurham. 1939. *Mental Disorders in Urban Areas.* Chicago: University of Chicago Press.

Goldberg, Steven. 1973. *The Inevitability of Patriarchy.* New York: Morrow.

Gough, Kathleen. 1971. *"The Origin of the Family."* In *The Human Experience* (1st ed.), David H. Spain, ed., pp. 181–191. Homewood, Ill.: Dorsey Press.

Hirschfeld, Lawrence A., James Howe, and Bruce Levin. 1978. "Warfare, Infanticide, and Statistical Inference: A Comment on Divale and Harris." *American Anthropologist* 80:110–115.

Hollingshead, Hugh, and Frederick C. Redlich. 1958. *Social Class and Mental Illness.* New York.

Hunt, Robert C. 1973. "Power in the Domestic Sphere." *Science Journal* 6:68–72.

Janeway, E. 1971. *Man's World, Woman's Place.* New York: Dell.

King, Mark. 1974. "Sex Differences in Self-Actualization." *Psychological Reports* 35:602.

Krauss, Irving. 1976. *Stratification, Class and Conflict.* New York: Free Press.

Lancaster, Chet, and Jane Beckman Lancaster. 1978. "On the Male Supremacist Complex: A Reply to Divale and Harris." *American Anthropologist* 80:115–117.

Lenski, Gerhard. 1966. *Power and Privilege: A Theory of Social Stratification.* New York: McGraw-Hill.

Levinson, Andrew. 1974. *The Working Class Majority.* New York: Coward, McCann and Geoghegan.

Lewis, Diane K. 1977. "A Response to Inequality: Black Women, Racism and Sexism." *Signs* (Winter):339–361.

Maslow, A. H. 1963. "Self-Actualizing People." In *The World of Psychology* (Vol. 2), G. G. Levitz, ed. New York: Braziller.

McKee, J. P. 1959. "Men's and Women's Beliefs, Ideals, and Self Concepts." *American Journal of Sociology,* p. 64.

Miller, S. M., and Pamela A. Roby, 1977. *The Future of Inequality.* New York: Basic Books.

Murdock, G. P. 1937. "Comparative Data on the Division of Labor by Sex." *Social Forces* 15:551–553.

Murdock, George P., and Catherine Provost, 1973. "Factors in the Division of Labor by Sex: A Cross Cultural Analysis." *Ethnology* 12:203–225.

Parker, Seymour, and Hilda Parker, 1979. "The Myth of Male Superiority: Rise and Demise." *American Anthropologist* 81 (2, June):289–308).

Parsons, Talcott, 1955. "Family Structure and the Socialization of the Child." In *Family Socialization and Interaction Processes,* Talcott Parsons and Robert F. Bales, eds., pp. 35–131. Glencoe, Ill. Free Press.

Romney, A. 1965. "Variations in Household Structure as Determinants of Sex-Typed Behavior." In *Sex and Behavior,* F. Beach, ed., pp. 208–220. New York: Wiley.

Rowbotham, Sheila, 1974. *Woman's Consciousness, Man's World.* Harmondsworth: Penguin Books.

Sewell, William H. 1971. "Inequality of Opportunity for Higher Education." *American Sociological Review,* pp. 793–809.

Sexton, Patrician, and Brendan Sexton, 1971. *Blue Collars and Hard Hats: The Working Class and the Future of American Politics.* New York: Random House.

Smelser, Neil J. 1963. *The Theory of Collective Behavior.* New York: Free Press.

Staples, Robert, 1979. "The Myth of Black Macho: A Response to Angry Black Feminists." *The Black Scholar* (March/April):24–36.

Stephens, William, M. 1963. *The Family in Cross-Cultural Perspective.* New York: Holt, Rinehart & Winston.

Tiger, L., and J. Shepher, 1975. *Women in the Kibbutz.* New York: Harcourt Brace Jovanovich.

Tumin, Melvin M. 1967. *Social Stratification: The Forms and Functions of Inequality.* Englewood Cliffs, N.J.:Prentice-Hall.

Turner, Jonathan H., and Charles Starnes, 1976. *Inequality: Privilege and Poverty in America.* Pacific Palisades, Calif: Goodyear.

U.S. Bureau of Prisons, 1978. *Annual Statistical Report Series.* Washington, D.C.

U.S. Bureau of the Census, 1979/80. U.S. Department of commerce, Current Population Reports Consumer Income Services P-60, No. 125. *Money Income and Poverty Status of Families and Persons in the United States* (October), p. 7.

U.S. Department of Health, Education, and Welfare, 1975. Public Health Service Publication No. 100, Series 10, No. 58. *Vital and Health Statistics.* Washington, D.C.: U.S. Government Printing Office. 1976 Public Health Service. *Health-Status of Minorities and Low Income Groups.*

U.S. Department of Justice, 1978. *National Crime Survey.* Washington, D.C.: Law Enforcement Administration. 1979

Social Policies, Black Males, and Black Families

Bogart R. Leashore

The convergence of some socioeconomic indicators between Blacks and whites over the last few decades has prompted some social scientists and others to conclude that the significance of race has declined in the United States.[1] Statistically significant differences between Blacks and whites on several socioeconomic measures have declined.[2] However, it is erroneous to conclude therefore that racial inequality no longer exists in the United States. For example, in April 1985 the net seasonally adjusted unemployment rate for Blacks age 16 to 19 years was 37 percent, compared to 14.4 percent for whites in the same age group.[3] Similarly, significant differences exist between Blacks and whites on family income, infant mortality, life expectancy, incarceration, the number of children living in poverty, and in other areas.[4] As was recently observed by a white U.S. journalist:

> *It was only yesterday that racial discrimination was legal in vast parts of the country. . . . Racism remains a fact of life in this country—it may be abating, it may be weakening, but it certainly not ready to be mounted for the Smithsonian.*[5]

In short, race remains a critical factor in the quality of life in the United States.

This chapter draws attention to the roles played by social policies in maintaining racial inequality, particularly with respect to Black males; why and how this has occurred; and how social policies might be altered to enhance the well-being of Black males. Black families, and other Americans as well Black males are of special interest because of the high risk status they face compared to white males, and the significant roles they continue to assume in Black family life despite the ''feminization of poverty.''[6] . . .

TAX INCREASES AND BUDGET CUTS

A comprehensive analysis of U.S. domestic policies observed that between 1980 and 1984 Black families, regardless of the presence or absence of a male head, were helped less than or hurt more than were white families.[7] Analysis of the current U.S. tax system indicated that the federal government is taxing the poor at levels "without equal in history."[8] A disproportionate number of blacks—males and females—are low wage workers, or working poor and near poor. This group has experienced the sharpest increases in taxes over the past few years, as well as the sharpest cutbacks in social programs. Further, prior to the 1981 tax act, most families in poverty were exempt from federal income tax. In 1978, a family of four at the poverty line paid only $269 in federal taxes, which increased to $460 in 1980. by 1984, a family of four at the poverty line paid $1,076 in taxes.[9]

Since 1980, budget cuts in social programs designed for those with low and moderate incomes have been greater than cuts in programs not designed for this group. Programs designed for low and moderate income persons represented less than one-tenth of the federal budget, yet these programs accounted for close to one-third of the total number of cuts in all federal programs. Black Americans comprise 30 percent to 40 percent of the beneficiaries of most of the low income programs that received the greatest cuts. It has been shown that the 1981 budget cuts cost the average Black family three times as much in lost income and benefits as they cost the average white family. This has been attributed to cuts in programs with high participation by Blacks. For example, as shown in Table 1, employment and job training programs received the greatest cuts in 1985—and more than 30 percent of the participants in these programs were Black.[10]

Table 1. Budget Cuts in Programs with High Black Participation

Program	Degree of Black Participation	Budget Cut
Public Service Employment (CETA)	30%	–100%
Employment and Training	37	–39
Work Incentive Program	34	–35
Child Nutrition	17	–28
Legal Services	24	–28
Compensatory Education (Title I)	32	–28
Pell Grants and other Financial Aid for Needy Students	34	–16
Food Stamps	37	–14
Aid to Families with Dependent Children	46	–11
Subsidized Housing	45	–11

Source: Center on Budget and Policy Priorities. *Falling Behind: A Report on How Blacks Have Fared under the Region Policies* (Washington, D.C.: Author, October 1984), p. 12.

RACISM, SOCIAL DARWINISM, AND LAISSEZ-FAIRE IDEOLOGY

The social welfare policies of the United States lag significantly behind those of many countries of the world.[11] For some, the existence of this lag is deliberate and is not coincidental. Claiming that race impacts on the development as well as the implementation of social welfare policies can be a highly controversial position. Nevertheless, it seems clear that Blacks disproportionately have to turn to social programs for assistance in providing for their daily needs. Drawing on the premises of social Darwinism and laissez-faire ideology, some social and behavioral scientists, policy makers, and others attribute this disproportionate reliance to the failure of individuals and tend to absolve government from sharing any responsibility.[12] The paradox of these circumstances becomes more apparent when recognition is given to the role the U.S. government has historically played in promoting and maintaining racial inequality. For example, little more than a decade go, federal state, and local governments knowingly participated in and supported a racist medical experiment on uninformed Black males. The experiment was conducted from 1932 to 1972 and is documented in the work *Bad Blood: The Tuskegee Syphilis Experiment.*[13] More recently, national efforts have turned to child support enforcement in response to the increasing numbers of families headed by women.[14] Rooted in coercive and punitive social policy, Black males are more likely to be the victims of child support enforcement programs because they experience a higher rate of unemployment, receive lower wages, and are therefore less likely able to pay than white males. . . .

With specific reference to Blacks, conservatives and some liberals raise their voices against affirmative action and other federal interventions to promote racial equality. There is an insistence that adequate opportunities are available for those who are motivated toward individual achievement. Pathological views of Blacks and the poor suggest that the problems of poverty are rooted in individual deficits, such as indolence. Futile and endless rhetoric continues about the deserving and nondeserving poor. It is assumed that people are poor because they don't try, that governmental assistance is more of a hindrance than help, and that little can be done to improve "the lot of the less fortunate." Little regard is given to the demographics of poverty, which include the following facts: close to one-half of the adult non-aged poor work part time or full time but do not earn enough to escape poverty; others, for health or child care reasons, cannot enter the labor force; and most poor families do not remain in poverty for prolonged periods nor do they perpetuate a "culture of poverty" from one generation to the next. It has been stated that conservative attacks on government-sponsored social programs are "redoubtful assumptions" and that these conservatives "offer no alternative means of bolstering opportunity and advancement for the nation's disadvantaged and working poor."[15]

MOBILIZING FOR ALTERNATIVE SOCIAL POLICIES

Although the United States is hailed as the land of opportunity, and indeed is so for some, too many Black Americans continue to face structural barriers that block their entry into the socioeconomic mainstream of the society. Joblessness, low wages, poverty, inadequate medical care, substandard housing, poor education, and incarceration are conditions of life that need to be addressed if the defeminization of poverty is to occur. Too often, these conditions of living have reduced the family availability of many Black males. . . .

The probability of being able to function as family provider is related to opportunities for working and receiving adequate financial compensation. Given these highly probable relations, it seems that serious attention should be given to the life circumstances of Black males. In the context of social policies, efforts should be directed toward the elimination of social welfare assaults on Black males and others. Special emphasis should be given to the following areas: health care, employment, wages and income support, and crime and justice.

Health Care Policy

The overall health status of U.S. Blacks continues to lag behind that of whites on several measures. These include higher rates of infant and maternal mortality and shorter life expectancy. Research has shown that Black women are more likely than white women to die because of childbirth complications; that low birth weight is more prevalent among Black than white infants; that Blacks in general and Black males in particular live shorter lives than whites; and that whites receive considerably more preventive and routine medical care than Blacks.[16] These results ring clear the need for an effective program of national health insurance.

Historically, health care policy has focused on three issues: access to care, quality of care, and cost of care. However, preoccupation with cost has resulted in less interest in access and quality of care. For example, profit-oriented hospitals have been shown to be more expensive than nonprofit or public institutions. Those most likely to be without health insurance including Medicaid are women, people of color, and older people. If they cannot pay, health services are not accessible. If they have little to pay with, the quality of care is likely to be what has been characterized as "junk medicine"—for example, unnecessary tests and procedural duplications.[17]

Politicians, labor, religious, service, and charitable organizations, and consumer groups should reassert the need for a program of national health insurance with wide coverage and a larger federal financial role. These forces must seize control of the health care industry from the hands of physicians, private hospitals, and private health insurance companies.[18] A universal program of quality health care that is attractive to the nonpoor, as well as the poor, is needed. Broad benefits, public financing, and administration by the federal government should be key features of social policy for national health insurance.[19] Various industrialized nations of the world have implemented a range of programs that guarantee equal access to medical care as a citizen right.[20] That the United States remains without such a health care policy not only defies reason, but also continues to be a source of international embarrassment.

Employment and Income Support Policies

Poverty statistics, economic, and employment differences between Blacks and whites have been established. What seems needed are social policies that will reduce and eliminate economic inequality, which is deeply embedded in the structure of U.S. society. Programs increasing the taxes of those with low and moderate incomes while reducing the tax burden of the affluent and big business have done little to improve the U.S. economy. The failure to ensure equal job opportunities for Blacks have placed them at the bottom of the U.S. socioeconomic structure. Weakened commitments of government to civil rights and affirmative action have only worsened the situation. Federal policies to create jobs can reduce unemployment and ensure minimal adequate incomes. Moreover, tax credits and wage subsidies designed for low income and low skill workers can be as economically efficient as public employment policies.[21]

Classical economic theory accuses trade unions of pushing wages up, which prices workers out of jobs and thereby keeps unemployment high. On the contrary, other evidence indicates that productivity can be improved by giving workers a formal voice in the workplace. If unions coalesced, broadened their interests, and shifted pressure for wage increases, they could become a greater positive force for full employment. In lieu of shortrun wage increases, and organized and cohesive labor movement, egalitarian wage distributions, opportunities for retraining, workplace enrichment, and welfare objectives.[22]

Aid to Families with Dependent Children (AFDC) has long been stigmatized as a program for those who do not want to work. As a means-tested program, it separates "them" from "us" and has a history of contributing to father absence and family breakup. Family allowance and cash housing allowances based on family size and family income exist in much of Europe. They are available to all moderate income families as well as to the poor. The combined allowance have been considered an income support system that guarantees a higher standard of living, especially for those families with special needs (e.g., female-headed families.)[25]

As an expression of important U.S. values, the development of AFDC policy has been consistently directed toward punishing poor parents, especially single mothers, while moving away from promoting the well-being of dependent children. Specifically, values related to capitalism, liberalism, and positivism have been influential in the development of AFDC. The work ethic, individualism, personal freedom, the free market, and the worthiness of individuals have greatly influenced AFDC policy. Racial discrimination against Black families in the early days of AFDC further contributed to the humiliating welfare system of today.[24]

A recent historical study of the Social Security system in the United States vividly depicts the process of institutionalizing antipoor biases in the system. Among other things, it is shown why and how the phrase *social security* has come to mean social insurance even though the legislation of 1935 included public assistance. It is concluded that policy developments relative to public assistance were so constrained that many of the needy went without adequate support.[25] Critical assessments of the Social Security Act of 1935 have posited several relations between the state and the economy, or how political power gets translated into economic power. A recent assessment concludes that

> *in a hierarchical state structure, capitalist groups with varying economic interest exerted their influence at different levels in the hierarchy. . . . Economic power then gets translated into political power through the direct intervention of corporate liberals and through the hierarchical structure of the state, which allows competing factions to petition state managers for direct agendas in social policy.*[26]

Actions for Social Security reform should include a comprehensive analysis of the age requirement for receipt of benefits. Particular attention should be given to any disparities between males of color and white males relative to life expectancy and the age at which benefits can be received. Should Black and other males of color be eligible for Social Security benefits at an earlier age than white males because the latter have a longer life expectancy?[27] Relative to AFDC all states should be prohibited from using the absence of father in families as an eligibility requirement. In the case of child welfare, federal and state legislation and policies should be modified to include subsidized and legal guardianship as another plan of care for abused and neglected children, in addition to foster care and adoption. Far too many Black children, as well as others, linger in foster care.[28] More importantly, efforts need to be directed toward eliminating circumstances that necessitate taking children from their biological families, especially inadequate income and housing. Entitlement programs of the federal government for children, specifically AFDC, continue to lag behind those for other groups (e.g., veterans, the aged, the disabled, and those who are retired). Equal treatment for children through some form of federalized payments is not beyond the capacity of our government.[29]

Cutbacks in federal funds for child day care and nutrition should not only be restored, but increased. Similarly, federal aid for low and moderate income college students and food stamps should be restored and/or increased.

Crime and Justice

One of the most glaring differences between Blacks and whites in the United States is the disturbingly higher involvement of Blacks as compared with whites in the criminal justice system. . . .

Conditions of prison overcrowding, environmental conditions, idleness, violence, limited staffing, and inadequate medical care characterize many state prisons. Resulting court actions have included orders to reduce prison populations, to provide meaningful work, to provide meaningful opportunities for educational and vocational training, to expand prerelease transition programs, to provide medical care and staffing that meet certain standards, and to prevent violence.[30] With specific reference to Black homicide, the highest rates have been found among unemployed and underemployed Black youth and young adults. Thus, it can be argued that, like reduction of poverty and other social problems, homicide reduction can be achieved through major political and social changes.[31]

Given the high incarceration rate for Black males, new policy initiatives need to be established. These should include sentencing reform, plea bargaining, and employment opportunities for ex-offenders. Regarding the latter, any significant reduction in crime will require better employment opportunities for ex-offenders as well as for delinquents. New policy initiatives for the employment of ex-offenders can be specifically designed for ex-offenders, or created in conjunction with new programs for the employment of disadvantaged workers in general.[32] Suggested areas for prevention and intervention concerning homicide include gun control, community organization and education, and more effective responses to prehomicide behavior.[33]

SUMMARY AND CONCLUSIONS

This chapter has focused on social policies and how they have had an impact on Black males in particular and Black families in general. It is shown how domestic policies related to taxes and budget cuts have differentially affected Black families and how racism and ideologies have influenced the development and implementation of social policies in the United States. Attention is called to three areas in which there is a need for alternative social policies: (1) health care, (2) employment and income support, and (3) crime and justice. National and local efforts are needed to provide an effective program of national health insurance, full employment, family allowances, and actions to reduce incarceration.

The achievement of the social policy initiatives presented in this chapter will require deliberative efforts on the part of many parties, including Blacks and their people of color and supportive whites. In so doing, system-challenging political strategies should be used both within and outside of social institutions. Mass actions and collective efforts by multi-ethnic liberal challenging coalitions can result in social change for female-headed families and others who do not have basic power resources. Strategies that can be used include demonstrations, congressional lobbying, and voting. Black leaders and organizations can function in a national leadership capacity to achieve desired social change.[34] In the meantime, fraternal, business, and religious organizations should implement broad-based supportive and educational programs targeted for Black males including those who are institutionalized (e.g., those in prison).

Several conscious strategies should be developed within the Black community. These should include an internal Black agenda with a recommitment to Black community development or institution building. Further, Blacks can generate an internal economy with a capacity to absorb the marginally unemployed. Resources can be pooled into economic development institutions that go beyond providing technical assistance to small businesses but can also provide capital for large-scale enterprises that contribute to meaningful employment. An economic development institution could plan the organization and distribution of financial resources in order to promote economic stability and security within Black communities. Political activities should include mobilizing the voting power of the Black community so that officials are elected who are sensitive to and understand their needs. Black institutions such as churches can establish *priorities* of social needs and can commit resources toward designated ends—as has been the case with a national network of Black churches that was organized to provide financial assistance to needy. Black college students. This requires the involvement of organizations cutting across special interests, social classes, and resources so that a sense of community is restored. Special uses of mass media can be applied in order to bring leadership together to plan and promote goals and strategies. Local needs should be clearly linked to national issues; similarly, national activities should involve local programming.[35]

The mobilization of people of color and others for meaningful social change requires removal of blocks or barriers to power including internal and external political and economic forces that serve to maintain powerlessness among oppressed groups. Through the process of empowerment, Blacks and others can exert influence and overcome obstacles to meeting their needs. Basic to the process of empowerment, Blacks and others must understand the consequences of powerlessness. Moreover, there should be an understanding of and an appreciation for the capacity to bring about change.[36] With particular reference to Black males, it has been suggested that myths have been perpetuated in response to "an unmitigated fear of black male power."[37] Intertwined with racism and other factors, this fear has resulted in a range of social and economic assaults, which have been operationalized through punitive and coercive social policies and social services.

Black social and behavioral scientists as well as others, should draw attention to research that supports the need for new social policy initiatives. Black scholars and researchers can ill afford the luxury of academic isolation, lest their contributions be minimized. Fresh perspectives and progressive thinking are needed for examining social issues related to the well-being of Black people and that of all Americans. This should include a more balanced view of racism that analyzes not only the consequences for the victim, but also the motivations of the perpetrator. Knowledge and understanding is needed regarding why and how racism is nurtured and sustained in the United States, and what mechanisms can be used to eliminate it. In addition, white Americans should be educated about the social benefits which they stand to gain through the enactment of constructive social policies.

FOOTNOTES

1. William Julius Wilson, *The Declining Significance of Race: Blacks and Changing American Institutions* (Chicago: The University of Chicago Press, 1980); Michael Hout, "Occupational Mobility of Black Men: 1962 to 1973," *American Sociological Review,* 49 (June 1984), pp. 308–322.
2. Reynolds Farley, *Catching Up: Recent Changes in the Social and Economic Status of Blacks* (Cambridge: Harvard University Press, 1983); Richard B. Freeman, *The Black Elite* (New York: McGraw-Hill, 1976).
3. U.S. Department of Labor, Bureau of Labor Statistics, USDL85–184, Washington, D.C. (May 1985), Table A-3.
4. Theodore Cross, *The Black Power Imperative: Racial Inequality and the Politics of Nonviolence* (New York: Faulkner Books, 1984); Children's Defense Fund, *Portrait*

of Inequality: Black and White Children in America (Washington, D.C.: Children's Defense Fund, 1980); National Urban League, Inc., *The State of Black America,* 1984 (New York: National Urban League, 1984).

5. Richard Cohen, "Racism Recollected," *Washington Post,* August 10, 1985, p. A19.
6. Lawrence E. Gary and Bogart R. Leashore, "High Risk Status of Black Men," *Social Work,* 27 (January 1982), pp. 54–58; Gary and Leashore, "Black Men in White America: Critical Issues," in Color in a White Society, Barbara White (ed.) (Silver Spring, Md.: National Association of Social workers, 1984). pp. 115–125.
7. John L. Palmer ad Isabel V. Sawhille, *The Reagan Record: An Assessment of America's Changing Domestic Priorities* (Cambridge, Mass.: Ballinger, 1984).
8. Daniel Patrick Moynihan, "Family and Nation," Cambridge, Mass.: Harvard University, the Godkin Lectures, 1985).
9. Center on Budget and Policy Priorities, *Falling Behind: A Report on How Blacks Have Fared under the Reagan Policies* (Washington, D.C.: author, October 1984).
10. Ibid.
11. Robert Kuttner, *The Economic Illusion* (Boston: Houghton Mifflin, 1984).
12. Ibid.; Sar A. Levitan and Clifford M. Johnson, *Beyond the Safety Net: Reviving the Promise of Opportunity in America* (Cambridge, Mass.: Ballinger, 1985), pp. 6–18.
13. James Jones, *Bad Blood: The Tuskegee Syphilis Experiment* (New York: Free Press, 1981).
14. Joyce E. Everett, "An Examination of Child Support Enforcement Issues," in Harnette McAdoo and T. M. Jim Parham (eds.), *Services to Young Families Program Review and Policy Recommendations* (Washington, D.C.: American Public Welfare Association, 1985), pp. 75–112.
15. Levitan and Johnson, *Beyond the Safety Net,* pp. 6–18.
16. *A Dream Deferred: The Economic Status of Black Americans, a working paper* (Washington, D.C.; The Center for the Study of Social Policy, 1983).
17. Michael Clark, "What Hath Reagan Wrought," *Health PAC Bulletin,* 15 (July–August 1984, pp. 3–4.
18. Kuttner, *The Economic Illusion,* pp. 249–250.
19. Theodore R. Marmor, Judith Feder, and John Holahan, *National Health Insurance: Conflicting Goals and Policy Choices* (Washington, D.C.: The Urban Institute, 1980).
20. Kuttner, *The Economic Illusion.*
21. Irwin Garfinkel and John L. Palmer, "Issues, Evidence, and Implications," in *Creating Jobs: Public Employment Programs and Wage Subsidies* (Washington, D.C. The Brookings Institution, 1978).
22. Kuttner, *The Economic illusion,* pp. 136–186.
23. Kuttner, *The Economic Illusion,* pp. 243–247.
24. Jan Mason, John S. Wodarski, and T. M. Jim Parham, "Work and Welfare. A Reevaluation of AFDC," *Social Work,* 30 (May–June 1985), pp. 197–203.
25. Jerry R. Cates, *Insuring Inequality: Administrative Leadership in Social Security, 1935–54* (Ann Arbor: The University of Michigan Press, 1983).

26. Jill S. Quadagno, "Welfare Capitalism and the Social Security Act of 1935." *American Sociological Review,* 49 (October 1984), p. 645.
27. Gary and Leashore, *Social Work,* 27 (January 1982), p. 57.
28. Bogart R. Leashore, "Demystifying Legal Guardianship: An Unexplored Option for Dependent Children," *Journal of Family Law,* 23 (1984), pp. 391–400.
29. Moynihan, "Family and Nation," pp. 43–44.
30. Alvin J. Bronstein, "Prisoners and Their Endangered Rights," *The Prison Journal,* LXV (Spring–Summer 1985), pp. 4–5.
31. Darnell F. Hawkins, "Black Homicide: The Adequacy of Existing Research for Devising Prevention Strategies," *Crime and Delinquency,* 31 (January 1985), p. 94–97.
32. James B. Jacobs, Richard McGahey, and Robert Minion, "Ex-Offender Employment, Recidivism, and Manpower Policy: CETA, TJIC, and Future Initiatives," *Crime and Delinquency,* 30 (October 1984), pp. 486–503.
33. Hawkins, "Black Homicide," p. 96.
34. Ronald Walters, "Imperatives of Black Leadership: Policy Mobilization and Community Development," *The Urban League Review,* 9 (Summer 1985), pp. 20–41.
35. Ibid.
36. Barbara Bryant Solomon, *Black Empowerment: Social Work in Oppressed Communities* (New York: Columbia University Press, 1976).
37. Robert Staples. "The Myth of Important Black Male," in *The Black Family: Essays and Studies* (2nd ed.) (Belmont, Calif.: Wadsworth, 1978), p. 99.

The Dilemma of Growing Up Black and Female*

Algea O. Harrison

The purpose of this paper is to discuss how Black females attempt to resolve the dilemma of femininity and high achievement goals. Generally there has been a reverse relationship between femininity and high need achievement. The objective of this report is to review the nature of the relationship between femininity and high need achievement. The objective of this report is to review the nature of the relationship for Black females. Since the young Black female is presented with different models of life style for womanliness it is expected that her femininity may develop differently from that of her white counterpart. The Black female becomes cognizant of the fact early in life that she will not be able to achieve the culturally imposed goals of being soft, clinging and dependent to obtain a man who will support her and provide an array of material possessions. How will she attempt to incorporate femininity as defined by the dominant culture into her own culture's definition of the female role?

CHARACTERISTICS OF FEMALES

A sex role standard has been defined as a belief shared by the members of the culture regarding the characteristics that are appropriate for males and females (Kagan 1971). Specific behaviors have been ascribed as distinctive of females, i.e., dependency, passivity, conformity, nurturance, submissiveness, etc. A series of studies of overt behavior and/or story telling responses indicate more occurrence of affiliative and nurturant behavior and concern with interpersonal relationships among girls than boys (Kagan 1971). An expressive role, skills in dealing with people, has also been prescribed for women (Reiss 1966). They seem to be better and earlier trained for a commitment to and capacity for romantic love and the subtleties of emotion that lead to strong heterosexual attachments (McCandless and Evans 1973). Therefore, it is not surprising that most studies report greater dependency, conformity, and social passivity for females than males at all ages (Kagan 1971).

Generally, girls are less active physically, displaying less overt physical aggression, are more sensitive to physical pain, have significantly less genital sexuality,, display greater verbal, perceptual and cognitive skills, and are better at analyzing and anticipating environmental demands than boys (Bardwick and Douvan 1971). Girls perform less initiative aggression than boys after being exposed to aggressive models (Bandura 1965). they usually show more prosocial aggression; however, when anonymity is guaranteed girls are as capable as boys of delivery aggressive consequences such as electric shock in laboratory experiments (McCandless and Evans 1973).

The role standard has had its most notable effect on the mastery of specific cognitive skills. From kindergarten through grade four, the girl typically outperforms the boy in all areas and the ratio of boys to girls with reading problems ranges from 3 to 1 to 6 to 1 (Bentzen 1963). There seems to be a developmental shift and in the adolescent years, academic and vocational success is viewed as masculine and inappropriate for females. Problems of involving spatial and mechanical reasoning, physics, science, logic, and mathematics are viewed as more appropriate for boys than for girls. Whenever adolescent or adult subjects are tested on these skills males consistently obtain higher scores than females (Kagan 1971). The adolescent girl, her parents, her girl friends, and her boy friends perceive success as measured by objective, visible achievement as antithetical to feminity (Bardwick and Douvan 1971). It is in the are of need achievement that the Black female differs from the general society's expectations of what is appropriate feminine.

BLACK FEMALE'S ASPIRATIONS AND ACCOMPLISHMENTS

In spite of the difficulties presented by sex typing the Black female has generally emerged with a positive self-concept and high aspirations and expectations. Although a negative self-image appeared to be more characteristic of the Black child than of the white child, the Black female had more positive self-attitude than the Black male (Dreger and Miller 1973). Dreger and Miller (1973:151), in reviewing such studies, found that "Black girls have higher educational hopes than do Black boys . . . Black high school seniors in Kentucky set occupational goals similar to those of whites with the exception that the Black female has higher expectations. The Black girls concentrated their occupational expectations among the professions and usually rejected the traditional role of housewife. Out of a total of 52 Black female subjects not one wanted to be a housewife. Out of a total of 52 Black with 25 percent of the white girls . . . an ambitious pattern of aspiration and expectation among Black girls was reported with a much greater percentage of Black girls than boys actually enrolled in college preparatory programs." In studies designed to measure generalized achievement motivation using the McClelland method it has been found that the Black female's achievement motivation is greater than the Black male (Smith and Abramson (1962).

In a study conducted by Brazziel (1971), 262 Black students completed the Edwards Personal Preference Schedule. The sample was divided geographically into lower-South (rural and urban students) and upper-South (residents of a large metropolitan area). When sex comparisons are made for the lower-South group, females exhibit significantly higher needs for achievement, endurance and intraception, but are lower in deference, autonomy and heterosexuality. On the other hand, there are only two significant differences between the sexes in the upper-South sample, the females score lower on needs for dominance and heterosexuality. What is noticeable is the relative absence of sex differences in this group when compared to the norm group. Sex differences are present in twelve of fifteen variables in the general college norm but are revealed in only two instances in the upper-South and six instances in the lower-South.

Sex differences by social class were not pronounced, in the lower-South, both classes revealed higher female needs for achievement. Middle income females in the lower-South group revealed higher needs for nurturance and middle-income males in the upper-South groups scored higher on dominance.

The high need for achievement and higher educational aims among Black females has historically resulted in more Black girls enrolled in college than boys. In recent years Jackson (1973:57) notes "Black women and men 25 years of age and older were closer together in 1970 than in 1960 in average number of years of schooling. In the category of college education, however, there were more women. In 1960 the ratio was 100 males to 156 females. In 1970 the ratio rose to 100 males to 161 females." The sex difference in educational achievement varies according to the geographical region. When national statistics are considered Black women have completed a median of 8.7 school years and men 7.7. In the North there was no difference between the sexes in 1950 and by 1965 men were ahead of the women. In the South women still are more highly educated (Billingsley 1968).

Epstein (1973:916) notes that seemingly contradictory figures are reported concerning the total number of graduate and professional degrees earned by Black men and women.

> *A study of Negro colleges where the majority of blacks have earned their graduate degrees (Blake, 1971, p. 746) shows that Black women earned 60% of the graduate and professional degrees awarded in 1964–65. However, a Ford Foundation study (1970) of all Black Ph.D. holders in 1967–68 indicated that of a 50% sample of the total, only 21% were women. Another source covering Black colleges in 1964 lists more women than men earning M.A.'s but more men than women earning Ph.D's (Epstein, 1973:916).*

In most professional groups, Black women constitute a larger proportion of the women than the proportion of Black men of the men (Epstein 1973). From 1880 to 1960 there has been a larger percentage of Black females classified as in professional service than Black males, except in 1880 when the percentage of male teachers, 66.4 percent, was greater than female, 33.6 percent (see United States Census, 1880–1960). In the United States as a whole, Black women out-number men in the highest job categories, with 10.8

percent of them compared to 8.2 percent of male workers. When we consider the North and West, men slightly outstrip women, but in the South, where schoolteaching has been traditionally open to Black women, the 11.9 percent of women in professional, technical, and managerial jobs considerably outstrips the 6.4 percent of Black men. Occupational opportunities are greater for Black workers in the North than in the South, and in the South, particularly, they are better or Black women than for Black men (Billingsley 1968).

It must be remembered that a very small percentage of the Black women employed are professional workers, over half are classified as in domestic and personal services (U.S. Bureau of the Census 1969). It is only when the statistics refer to *nonwhite* employed is there a decrease in numbers of females employed as private household workers. In 1969, 12 percent of *nonwhite* females employed were in professional, technical, and managerial fields as compared to 11 percent *nonwhite* MALES (U.S. Bureau of the Census 1969).

In 1967 the median income for Black females was $3,268 and $4,837 for Black males (U.S. Bureau of the Census 1972). At all educational levels the Black female's income is approximately $1,000 to $2,000 less than the Black male of equivalent education (U.S. Bureau of the Census 19072). This difference in income is most notable when we compare median income of the Black female head of family, $3,341, with that of the Black male head of family, $7,329 (U.S. Bureau of the Census 1972). These findings suggest that although there are slightly more Black female than Black male professionals, the females are mainly employed in the low-paying and low status professional jobs, i.e., teaching, nursing, etc.

The unemployment rate is also a reflection of difficulties in the labor market for Black females. Unemployment was lowest for white adult males, 4.0 percent, and highest for minority teenage girls, 35.5 percent (U.S. bureau of the Census 1972). Minority adult women had an unemployment rate of 8.7 percent compared to 7.2 percent for minority men. Harwood and Hodge (1971) skillfully denounce the myth that Black females have had an advantage in the job market when she had to work. Actually, she found a limited range of low paying jobs to choose from, mainly as a servant in a private household. The census data reveal that since 1890 Black men have enjoyed a greater diversification of jobs than Black women.

Black families have been accused of traditionally encouraging their girls to high achievement at the expense of the boys. This practice of stressing achievement for girls has been defended by Grier and Cobb (1968). The Black family was concerned about the physical safety and protection they could offer their children. The sons were taught to avoid open conflict with white people and they had to curb their aggression and other behavior considered masculine in American society. For their daughters, the aim was to protect them from the sexual exploitation they might suffer if forced to work as domestics. The families sought to give them economic freedom through education. Schools were seen as a refuge for the daughter from what was considered a "traditional way of life." Grier and Cobb (1968:124) notes: "If school is seen as a refuge from the white aggressor, and if the Black family places its women and children within such safe confines, and if the men turn to face the enemy—pray show me that critic of the 'weak' Negro family." In addition the Black family's major occupation after emancipation was farming and share-cropping and male offspring were necessary to provide a basic economic support for the family. Therefore, the family's educational aspirations were generally centered around the females. The financial resources of the family were limited and in order for a member of the family to attend school, the others had to labor to provide the money. This usually meant that the males of the family pooled their resources and sent the females to school.

The attitude of the current Black family has changed very little. Girls are still encouraged to stay in school in the South and urban ghettos as a place of refuge from the problems of modern day society. These personal and familial aspirations for achievement of Black females have materialized somewhat as expected.

In discussing the role of the Black female the issue of Black matriarchy has been listed as a source of conflict with the implication being that the Black female's dominance has been destructive to the Black community. Robert Staples (1970:8) dismissed this cruel thesis by noting:

> *For the Black female, her objective reality is a society where she is economically exploited because she is both female and Black; she must face the inevitable situation of a shortage of Black males because they have been taken out of circulation by American's neo-colonialist wars, railroaded into prisons, or killed off early by the effects of ghetto living conditions. To label her a matriarch is a classical example of what Malcolm X called making the victim the criminal.*

BLACK AND WHITE FEMALE DIFFERENCES

The conflict over sex role identity and high need in social achievement distinguishes the Black and white females. Generally, females in American society have exhibited lower occupational and educational aspirations. Females have been socialized to succeed in the traditional sex roles and do not maximize the personality traits that are essential for success in the real world, i.e., independence, aggression, competitiveness, leadership, etc. Society does not stress these personality characteristics for females and therefore very few have succeeded in the business and professional world where these skills are essential. There is a difference, however, for Black females.

Horner has attempted to explain the phenomenon of low motive to achieve for females in general. Horner (1968) hypothesized the existence of a motive to avoid success (M_{-S}) which she defined as the expectancy of anticipation of negative consequences as a result of success in competitive achievement situations. Weston and Mednick (1973) investigated the relationship between Horner's postulated motive and race and social class. Subjects were undergraduate women and the verbal TAT cues such as those used by Horner and a brief questionnaire requesting socioeconomic information were administered. It was found that Black college women exhibited fewer M_{-S} responses than white college women. There was no social class differences for the Black female on the number of M_{-S} responses. White lower class females were not included in the study and no class comparisons were made for whites. Bager (1972:605) found that Black college women tended to have higher educational aspirations than white college women.

In somewhat related research (Iscoe, Williams and Harvey 1964) it was found that Negro females (7, 9, 12, and 15 years) were less conforming than white females of the same age when subjected to highly speculative and questionable, i.e., Negro mothers are chief source of authority, Negro females can get away with nonconformity more than can a white female, Negro females are more independent in dealing with whites than are Negro men, etc. Nevertheless, it does suggest that early in life Black females probably will be more resistant to efforts to get them to conform to the traditional sex role standard.

In the area of professional success Black career women have exceeded their white counterparts. Black women constitute a larger proportion of the Black professional community than white women in the white professional community. Only 7 percent of white physicians are women, but 9.6 percent of Black doctors are women; Black women make up 8 percent of Black lawyers but white women constitute only 3 percent of all white lawyers; Black women accountants, musicians, professional nurses, and social workers exceeded their white female colleagues in earnings (Epstein 1973). Black women are more likely to be employed than the white female with equivalent education.

One of the most obvious differences between Black and white females is the economic necessity of Black females working in order for the family to maintain a middle-class standard of living. Because of the racist economic practice in the general society Black men do not have access to higher paying occupations nor do they have any oral control over the economic base. The source of high need achievement for Black women may not be solely due to personal aspiration but also economic need. The Black female's role in the economic survival of the Black community may be compared to that of other women in pre-industrialized and less technologically advanced societies and/or to industrial societies during their pre-industrialized stage of development. Women were generally called upon to work in those societies, i.e., pioneer women, Russia, China, etc. Historically Black women have had the role of worker with very few accrued benefits.

BLACK FEMALE'S SEX-ROLE IDENTITY

There are two possible explanations of why a larger percentage of Black females than white strive toward goals and appear to comfortably function in roles that are viewed by the general society as anti-feminine. One approach is to view her strivings as a result of her feelings of rejection by society. Another view is to see her aims of accomplishment as a result of being exposed to successful, competent, female models in the Black community.

The first possibility may result because the Black female will encounter problems establishing her sex role that are different from her white counterpart largely because of society's view of what is desireable in womanhood. As Grier and Cobb (1968:32) noted "the first measure of a child's worth is made by her mother, and if, as is the case with so many Black people in America, that mother feels that she, herself, is a creature of little worth, this daughter, however valued and desired, represents her scorned self." The Black woman is the antitheses of America's idea of a beautiful ideal woman as communicated throughout all strata of society. The ideal all-American is a blond, blue-eyed, white-skinned girl with regular features. This prevailing ideal of womanhood presents problems for Black girls as can be easily seen in this typical self-revealing comment:

> *Because I was dark I was always being plastered with vaseline so I wouldn't look ashy. Whenever I had my picture taken they would pile a whitish powder on my face and make the lights so bright I always came out looking ghostly. My mother stopped speaking to any number of people because they said I would have been pretty if I hadn't been so dark. Like nearly every little Black girl, I had my share of dreams of waking up to find myself with long blond curls, blue eyes and skin like milk (Marshall 1970:26).*

The patterns of marriage in the Black community also perpetuate the rejection of the Black female. The light-skinned female was viewed as the most desirable marriage partner for Black men (Staples 1973a). Interestingly, the reverse skin color was viewed as most sought after by Black females. The dark skin Black male was preferred more than the light skin who was viewed as self-centered and closely resembling the oppressive white male.

There was no way for the Black female to be transformed into a lovely white maiden, hence she did the next best thing. She ascribed to those characteristics that are viewed by society as valuable and she could obtain. Most personality characteristics that are valued by society are possessed by successful persons, usually males, i.e., independence, need for success, self-assertion, ambition, drive, etc. These qualities are earned and acquired and not controlled by the genes like color of skin, texture of hair, physique, etc. If she could not gain acceptance in the traditional female manner she would have to be acknowledged for her possession of the other traits on which society places a premium. As a result of society's rejection of her Black womanliness she strove for acceptance through avenues that would demand recognition, acquiring some of the traditionally male personality traits.

It has been suggested that a successful woman may be an economic asset and attractive and therefore not as threatening to a Black male (Weston and Mednick 1973). Most Black families, whether low-income or note, are characterized by an equalitarian pattern in which neither spouse dominates, but share decision-making and the performance of expected tasks (Hill 1972). Her unique qualities facilitated economic gains and made it possible for increasing numbers of Black families to move into the middle class. In the professional employment market Black females are frequently viewed as less threatening than Black males and employers, if they have to hire a Black, sometimes preferred females (Epstein 1973 and Jackson 1973). Therefore it was possible for her to obtain measures of success because of her unique position in society.

The attainments of success for the professional Black woman seems to have been a double-edged sword. There is a higher rate of divorce and low incidence of marriage for this category of women for various reasons. The major problems seem to be the lack of a large number of equivalently educated Black males from which to select a mate, characteristics of females preferred for wives by Black male professionals, marital partners with less education, Black males marrying white females, etc. (Jackson 1973, Epstein 1973, and Staples 1973a). Bager (1972) conducted a survey of institutional variables predicting marriage for women. He found that for Black women in a predominantly black institution, being nonwhite and having high degree aspirations were both negatively related to getting married during the undergraduate years (Bager 1972:605). It seems as if the acquisition of "non-feminine" type personalities has presented some difficulties for Black females.

Another possible reason for the Black female's striving toward success is the type of models she is exposed to in the Black community. Modeling is most effected when there is a close similarity between the modeler and the modelee (Bandura 1965). The Black models in her community are of women obtaining success in business and professional careers, mothers who are heads of households coping with the many problems of being poor in urban America, and just a daily contact with women who are leading useful productive lives in spite of the pervasive effects of racism in society. Although this is not the appropriate mechanism or time to review her long and rich history it is worth noting that in West African societies women by custom and tradition play a substantial role in the community. Her role as a mother was considered of primary importance in patrilineal or matrilineal society. Her treatment during slavery and reconstruction has been greatly documented and visibly evident in her present day descendents (Staples 1973a).

The important point is that females in the Black community are highly visible and noted for their strengths, accomplishments in the face of obstacles, and personal sacrifices for her family and the Black community. The young female, therefore, is exposed to successful females and has models to aspire to emulate. The Black female's view of what is appropriately female comes from her own community and not from feelings of rejection from the white world.

Ladner (1971) dismisses the idea that Black females depreciate themselves since they have a clear understanding of the root causes of their rejection and place the blame squarely where it belongs. She categorizes the self-hatred thesis as one of "many other myths that are propagated about Black people. It falls within the realm of institutional subjugation that is designed to perpetuate an oppressive class" (Ladner 1971:107). The urban lower-class adolescent girls that were the basis for her study has been exposed to women who played a central role in their households and community. Ladner (1971:132) notes that "it is against this backdrop that the symbol of the resourceful woman becomes an influential model in their lives."

IMPLICATIONS

The dilemma of being a female for the Black woman is that she is being urged by society in general to cultivate the traits that lend themselves to feminity, i.e. dependency, passiveness, submissiveness, etc. On the other hand, she is pressured by the political-economic system and survival needs of the Black community to develop those traits that are contrary to the ideas of womanhood as prescribed by the sex role standard, i.e., independence, self-assertion, persistence, etc.

Future research should be designed to provide insights into the psychological processes involved in the establishment of the Black female's sex role identity. It is obvious from her history of oppression and role in the Black community that there is similarity and dissimilarity with the white female. Is the major motivating factor feelings of rejection from the white sex role standard and/or identification with the model of her community?

Regardless of the specifics of the psychological process it is important that appropriate models should be provided by adult citizens. Exposure to and availability of successful Black females should be abundant in the young female's life.

The educational system should be aware when they are counseling young Black females that her aspirations and needs are different from the typical female's. Her historical role int he community and its impact on her developing personality have to be taken into consideration.

It is also important that the economic-political system acknowledge that in order for the Black community to survive Black males and females need higher paying jobs. When approximately one-third of the families have females as head of household, supportive systems have to be provided in the community. The status of the Black family has altered and public policy must reflect this change. This policy should include a guaranteed income, elimination of sexist discrimination in employment opportunities, community-controlled child care centers, safe and free contraceptives and abortions, and input from the Black community in policy making decisions (Staples 1973b).

NOTE

*A revised version of a paper presented at the Sixth National Convention of Association of Black Psychologists, August 25, 1973, Detroit, Michigan.

REFERENCES

Bager, A. 1972. "College Impact on Marriage." *Journal of Marriage and the Family* 34:600–610.

Bandura, A. 1965. "Influence of Models' Reinforcement Contingencies on the Acquisition of Imitative Responses." *Journal of Personality and Social Psychology* 1:589–595.

Bardwick, J. and Douvan, E. 1971. "Ambivalence: The Socialization of Women." In V. Gornich and B. Moran (Eds.) *Women in Sexist Society.* New York: Basic Books.

Bentzen, F. 1963. "Sex Ratios in Learning and Behavior Disorders." *American Journal of Orthopsychiatry* 33:92–98.

Billingsley, A. 1968. *Black Families in White America.* Englewood Cliffs: Prentice Hall.

Brazziel, W. 1971. "Correlates of Southern Negro Personality." In R. Wilcox (Ed.) *The Psychological Consequences of Being a Black American.* New York: Wiley: 401–408.

Dreger, M. and Miller, K. 1973. Comparative Psychological Studies of Negroes and Whites in the United States: 1959–1965." In D. R. Heise (Ed.) *Personality, Biosocial Bases.* Chicago: Rand McNally: 125–156.

Epstein, C. 1973. "Positive Effects of the Multiple Negative: Explaining the Success of Black Professional Women." *American Journal of Sociology* 78:912–935.

Grier, W. and Cobb, P. 1968. *Black Rage.* New York: Basic Books.

Harwood, E. and Hodge, C. 1971. "Jobs and the Negro Family: A Reappraisal." *The Public Interest* 23:125–131.

Hill, R. 1972. *The Strengths of Black Families.* New York: Emerson Hall.

Horner, M. S. 1968. *Sex Differences in Achievement Motivation and Performance in Competitive and Non-Competitive Situations.* Unpublished Doctoral Dissertation. University of Michigan.

Iscoe, I., Williams, M. and Harvey, J. 1964. "Age, Intelligence, and Sex as Variables in the Conformity Behavior of Negro and white Children." *Child Development* 35:451–460.

Jackson, J. J. 1973. "Black Women Created Equal to Black men." *Essence* (November): 56–72.

Kagan, J. 1971. *Personality Development.* New York: Harcourt, Brace & Javanovich.

Ladner, J. 1971. *Tomorrow's Tomorrow: The Black Woman.* Garden City: Anchor Books.

Marshall, P. R. 1970. In T. Cade (Ed.) *The Black Woman.* Signet Books.

McCandless, B. and Evans, E. 1973. *Children and Youth Psychosocial Development.* Hinsdale: Dryden.

Reiss, I. L. 1966. "The Sexual Renaissance: A Summary and Analysis." *Journal of Social Issues* 22:123–137.

Smith, H. P. and Abramson, M. 1962. "Racial and Family Experience Correlates of Mobility Aspiration." *Journal of Negro Education* 31:117–124.

Staples, R. 1970. The Myth of the Black Matriarchy. *The Black Scholar* (January–February). 1973a *The Black Woman in America.* Chicago: Nelson-Hall. 1973b "Public Policy and the Changing Status of Black Families." *The Family Coordinator* 22L345–351.

U.S. Bureau of the Census. 1969. *The Social and Economic States of Negroes in the United States, 1969.* Washington, D.C.: U.S. Government Printing Office:42. 1972. "General Social and Economic Characteristics." Final Report, D.C. C17–C1. *U.S. Summary* Washington, D.C.: U.S. Government Printing Office :1–379.

Weston, P. and Mednick, M. 1973. "Race, Social Class and Motive to Avoid Success in Women." In J. Rosenblith, W. Allinsmith, and J. Williams (Eds.) *Readings in Child Development.* Boston: Allyn and Bacon: 308–312.

CHAPTER FOUR

Primary Group Issues

Based on research findings, Jacquelyne Jackson presents some interesting ideas to contradict accepted stereotypes abut Black men in Black families and about Black husband-wife relationships. There seems to be a clear separation of roles in household activities, with joint decision making on more significant family responsibilities. Some differences exist between older and younger Black husband-wife families and the Black husband figure demonstrate signs of having a clearly defined role and significant power.

Lena Myers addresses the importance of affect in marital relations and suggests that marital success is based on the ability to define marital interaction goals and to establish opportunities to carry out these goals in an environment that is flexible without negating the positive aspects of conflict. These conclusions are supported by the perceptions of over 400 presently married or once married Black women.

Delores Aldridge provides significant information on interracial marriages in the United States covering such topics as incidence, causal factors, characteristics and consequences of interracial marriages concluding with an impressive bibliography to be drawn upon for additional research efforts.

Ordinary Black Husbands: The Truly Hidden Men

Jacquelyne Jackson

The apparent voluminousness of and persisting myths in most literature about black families have generally been effective in masking its actually sparse, fragmentary, and inconclusive status. For example, any serious search for concrete data and generalizations about ordinary blacks functioning effectively or normally as spouses, parents, and grandparents is almost in vain. The present paucity of much of that literature has been generated primarily by the "culture of investigative property." That is, most of its contributors have been unduly possessed by a homogeneous view of blacks; an overconcentration upon abnormality (and especially upon by-products of sexual intercourse or, indeed, upon the sexual act itself); an apathetic lack of interest in interdisciplinary research; a short attention span; an exaggerated masculinity in defense of their adolescent knowledge; and an inability to defer gratification, as evidenced by their relatively frequent utilization of inappropriate racial comparisons and insufficient data which of course,usually produce invalid conclusions.

Such traits, analogous in many respects to those commonly ascribed to the "culture of poverty," must be reduced to facilitate acquisition of realistic knowledge about black families in particular and families in general. One step in that direction is very simple: it is merely a description and uncomplicated statistical analysis of ordinary black family members. It recognizes the diversity of black, permits intragroup comparisons of blacks, and can eventually produce a baseline of normality from which deviations can be evaluated to determine f they are only "different strokes for different folks" or if they are inherently, structurally, or functionally deficient for their owners and those whose lives they affect.

This presentation is a humble step in that direction. It is merely a description and simple analysis of ordinary black husbands who, while numerically larger among black

Presented orally at the 1973 annual meeting of the American Orthopsychiatric Association, New York, this research was partially supported by NIMH Grant #MH16554.

men, represent the truly hidden men from the perpetrators of the "culture of investigative poverty." It is so ordinary, so routine, so humdrum until you may well be bored by the absence of titillation about school drop-outs, streetcorner winos, drug addicts, muggers, absent fathers, and revolutionaries.

More specifically, this exploratory comparison of instrumental and affective relationships between spouses as reported by two sub-sample sets (i.e., nonmanually and manually employed husbands, and employed and nonemployed or largely retired husbands) from a larger study of roles and resources of older blacks in a southern urban residentially segregated environment was particularly concerned about role allocations for ordinary household maintenance activities and about spouse unilaterality (i.e., decision-making by one spouse).

Following Adams' (1968) definition, *instrumental relationships* consisted of shared activities and mutual assistance patterns between subjects and spouses during the year immediately preceding the interview, with emphasis upon activity type and frequency of occurrence, while *affective relationships* were measured by *agreement* (i.e., responses to "Would you say you and your spouse agree about things you really consider important in life?" of no, very little, to some extent, to a great extent, or completely).

According to Blood and Wolfe (1963). *instrumental relationships* were also measured by ascertaining spouse dominance (i.e., husband only, husband more often than wife, husband and wife about equally, wife more often than husband, and wife only) in specific decision-making situations.

In the largest study, black interviewers, utilizing a modified Kinship Interview Schedule, modeled upon Adams (1968) and Blood and Wolfe (1963), collected data in 1968 and 1969 for approximately 73 percent of all male household heads or all males 21 or more years of age in an urban renewal area, as listed by the local Housing Relocation Office, and from 79 percent of adult male subjects randomly selected from designated blocks in areas peripheral to the urban renewal area, and produced a total of 170 male subjects married and living with spouse and included in this report.

Nonmanually (i.e., white-collar or salaried) and manually (i.e., blue-collar or wage-earning) employed subjects were similar in age (about 40 and 46 years respectively) and long-term or indigenous residence in the city. But, whereas well over two-thirds of the nonmanuals had completed or gone beyond high school, only about one-third of the manuals had achieved equivalent education. They also differed at the .05 level of confidence in that nonmanuals were less likely to be fathers (38 percent of the nonmanuals and 19 percent of the manuals were childless) and the manuals were somewhat more likely to be both fathers and grandfathers (true of approximately 35 percent of the manuals and 9 percent of the nonmanuals).

The mean age of nonemployed or largely retired subjects (about 61 years) was significantly higher than that of the employed subjects (about 45 years). Other significant differences at or beyond the .05 level of confidence also distinguished these two sub-groups: nonemployed subjects with less average education had longer community residence and more children and grandchildren, but they were more likely to be living only with spouse than were the employed subjects. All of these significant differences were, of course, expected, and they are normal.

Interview items, grouped under four major categories of (a) *household maintenance activities* (such as grocery shopping and breakfast preparation), (b) *household decision-making activities* (such as grocery budgeting and disciplining children), (c) *spouse interactive activities* (such as church attendance and family and commercial recreation), (d) *spouse affect* (i.e., agreement tabulated by response frequencies by (1) nonmanually and manually employed, and (2) employed and nonemployed or largely retired husbands, and chi-square analyses were utilized to test for significant differences.

FINDINGS

Nonmanually and Manually Employed Husbands

Among the 23 nonmanually employed husbands, about 70 percent had received more and 22 percent as much education as their wives, whereas approximately 52 percent of the manually employed husbands had received somewhat less education than their wives. Nevertheless both sets of husbands were not significantly different in their responses about *household maintenance activities.* Approximately three-fourths or more of both groups reported the wife as usually preparing her husband's breakfast, and washing, ironing, dishwashing, and housecleaning for the family, whereas 90 percent or more of the husbands usually performed the yardwork and household repairs. About 59 percent of the manually employed husbands reported that they most often performed grocery shopping as a couple, whereas about 57 percent of the wives of the nonmanually employed spouses were reported as usually doing the grocery shopping. About 61 percent of the nonmanually and 52 percent of the manually employed couples usually paid bills jointly.

Less role segregation was apparent in *household decision-making activities.* The majority of nonmanually and manually employed husbands reported husband-and-wife joint decisions in deciding about grocery budgets, insurance purchases, physician selections, and residential locations. About 61 percent of the nonmanually and 57 percent of the manually employed husbands also reported joining disciplining of children, but where joint discipline was generally absent, then husbands—and not mothers—most often served as disciplinarians for their offspring.

Whereas approximately 70 percent of the nonmanually and 76 percent of the manually employed husbands reported that they determined for themselves whether or not they would accept particular employment initially, a much smaller proportion (47.8 percent and 58.6 percent respectively) determined without spouse assistance if they would continue in that employment. A slightly higher percentage of the nonmanually (65.2 percent) than the manually (55.2 percent) employed husbands indicated that their wives only decided if and when they should work.

Among spouse interactive activities, where the activity had to have been engaged in jointly at least once during the year preceding the interview, nonmanually and manually employed husbands were indistinguishable only by church attendance with spouse. They differed, at or beyond the .05 level of confidence, in that nonmanually employed couples were much more likely to have shopped (other than grocery) or vacationed together, engaged in family or commercial recreation, visited relatives jointly, or engaged in other activities.

Manually employed husbands were also significantly more likely to report their wives as usually doing the family letter-writing (72.4 percent) than were nonmanually employed husbands (3.48 percent), and partial factors accounting for that difference may well include differential levels of education and employment statuses among the involved spouses. Although manually employed subjects reported their wives as those most likely to perform family letter-writing, they were not reported as those who usually telephoned relatives. Only about 45 percent of the spouses fell in that category. Among the nonmanually employed spouses, a slightly higher percentage (39.1 percent) were reported as those who usually telephoned relatives than those who usually engaged in family letter-writing.

About 57 percent of the manually and 49 percent of the nonmanually employed husbands reported themselves and their spouses incomplete agreement about the most important things.

Employed and Nonemployed or Retired Husbands

Among the 52 employed subjects (which includes both nonmanually and manually employed subjects compared above), about 46 percent had received more education than wives, as had about 30 percent of the nonemployed or retired husbands. In almost all of the remaining cases, husbands and wives had received equal education. Although educational levels of spouses among the employed group were higher than those among the nonemployed, the two groups were indistinguishable by differences in educational level between husbands and wives in each group.

The typical patterns of *household maintenance activities* reported for nonmanually and manually employed subjects also characterized those employed and not employed. Obviously, similarities would appear for the employed subjects, but what is most interesting is that they also tended to appear for the largely retired group who were older, had less education, and were most often no longer active in the labor force, as compared with employed subjects. Wives were most often reported as usually preparing their husbands' breakfasts and performing the family's laundry, dishwashing, and household cleaning chores. But two significant differences at or beyond the .01 level of confidence did emerge between the two groups: employed subjects were less likely to report their wives as usually performing household cleaning tasks and more likely to report them as dishwashers. Whereas almost all of the employed husbands reported themselves as the usual person responsible for yardwork and household repairs, a smaller percentage (but still a hefty majority) of the largely retired subjects fell within those categories. About 53 percent of the largely retired subjects reported their wives as the usual grocery shoppers, but the model response (46 percent) to this inquiry from employed subjects was husband and wife, a difference significant at the .01 level of confidence. About 40 percent of the largely retired subjects indicated that they most often paid bills, whereas the corresponding modal response from employed subjects (55.8 percent) was husband and wife. Although these two groups were statistically indistinguishable in their reports of the spouse most often paying the bills (irrespective of the source of monies), greater spouse unilaterality was present among the largely retired.

For household *decision-making activities,* employed and nonemployed subjects of resembled each other in spouse responsibility for grocery budgeting, deciding where to live, disciplining children, and physician selection. Joint decisions were most frequent among both groups for living locality and choice of physician. Those about grocery budgeting were much more characteristic of employed (56 percent) than the nonemployed (35 percent), which again reveals some greater spouse unilaterality among the latter.

These two sets of husbands differed critically by employment and insurance decisions. Nonemployed husbands reported greater unilateral power in decisions about their employment for their wives. They also differed in spouse power regarding purchase of life and burial insurance. About 65 percent of the employed and 52 percent of the nonemployed reported joint decisions, while about 35 percent of the former and 30 percent of the latter reported husband only or husband mostly. None of the employed husbands reported wife only or wife mostly, but almost 18 percent of the nonemployed husbands placed their wives in that category.

Statistically significant differences were most apparent in a comparison of *spouse interactive activities*. Employed subjects were much more likely to report attending church, shopping, vacationing, family and commercial recreation, and other activities with their spouses. Although not statistically significant, they also visited relatives more frequently with their spouses. Their wives were usually more responsible for family letter-writing (53 percent) and somewhat less responsible for telephoning relatives (42 percent), with the reverse pattern typifying nonemployed husbands, where about 47 percent of their wives were usually responsible for family letter-writing, and about 56 percent for telephoning relatives.

Modal *spouse affect* responses were complete agreement for employed (53 percent) and great agreement for nonemployed (58 percent) husbands. Fewer than four percent of both employed and nonemployed husbands indicated less than great agreement with spouses about the most important things in life.

DISCUSSION

In general, this description of instrumental activities and perceived spouse agreement revealed the expected conjugal role segregation in household maintenance activities performed within or around the home. Wives engaged in traditional "women's work," and husbands in "men's work." Wives of nonmanually employed and of largely retired husbands were more likely to shop for groceries without their husbands than were their respective counterparts. Spouses were most often jointly involved in paying bills except among the largely retired group.

The reported pattern of household decision-making activities most often indicated joint spouse participation, particularly in activities directly affecting all family members.

Data collected about parental responsibility for disciplining children suggested that fathers—and not mothers—in older black husband-wife families most often performed that function. Among younger families, there appeared to be a greater shift toward joint parental responsibility. Such data contradict the usual stereotype of the relative insignificance of the father in black families, and, perhaps more important, the extent of his power within his family. Undue emphasis upon matriarchal black families, e.g. has overshadowed patriarchal black families. In a recent comparison of selected research studies about black and white families between 1966 and 1970, it was noted that

> *When the concept of matriarchy is restricted to wife dominance in husband-wife families, existing evidence suggests strongly that matriarchy is most characteristic of white, professional families with unemployed wives. Lower-class, intact black families appear to be even more patriarchal (i.e., male dominated) than their white counterparts. That is, black males tend to exercise stronger power within their families than do white males. Clearly, among working-class and middle-class families, black or white, equalitarianism tends to be the dominant pattern, or at least there appears to be a shift towards that pattern (Jackson 1973:437–438).*

Greater spouse unilaterality about employment statuses for husbands and wives was also more common among older than younger husbands.

With the exception of family letter-writing and telephoning relatives, the data clearly followed expected patterns of greater or more frequent spouse involvement in interactive activities among those in nonmanual than manual employment, as well as among those employed than those not employed. Such differences, of course, are functions of socioeconomic and health variables.

Perhaps most interestingly was the striking amount of agreement reported by these husbands between themselves and their wives on the most important things in life. While these subjects were not asked specifically if they loved their wives, many of them volunteered sentimental comments about their wives to the field interviewers. My impressionistic judgments of many married black couples lead me to believe that love is valued. If so, we must question the validity of such assumptions about love and black couples as that given by Bell (1971:250).

> *There have been a number of studies indicating that husband-wife roles and patterns of interaction in the lower class are quite different from those of the middle class. In the Black lower class the notion f love as a prerequisite to marriage and as a condition for its successful maintenance is not a strong value. There is also strong evidence that companionship in marriage is not a strong value or behavior pattern in the lower class. Lack of marital companionship is reflected in the general patterns of sex-segregated activities. For example, lower-class partners tend to maintain old friendship and kinship ties rather than reorganize ties after marriage to make the spouse a part of one social network.*

Bell (1971:250) further indicated that "Recent research indicates that the lower-class husband is not only tangential to family functioning but that very often his wife prefers it that way." These exploratory data about ordinary husbands, as well as data collected from many of their wives, but not reported herein, contradict Bell. But they also underscore the problems involved in generalizing about blacks from data unrepresentative of blacks.

Thus, in addition to this description of ordinary black husbands constituting the truly hidden men, obscured, as it were by the "culture of investigative poverty," perhaps the primary purpose of this presentation could well have been that of calling attention anew to the critical need to accumulate meaningful and valid data about the diversities of black families. Except for purposes of demonstrating clearly racial discrimination and its consequences, the current paucity of our knowledge about black families mandates greater concentration upon comparisons of black families with black families, and not with white families.

In any case, these findings, while applicable only to the sample, could well be taken as hypotheses for future investigations of patterns of interaction between black husbands and wives.

REFERENCES

Adams, Bert N. 1968. *Kinship in an Urban Setting.* Chicago: Markham.

Bell, Robert R. 1971. "The Related Importance of Mother and Wife Roles among Black Lower-Class Women." In *The Black Family, Essays and Studies,* ed. by Robert Staples. Belmont, California: Wadsworth, 248–255.

Blood, Robert, and Donald M. Wolfe. 1963. *Husbands and Wives: The Dynamics of Married Living.* New York: Free Press.

Jackson, Jacquelyne J. 1973. "Family Organization and Ideology." In *Comparative Studies of Blacks and Whites in the United States,* ed. by Kent S. Miller and Ralph Dreger. New York: Seminar Press, 405–445.

On Marital Relations: Perceptions of Black Women

Lena Wright Myers

During the past few years, a number of books have been written about different aspects of human sexuality. "How-to-do" manuals have become best sellers, and books on sex roles and the psychology or social psychology of women (usually whites) have become household items. Recently, a few authors have started discussing the many supposedly profound and difficult dilemmas of intimate relationships and love that are evolving between men and women. And the latter term, love, has been claimed to be so subjective and so elusive that it defies definition. As a matter of fact, there are almost as many ways to love as there are people in the world to be loved or not loved. It is true that expressions of love vary from culture to culture, era to era, and person to person. In some centuries, "real love" had to be romantic and free of the "ugliness" of sex. In other periods of time, sexual expression was considered the most important ingredient of love.

Attitudes toward intimate expression in the western world have varied between the extreme of an almost total suppression of sexuality—at least on the surface—and a public tolerance of all varieties of intimate expression. The mass media have given emotional expressions with overtones of sexuality the hard sell, processing and packaging it in a variety of styles.

One may review magazine articles to see how the stars intimately express themselves. Another person may examine orthodox cases of intimacy by various groups. Others may seek the norms of close friends or peers, or revert to parental norms regarding intimate expressions. But all of us must set our own course for expressing ourselves in an intimate relationship.

AUTHOR'S NOTE: The research reported in this chapter was supported by a Ford Dissertation Fellowship in Ethnic Studies, 1972–1973, and a National Science Foundation Research Grant, 1974–1976.

Maybe some people are "on the fringes" in search of their own personal emotional expressions of sexuality (Masters and Johnson, 1974:86)

This study is not an effort to define love among Black men and Black women, nor is it an attempt to provide a "how-to-do-it" (whatever is that you are doing at a given time) manual. It is simply a descriptive account of social and/or symbolic interaction among Black couples as told by 400 Black women. Now, what is meant by social and/or symbolic interaction?

Developing and weaving related concepts. Mead (1934) noted that social interaction may be viewed as a conversation of gestures. He suggested that a conversation of gestures includes the mutual adjustment of behavior, where each participant uses the *first* gesture of the other participant's action as a cue for her or his own action. Thus, her or his response becomes a stimulus to the other participant, prompting either a shift in the other's attitude or the completion of the originally intended act. One person may unconsciously respond to the tone of voice or facial expression of the other person with whom he or she may be interacting and the other person may be unaware at a given time. This is called unconscious or nonsignificant conversation of gestures and consists of simple stimulus and response. But most human interaction through the process of socialization becomes symbolic depending upon shared understandings about the meanings of gestures. People respond creatively to the environment which they are a part of through the interpretive process. They do not respond mechanically to the intrinsic qualities of situations. Instead, they assign meanings to the given situations and respond in terms of those meanings (Blumer, 1966). The ability to assign meaning to given situations is learned by persons while interacting with other persons. Since each person will respond to events in terms of the meanings he or she assigns to them, each person's action is comprehensible and predictable to others only to the degree that the underlying meanings are *known* (Lauer and Handel, 1977).

Social and/or symbolic interaction is defined in this chapter as a social process which stresses communication through language and gestures (body talk) in the formation and maintenance of personality and social relationships among Black men and Black women. There are many things that are left *unsaid* among Black women and men; this may even complement the old cliche that "action speaks louder than words." Some things need to go *unsaid* and *unacted*, too, if there is not shared symbolic meaning among women and men i the form of language and gestures. However, if there are shared symbolic meanings, both verbally and nonverbally, more positive relationships may exist between Black women and Black men.

Most Blacks do not marry in pursuit of a secure financial status, as do whites. However, when they do, they could end up as Ladner (1972) describes:

> *It could be that when Blacks fall into the "trap" of using the dominant society's reasons for marriage, they become "ipso facto" prone to failure, because in this kind of environment, emotional love cannot counteract joblessness and the multitude of tensions which are frequently present.*

For many Blacks the realities of the world cause frustrations that may affect their love lives. Therefore, it may be necessary to find alternatives for coping with the negative influences of society. Let us assume that a kind of symbolic or vicarious intimacy ensues which creates an unconscious desire for Black married couples to retain their marital relationships rather than resolve them. This form of symbolic intimacy may ensue in spite of negative environmental influences and traditional norms.

In an attempt to explore how Black women perceive their relationships with Black men in a marital situation, I used interview data which I collected from two separate, simple random samples, each of which included 200 Black women from Michigan and Mississippi (N=400) in 1972–1973 and 1974, respectively. These were women who (1) had lived with their husbands for 5 years or more and (2) were divorced or separated. They were 20 to 81 years old. Their educational level ranged from third grade to masters degrees and above. These women had 1 to 15 children, with monthly *family* incomes ranging from $60 to $2,500. The length of residence in the respective areas ranged from 1 to 81 years.

This study describes how these Black women saw their social and/or symbolic relationships with their husbands or former husbands.

One of the expressive gratifications sought by married couples is cathectic affection. In order to examine how satisfied were Black women with their cathectic affection, the following question was asked:

> *Cathectic affection has to do with feelings or emotions pertaining to the physical aspect of married life. These may range from the most innocent to the most intimate demonstrations of affection. Now, then, are you generally satisfied—or dissatisfied—with this aspect of your marriage or former marriage?*

Table 1 shows the data obtained from the above question. For both samples, the married women appear more satisfied with the cathectic aspect of their marriages than do the women who are separated or divorced. The difference between the married women and the single women (separated or divorce) of the Mississippi sample is only slight (94 percent and 41 percent, respectively). But for the Michigan sample, the difference between the married and single women is much greater. Ninety-six percent of the married women expressed general satisfaction with their cathectic affection, while 68 percent of the single women expressed the same.

A clearer understanding of cathectic affection may be found in the examples which follow.[1]

> *Fay is a 47-year-old married woman with four children who lived in Mississippi. With a ray of self-confidence which even the most non-perceptive individual should be able to grasp seemingly she had no problems with talking about her marital relationship with Melvin. She said, "Melvin has a way of looking at me that tells me that he wants to be with me, without having to say one word." She also said that he had another way of looking at her that let her know he did not want to be bothered at times.*

Table 1. Perceived Satisfaction with Cathectic Affection

MICHIGAN	**Generally Satisfied**		**Dissatisfied**		**Total**	
	N	**%**	**N**	**%**	**N**	**%**
Married	80	96	3	4	83	100
Separated or divorced	48	68	23	32	71	100
MISSISSIPPI						
Married	103	94	7	6	110	100
Separated or divorced	68	91	7	9	75	100

Somewhat similar is the example of Gerri, a native of Michigan, age 30, a divorcee, and the mother of one child. She talked about how "touchy-feely" both she and Paul (her former husband) were Gerri made it very clear that the lack of cathectic affection was not the reason for their marriage ending in divorce. As a matter of fact, she stated, "that is one of the things that I miss the most about Paul and my relationship . . . we could understand and feel each other."

Both cases indicate shared meanings and understandings of emotional expressions between Black women and their husbands or former husbands. Even though Faye may not have been very pleased about the way Melvin looked at her that told her he did not want to be bothered at the moment, she must have understood that nonverbal gesture and likely behaved accordingly. An understanding of such a gesture could also have aided her in not becoming a "clinging vine" in the marital relationship, as some women do and which some men resent.

For Gerri, the nonverbal communication between her and Paul appeared to have been of great importance to their relationship. Being "touchy-feely" toward each other seems to suggest shared meanings and understanding through and about touching.

The fact that Black women were satisfied with physical affection shown by their mates is symbolic in that there must have been shared understanding about the meaning of gestures. Satisfaction received from expressions of physical affection has meaning and arouses meaning in the partners to whom these expressions are communicated. This sharing is essential to communication in the symbolic interactionist process. As one writer puts it:

Each part of the body speaks a silent but intimate and revealing language. More than mere words—a wink, a shrug, or a handclasp can be the best clue you'll ever get to a person's innermost feelings [Callum, 1972].

The key to nonverbal communication of emotional expression is understanding the *clues*, and one need not be a sociologist or psychologist to do so. Black people are an expressive people. Data in Table 1 indicate that shared meanings and understandings about such clues did exist between Black women and their husbands or former husbands as perceived by the women.

The emergence of body language depends upon an already established form of interaction with the other in a marital situation. The other is the spouse. It is only to language that the individual using the gesture responds int he way the other individual does. In other words, the meaning of what one is saying includes the tendency for the other person to respond to it. As hope to arouse. Each gesture or word serves as a stimulus to them as well as to their spouses. Now, let us examine the women's perception of freedom to communicate with their husbands or former husbands.

Assuming that the "significant other" within a marital situation, at a given time, is the spouse, the women of these samples were asked the following question:

Do you feel very free _____free _____ not so free _____ to confide, talk things over, or discuss anything with your husband or former husband?

Table 2. Perceived Satisfaction With "Freedom" to Communicate With Spouse

MICHIGAN	Very Free or Free		Not so Free		Total	
	N	%	N	%	N	%
Married	75	89	9	11	84	100
Separated or divorced	40	55	33	45	73	100
MISSISSIPPI						
Married	82	74	28	26	110	100
Separated, divorced or widowed	37	49	38	51	75	100

In observing the data in Table 2, we find that the married women of both the Michigan and Mississippi samples felt freer than the separated or divorced women (when these women were married) to communicate with their spouses. Conversely, the separated or divorced women felt less free to communicate with their spouses than did the married women. It is interesting to note that the married women of Mississippi felt less free than the married women of Michigan to communicate with their husbands. Could this difference be accounting for by region or social class? This question cannot be answered by this analysis, but is an interesting question to be pursued in the future.

Examples of freedom or lack of freedom to verbally communicate with husbands or former husbands are as follows:

Ellen is a 68-year-old mother or four from Mississippi who has been married to George for 47 years. She said, "I never believed in the old saying that woman should be seen but not heard—like some people say about children . . . and George knows that."

However, Annette, a 28-year-old mother of two from Michigan, offered an opposing view. She has been separated from Ray for almost three years. "He never wanted me to say much of anything unless he asked me something." Annette said. The lack of verbal communication between Annette and Ray is obvious in that Ray seem to want Annette to do little or no talking to him. One-way verbal communication (as in this case) must have been extremely frustrating—especially for the listener. This alone could account for Annette having felt "not so free" to confide, talk things over, or discuss anything with her former husband.

What does this imply? It could be that a distinction between verbal and nonverbal communication did not occur among the separated or divorced women and their former spouses. Or, it may be that if distinctions were made, neither form of communication was utilized to its fullest, which may have accounted for their marital relationships having been resolved.

In an effort to assess the husbands' readiness to understand what their wives say to them during the process of interacting, data were obtained from the following question:

Do you feel that your husband/former husband very readily _______ readily ________ not so readily ________ received or understands what you are trying to say?

From Table 3 one can observe that for both samples a greater proportion of the married women than the separated or divorced women said that their husbands very readily received or understood what they were trying to say to them. Conversely, a greater proportion of the separated or divorced women than the married women indicated that their former husbands did *not* so readily receive or understand what they were trying to say to them.

Table 3. Spouses' Readiness to Receive and Understand What Respondents Were Saying

MICHIGAN	**Very Readily or Readily**		**Not so Readily**		**Total**	
	N	**%**	**N**	**%**	**N**	**%**
Married	71	85	13	15	84	100
Separated or divorced	32	42	44	58	76	100
MISSISSIPPI						
Married	50	49	52	51	102	100
Separated, divorced, or widowed	29	40	44	60	73	100

The difference between the married women and the separated or divorced women is much greater in the Michigan sample than in the Mississippi sample. In other words, the Mississippi women, married as well as separated or divorced, have more in common (49 percent, 40 percent) than do the Michigan women (85 percent, 42 percent) with regard to perceptions of their husband's empathy.

Companionship is a form of expressive gratification which is sought in a marriage. In order to test this, the following question was asked the respondents:

> *Companionship has to do with shared leisure or non-work time activities, e.g., movies, picnics, parties and dancing. Are you generally satisfied—or dissatisfied—with this aspect of your marriage or former marriage?*

Table 4 shows that a greater proportion of married women were satisfied with the companionship in their lives than women who were separated or divorced for both the Michigan and Mississippi samples. Conversely, divorced or separated women were more dissatisfied with their companionship than married women. Here, we observe that the difference between married and single women is greater in the Michigan sample (90 percent and 56 percent, respectively). A 52-year-old divorcee from Michigan said that her former husband was never home long enough to do anything with her and their six children, even when not working. This confirms a common expectation—if separated or divorced women were satisfied with their marriages, they would still be married, especially since companionship is the essence of marriage.

Table 4. Perceived Satisfaction With Companionship

MICHIGAN	Generally Satisfied		Dissatisfied		Total	
	N	%	N	%	N	%
Married	76	90	8	10	84	100
Separated or divorced	40	56	32	44	72	100
MISSISSIPPI						
Married	72	67	35	33	107	100
Separated, divorced, or widowed	37	49	38	51	75	100

Interacting individuals in any situation most constantly interpret the gestures of others and, in so doing, arrest, recognize, and adjust their own intentions, wishes, feelings, and attitudes. Similarly, they have to judge the fitness of norms, values, and group prescriptions from the situation indicated by the acts of others. This process of interpretation and redefinition relates to all kinds of interpersonal situations, whether they involve cooperation, love, conflict, hostility, or anger. This notion is examined by using the following questions:

How often would you say that you and your husband/former husband had a big "blow up" and really got angry with each other?

_____ *never*

_____ *seldom*

_____ *sometimes*

_____ *often*

_____ *very often*

Table 5 shows that married women in the Michigan sample are more likely than the separated or divorced women to never have marital conflicts. On the other hand, separated or divorced women were more likely to have had conflicts with their former husbands. This conforms to a common-sense expectation. Conflict is negatively related to marital disruption, although some conflict is positively related to a marriage.

Table 5. Frequency of Conflict During Marital Relations

MICHIGAN	**Never**		**Seldom or Sometimes**		**Often or Very Often**		**Total**	
	N	**%**	**N**	**%**	**N**	**%**	**N**	**%**
Married	12	15	63	77	7	8	82	100
Separated or divorced	2	2	31	40	45	58	78	100
MISSISSIPPI								
Married	0	0	59	74	21	26	80	100
Separated, divorced, or widowed	0	0	20	48	22	52	42	100

In the Mississippi sample, we find that neither married nor single women (separated or divorced) had no marital conflicts. The married women (26 percent and 52 percent, respectively).

The notion of conflict in a marital relationship brings to mind an article entitled "Problems Remain the Same" which appeared in a well-known magazine some time ago, noting a request for advice from a marriage counselor:

After ten years of marriage, our problems today are the same as at the beginning. It seems that there can be no compromise. Briefly, our problems are:

1. *He thinks I talk too much detail. He tunes me out, and does not remember things I have told him.*
2. *He says I depend on him too much for little decisions.*
3. *I don't like to argue. I used to cry over misunderstandings, which disgusted him. Now I sulk.*
4. *I have always been more affectionate than he—sometimes too aggressive, which annoys him. I have restrained myself, but this has not made him more affectionate. Signed, Lonely [Home Life, 1972]*

Conflict is often viewed negatively. However, some theorists suggest that conflict has some positive aspects (Simmel, 1955). It can serve as a force which integrates people on opposing sides, bonding them firmly into a group. Granted, this also applies to at least two people interacting. Thus, conflict may be advantageous to some Black married couples in that they may refrain from personal abuse and confine a quarrel to issues, thus eliminating points of tension. In addition, it may serve to bring husbands and wives into communication with one another, forcing them to face up to their problems.

In examining reasons for conflict among the women and their husbands or former husbands, the following questions were asked:

What is/was this usually about?

occupational and financial matters or other matters

Thinking back over your married life, what was or is the one thing that you and your husband or former husband have disagreed about most?[2]

Table 6 shows the issues over which women had marital conflicts. For the Michigan married women, "suspicion of husband playing on wife," followed by occupational or financial issues were those over which they had the greatest conflicts. The issues over which they had the least conflicts were discipline of children and infrequent sexual activity on the part of the husband (11 percent each). For the single women, the reverse was true. The greatest conflict occurred over occupational or financial issues, followed by "suspicion of husband playing on wife." The issues which caused least conflict for single women were "infrequent sexual activity on the part of the husband" followed by discipline of children.

In the Mississippi samples, we find some variations from the Michigan sample. Mississippi married women's greatest marital conflicts appeared to be over child discipline, followed by suspected infidelity by the husband. The issue of child discipline caused less marital conflict int he Michigan sample. The issue over which the least conflict occurred was "infrequent sexual activity on the part of the husband." For the single women, the conflict occurred most frequently over "suspicion of husband playing on wife," followed by occupational or financial issues. The issues over which they had the least conflict were discipline of children and husband's infrequent sexual activity.

Table 6. Major Reasons for Conflict During Marital Relations

MICHIGAN	Occupational or Financial		Suspicion of Husband "Playing" on Wife		Disciplining Children		Infrequent Sexual Activity —Husband		Total	
	N	%	N	%	N	%	N	%	N	%
Married	24	35	30	43	8	11	8	11	70	100
Separated or divorced	47	61	22	29	5	7	2	3	76	100
MISSISSIPPI										
Married	17	28	20	34	23	38	0	0	60	100
Separated or divorced	15	35	23	55	2	5	2	5	42	100

SUMMARY AND CONCLUSION

This study is by no means exhaustive—it is merely an effort to describe the social and symbolic interaction among 400 Black women who were either married, separated, or divorced. Specifically, we were concerned with the interpersonal behaviors that affect the maintenance of marital relationships. From the empirical findings, one may conclude that alternatives utilized by Black married couples in retaining their marital status include perceptions of cathectic affection, perceptions of the opportunity to relate to their husbands (thus having them favorably respond), perceived degree of satisfaction with companionship, and the ability of both partners to use conflict to their advantage in the relationship.

In conclusion, Black married and unmarried women may see one function of social and symbolic relationships in marriages as an outlet of emotional support (support system) and concern of someone to confide in. Spouses (mates) seem to fulfill that need which cannot be found in the larger society due to its structure. Let us also realize that being divorced or separated does, in many instances, eliminate social and symbolic interaction between Black women and Black men in a living arrangement. Although sometimes misunderstood by outsiders, memories of this relationship can remain a part of a former Black mate's entire life. This was suggested by the 400 Black women from Michigan and Mississippi.

Black women and Black men, as reasoning creatures, can relate to each other verbally and through self-disclosure, can learn something about each other and about our own identities as well. In addition, as sexual creatures, we have the ability to express ourselves, our feelings, thoughts, and even our fantasies through physical (nonverbal) communication. It simply becomes an ongoing process of relating, sharing, and communicating.

NOTES

1. Pseudonyms are used to identify the women and their husbands or former husbands for each example, since names of the respondents were not secured to assure confidentiality.
2. It is important to note that open-ended responses to this question were also used in pursuing data on "communication" between the women and their husbands/former husbands, where responses regarding "communicating" occurred.

REFERENCES

Blumer, H. (1966) "Sociological implications of the thoughts of George Herbert Mead." American Journal of Sociology 71 (March.)

Callum, M. (1972) Body Talk. New York: Bantam.

Fullerton, G. P. (1977) Survival in Marriage: Introduction to Family Interaction, Conflict, and Alternatives. Hinsdale, IL: Dryden.

Green, E. J. (1978) Personal Relationships: An Approach to Marriage and Family. New York: McGraw-Hill.

Henley, N. M. (1970) "The politics of touch." Presented at the American Psychological Association Meetings, Miami Beach, Florida, September.

______. (1974) "Power, sex, and nonverbal communication." Berkeley Journal of Sociology 18.

Kogan, B. A. (1973) Human Sexual Expression. New York: Harcourt Brace Jovanovich.

Ladner, J. A. (1972) Tomorrow's Tomorrow: The Black Woman. New York: Doubleday.

Lauer, R. H. and W. H. Handel (1977) Social Psychology: The Theory and Application of Symbolic Interactionism. Boston: Houghton Mifflin.

Masters, W. H. and V. E. Johnson (1974) "The role of religion in sexual dysfunction," in M.S. Calderone (ed.) Sexuality and Human Values. New York: SIECUS/Association Press.

Mead, G. H. (1934) Mind, Self, and Society (C. W. Morris, ed.). Chicago: University of Chicago Press.

Myers, L. W. (1973) "A study of the self-esteem maintenance process among Black women." Dissertation, Michigan State University. (unpublished)

______. (1975) "Black women and self-esteem," in M. Millman and R. M. Kanter (eds.) Another Voice: Feminist Perspective on Social Life and Social Science, Garden City, NY: Anchor/Doubleday.

Simmel, G. (1955) Conflict and the Web Affiliations (K. H. Wolff and R. Bendix, trans.). New York: Free Press.

Walster, E. and G. W. Walster (1978) A New Look at Love, Reading MA: Addison-Wesley.

Interracial Marriages: Empirical and Theoretical Considerations

Delores P. Aldridge

Interracial marriages have garnered attention periodically since the turn of the century. However, sociopsychological research in the area of intermarriage continues to be scant in spite of increased contact between the races in the 1960s. Social scientists have maintained the study of intermarriage may provide a precise, quantitative measurement of crucial and related questions such as the process of assimilation, the degree of internal cohesion in individual racial, religious, and ethnic groups, and the extent of social distance between groups of these types (Barron, 1946: 249).

Little has been done, however, in the areas which promise so much in understanding social processes. What research that has been done has focused on: the incidence of interracial marriages; causal factors; sociopsychological characteristics; and, the problems encountered by the marriage partners and their children. This paper will summarize the small amount of research which has been done on interracial marriages in the areas mentioned in an attempt to update the body of information. It will also provide directives for future research which should lead to a better understanding of black-white marriages and their implications for black people and the larger society.

INCIDENCE OF INTERRACIAL MARRIAGE

The rate of interracial marriage has varied by state since many states prohibited interracial marriages until the Loving versus Virginia decision in 1967. With this decision all laws against interracial marriages were declared invalid.

Some evidence does exist which suggests that the rate of interracial marriage decreased in the first half of the century and prior to the 1954 Supreme Court decision declaring unconstitutional segregated public schools (Burma, 1962, Drake and Cayton,

JOURNAL OF BLACK STUDIES, Vol. 8 No. 3. March 1978 ©1978 Sage Publications, Inc.

1945; Lynn, 1953; Panunzio, 1942, Wirth and Goldhamer, 1944). However, data from California indicated that the rate of interracial marriage increased slightly following the court decision of 1954 (Barnett, 1963a). There are other fragmentary statistics which suggest racially mixed marriages may be on the increase in the United States (Powledge, 1963; Heer, 1966: 273; cf. Mayer and Smock, 1960). Data from another study conducted after the 1967 decision found a similar increase as the California study (Aldridge, 1973). Even though data have suggested increases, several surveys of attitudes of blacks prior to the seventies indicated a lack of eagerness for intermarriage. (Pittsburgh Courier, 1958). In the latter 1960s and into the 1970s the emphasis on black pride and racial solidarity has contributed to similar attitudes (Staples, 1973: 123).

CAUSAL FACTORS

Numerous social and psychological forces facilitating intermarriage have been set forth by various writers. For example, Barron (1946) took the position that an unbalanced sex ratio and numerically small representation lead some groups into considerable incidence of intermarriage. Another interesting and perhaps more thorough study dealing with causal factors was conducted by golden in 1959. He dealt with propinquity as a variable. Premarital studies indicate that young people of diverse groups are led into marital ties through residential propinquity, economic propinquity, and similarity, both occupational and spatial; by close association and common experiences in the amount, type, and locale of education; and by recreational contacts (Barron, 1946).

The intermingling of young adults of different races at the high school and college levels is widely expected to be reflected over the long run in an increased rate of intermarriage. Because of the continual lowering of the average age of dating and entering marriage, high schools will be increasingly faced with mixed racial associations (Barnett, 1963a). And the fact that large numbers of interracial couples meet on college campuses away from home reduces the amount of parental and community control over the choice of an individual's dating partners. Young people have revolted against traditional institutions and values which have led them to reject the taboos on dating across racial lines (Staples, 1973). While sociologists have theories and hypotheses on the rebellion-rejection theme explaining the occurrence of inter-marriage, no empirical studies appear to exist.

It seems only logical that an increase in interracial dating would result in an increase in interracial marriages. Using selective data, Heer observed an upward trend in black-white marriage in those areas where residential segregation by race is low and where there are minimal status differences between the white and black population.

While the proportion of black men dating interracially appears much higher than that of black women, the difference is not so great when it comes to interracial marriages as reflected in 1960 census data. While it appears that black women are deprived of many dates by white women, the vast majority of black males are still available to them for matrimony.

Until recently, many of the black men who married white women were of a higher social status than their wives. Because this social status differential was so common, a theory was formulated about it. Sociologists hypothesized that the black male traded his class advantage for the racial caste advantage of the white bride (Merton, 1941:361–374). But contemporary interracial marriages are more likely to involve spouses from the same social class (Pavela, 1964: 209). Furthermore, when intermarriages involved members of different social classes, there was a pronounced tendency for black women to marry up rather than to marry down (Bernard, 1966: 274–276).

Consequently, one reason that black women marry white men is to improve their social status. Of course, this applies to many homogamous marriages. One notable exception, however, are the marriages of black female entertainers to white men. Because of their close association with white males in the course of their jobs, many of them form interracial unions. Most of the celebrated cases in recent years involved famous black women who married white men who were not equally famous or wealthy (Staples, 1973: 121).

Various motives have been suggested to explain black women/white men marriages. Some students of the subject assert that uneven sex ratios are a basic cause. Wherever a group in nearness to another group has an imbalance in sex ratio, there is a greater likelihood of intermarriage. If the groups have a relatively well-balanced distribution of the sexes, members will marry their own group (Panunzio, 1942: 690).

In interracial marriages, there is the tendency to look for ulterior motives. It is a popular notion that people marry interracially because of rebellion against their parents,sexual curiousity toward racially different individuals, and other psychological reasons. It is commonly conceived that there are kinds of unconscious bizarre reasons which propel racially different individuals into marriages. People may marry their "own kind" for the most weird reasons, yet these reasons do not make each marriage suspect. Perhaps the imputation of ulterior motives to interracial couples says more about the individual making these interpretations and about the society we live in than about the couple who intermarry (Washington, 1970: 303).

CHARACTERISTICS OF INTERRACIAL MARRIAGE

Even though there is some consensus on certain aspects of the interracial marriage phenomenon (Barnett, 1963a), outright contradictions can be found in the literature. This may be attributed to the fact that several studies were conducted at different locales and at different times, and the referent group might be marriages, or married "couples," not randomly selected. Monahan (1970) stresses the point that there is disagreement even on such a fundamental point as to whether more black males than black females intermarry with whites more often than black females. But the 1960 census data on married couples show that slightly more black females had white spouses than black males had white spouses. Recently, Staples (1974: 6) stated that during the 1960s the black male-white female marriage was common, but the 1970s portend a significant increase in black female-white male marriages. He explains that much of this increase will occur in the South among the college-educated who now have greater opportunity for social interaction than in previous decades.

Pavela (1964) concluded from his Indiana study that, in many respects, the black-white marriages studied contradict the characteristics of such marriages in the public mind or even in much sociological literature. It would appear that such intermarriage now occurs between persons who are, by and large, economically, educationally, and culturally equal and who have a strong emotional attachment, be it rationalization or real. The following characteristics can generally be discerned from the literature.

(1) The religiously less devout marry persons of different races with a higher frequency than the religiously more devout (Schnepp and Yui, 1955)

(2) Persons who have experienced disorganized and stressful parental families are more likely to marry members of other races than those who were raised in cohesive and stable families (Hunt and Collier, 1957; Lynn, 1953; Schnepp and Yui, 1955; Strauss, 1954).

(3) Persons living in urban areas cross racial lines to a greater extent than persons living in rural areas.

(4) Persons crossing racial lines to marry generally chose partners who come from different religious backgrounds (Golden, 1953; Lynn, 1953) and apparently from different socioeconomic levels (Drake and Cayton, 1945; Golden, 1954; Wirth and Goldhamer, 1944); two studies (Lynn, 1953; Pavela, 1964), however, report that the majority of spouses in interracial marriages come from the same socioeconomic level.

(5) Nonwhite males undertaking an interracial marriage appear to have higher-than-average socioeconomic status, and the white male and female and the nonwhite female have a lower-than-average socioeconomic level (Drake and Caton, 1945; Golden, 1954; Wirth and Goldhamer, 1944). However, one study (Lynn 1953) reports that the upper class is greatly underrepresented and the lower class is slightly overrepresented in interracial marriages.

(6) In black-white marriages, it is the black male who marries the white female in the majority of cases (Barron, 1946; Burma, 1952; Drake and Cayton, 1945; golden, 1953; Lynn, 1953; Risdon, 1954; Wirth and Goldhamer, 1944). For contradictions see Monahan (1970: 62).

(7) Among those who undertake an interracial marriage, a greater-than-average number have been married previously (Golden, 1954; Pavela, 1964; Wirth and Goldhamer, 1944).

(8) Foreign-born white males more than native white males and native white females more than foreign-born white females, undertake black-white marriages (Wirth and Goldhamer, 1944).

(9) In black-white marriages, the family of the black spouse seems to be more willing to accept the couple than does the family of the white spouse (Golden, 1953).

(10) American males and females marrying out of their racial group are generally older than the average at the time (Blesanz, 1950; Burma, 1952; Golden, 1953, 1954; Lynn, 1953; Risdon, 1954; Strauss, 1954).

CONSEQUENCES

The fourth and last major kind of research intermarriage has dealt with the consequences of the practice on family life. How do interracial couples and their children fare in personality development and interpersonal relations and success or failure as measured by the criteria of divorce, desertion, and separation? What systematic and empirical data have researchers gathered about the consequences of interracial marriage?

The research is contradictory as to the degree of success attained by mixed marriages as measured by divorce. One study (Cheng and Yamamura, 1957) found that such marriages are less successful than marriages between persons of the same race, while a second study (Lynn, 1953) reported a failure rate for black-white marriages which was not greater than average. However, neither of the two studies dealing with the rate of divorce in mixed marriages found such marriages to fail less frequently than the average. It seems probable that marriages between whites and blacks would reflect the poorest outcome in view of the particular personal and social problems and the unusual difficulties which confront them, as indicated in many studies (Little, 1942; Drake and Cayton, 1945; Golden, 1951; Roberts, 1956; Smith, 1960; Powledge, 1963; Massaquot, 1965; Osmundsen, 1965). However, Pavela (1964) makes a point (based on his in-depth study of mixed married couples) that the external pressures faced by interracial couples are often great but certainly do not appear to be overwhelming. Further, except for some nonconfirming information on the state of Hawaii, nothing is known statistically to support the thesis of instability (Monahan, 1970).

The literature suggests that in black-white marriages contrary to what might be expected, children do not present a special problem. They are considered to be black by both the white and black communities. The youngsters generally make an adequate adjustment to the black community and thus their problems are the same as those of the children of two black parents (Drake and Cayton, 1945; Risdon, 1954).

The studies of interracial marriage have been fairly unanimous in their assessments of the outstanding problems encountered by couples who enter into such unions. The studies reveal such factors as housing, occupation, and relationships with family and peers as troublesome ones (Drake and Cayton, 1953; Golden, 1954; Risdon, 1954). Staples (1973) explained that among black peers, the sentiment today is clearly against interracial marriages. Many interracial couples are shut out of social life in black circles being forced to seek friends and social intercourse in all white or other interracial environments.

A preliminary survey of the literature on interracially mixed marriages has dealt with both theoretical and empirical considerations from four perspectives: first, the extent to which they occur; second, the causal factors associated with their occurrence; third, the characteristics obtaining for these marriages; fourth, the special problems or consequences of such marriages.

FUTURE CONSIDERATIONS

Though interest has seemingly always existed where interracial marriages are concerned, there continues to be a paucity of meaningful research available. It would be particularly relevant to assess the extent and nature of interracial marriages in the 1970s following the 1967 Leving versus Virginia case. But, perhaps more significant than the 1967 decision as a possible facilitator, is an analysis of interracial marriage with respect to the black movement of the 1960s emphasizing racial solidarity and ''black is beautiful.'' The question, ''Why are interracial marriages continuing to occur in the face of a more magnified emphasis on blackness?'' therefore, appears to be both apropos and timely.

Since studies are often in contradiction of each other, as earlier pointed out, there appears to be a need for examining in greater depth the rese4arch which has already been conducted on black-white marriages. For the most part, research studies from 1930 to 1975 have dealt with fragmented data rather than with a body of data reflecting the entire United States. It would appear, then, that a critical step in research should be to outline precisely the rates of interracial marriages from 1930 to 1975 for determining increases or decreases in racially mixed marriages. Further, research might be undertaken to determine whether the characteristics of interracial marriages approximate those of same-race marriages or appear significantly different. Future researchers might accomplish this by disaggregating data of the American population pertaining to interracial marriage by age, education, income, mobility, origin of birth, fertility and other relevant variables. This data could then be analyzed with respect to current theories and serve as a basis for generating new ones in an area which has not been studied systematically. But, even more importantly, black people will be in a position to determine whether the issue of black-white marriage is a serious threat to the black community and, if a threat, possible methods of amelioration.

REFERENCES

Aldridge, D. P. (1973) ''The Changing nature of interracial marriage in Georgia a research note.'' J. of Marriage and the Family 35 (November): 641–642.

Anderson, C. H. (1971) ''Toward a new sociology: a critical view.'' Homewood, IL: Dorsey Press.

Baber, R. E. (1937) ''A study of 325 mixed marriages.'' Amer. Soc. Rev. 2 (October) 705–716.

Barnett, L. D. (1963a) ''Research on international and interracial marriage. Marriage and Family Living 25 (February): 105–107.

______. (1963b) ''Interracial marriage in California.'' Marriage and Family Living 25 (November): 424–427.

______. and J. H. Burma (1965) ''Interracial marriage data discrepancy.'' J. of Marriage and the Family 27 (February): 97.

Barron, M. L. (1946) People Who Intermarry. Syracuse: Syracuse Univ. Press.

Beigel, H. G. (1966) ''Problems and motives in interracial relationships.'' J. of Sex Research 2 (November): 185–202.

Bernard, J. (1966a) ''Note on educational homogamy in negro-white and white negro marriages. 1960.'' J. of Marriage and the Family 27 (August): 274–276.

______. (1966b) "Marital stability and patterns of status variables." J. of Marriage and the Family 27 (November): 421–439.

Berry, B. (1965) Race and Ethnic Relations. Boston: Houghton Mifflin.

Besanceney, P. H. (1965) "On reporting rates of intermarriage." Amer. J. of Sociology 70 (May): 717–721.

Billingsley, A. (1968) Black Families in White America. Englewood Cliffs, NJ: Prentice-Hall.

Blau, P. and O. D. Duncan (1967) The American Occupational Structure. New York: John Wiley.

Blesanz, J. (1950) "Inter-American marriages on the Isthmus Panama." Social Forces 29 (December): 159–163.

Bogue, D. J. (1969) Principles of Demography. New York: John Wiley.

Brayboy, T. F. (1966) "Interracial sexuality as an expression of neurotic conflict." J. of Sex Research 2 (November): 179–184.

Brooks, M. R. (1946) "American Caste and class: an appraisal." Social Forces 25 (Decmeber): 207–211.

Brown, M. C. (1955) "The status of jobs and occupations as evaluated by an urban negro sample." Amer. Soc. Rev. 20 (October): 564–565.

Burma, J. H. (1963) "Interethnic marriage in Los Angeles. 1948–1959."Social Forces 42 (December): 156–165.

______. (1952) "Research note on the measurement of interracial marriage." Amer. J. of Sociology 57 (May): 587–589.

______. G. A. Cretser, and T. Seacrest (1970) "A comparison of the occupational status of intramarrying and intermarrying couples: a research note." Sociology and Social Research 54 (July): 508–519.

Calhoun, A. W. (1917) A Social History of the American Family. Cleveland. Clark Publishing.

Carter, L. F. (1968) "Racial caste hypogamy: a sociological myth?" Phylon 29 (Winter): 347–350.

Cash, E. (1955) "A study of negro-white marriages in the Philadelphia area." Ph.D. dissertation, Temple University. (unpublished).

Cavan, R. S. (1971) "Annotated bibliography of studies of intermarriage in the United States. 1960–1970 inclusive." Inter. J. of Sociology of the Family 1 (May): 157–165.

______. and J. T. Cavan (1971) "Cultural patterns, functions, and dysfunctions of endogamy and intermarriage." Inter J. of Sociology of the Family 1 (May): 10–24.

Centers, R. (1949) "Marital selection and occupational strata." Amer. J. of Sociology 54 (May): 530–535.

Cheng, C. K. and D. S. Yamamura (1957) "Interracial marriage and divorce in Hawaii." Social Forces 36 (October): 77–84.

Chilman, C. (1966) "Marital stability and patterns of status variables: a comment." J. of Marriage and the Family 27 (November): 446–448.

Collins, S. F. (1951) "The social position of white and 'half caste' women in colored groupings in Britain." Amer. Soc. Rev. 16(December): 796–802.

Cox, D. C. (1945) "Race and Caste a distinction." Amer. J. of Sociology 50 (March: 360–368.

______. (1942) "The modern caste school of race relations." Social Forces 21 (December): 226–281.

Das, M. S. (1971) "A cross-cultural study of intercaste marriage in India and the United States." Inter. J. of Sociology of the Family I (May):25–33.

Davis, A., B. B. Gardner and M. R. Gardner (1941) Deep South Chicago: Univ. of Chicago Press.

Davis, K. (1941) "Intermarriage in caste societies." Amer. Anthropologist 43: 376–395.

Day, C. B. (1932) A Study of Some Negro-White Families in the United States. Cambridge: Harvard Univ. Press.

Drachsler, J. (1921) Intermarriage in New York City. New York: Columbia Univ. Press.

Drake, S. C. and H. R. Cayton (1945) Black Metropolis. New York: Harcourt Brace & World.

Duncan, D. C. (1961) "A socio-economic index for all occupations." in A. J. Reiss et al. Occupations and Social Status. New York: Free Press.

Golden, J. (1959) "Facilitating factors in negro-white intermarriage." Phylon 20 (Fall): 273–284.

______. (1958) "Social control of negro-white intermarriage." Social Forces 36 (March): 267–269.

______. (1954) "Patterns of negro-white intermarriage." Amer. Soc. Rev. 19 (April): 144–147.

______. (1953) "Characteristics of the negro-white intermarriage in Philadelphia." Amer. Soc. Rev. 18 (April): 177–183.

______. (1951) "Negro-white marriage in Philadelphia." Ph.D. dissertation, University of Pennsylvania. (unpublished)

Gordon, A. I. (1964) Intermarriage: Interfaith, Interracial, Interethnic: Boston: Beacon Press.

Heer, D. M. (1974) "The prevalence of black-white marriage in the United States 1960 and 1970." J. of Marriage and the Family 35 (May): 246–258.

______. (1967) "Intermarriage and racial amalgamation in the United States." Eugenics Q. 14 (June): 112–120.

______. (1966) "Negro-white marriage in the United States." J. of Marriage and the Family 27 (August): 262–273.

______. (1965) "Negro-white marriages in the United States." New Society J. (August): 7–9.

Herbert,, L. (1939) "A study of ten cases of negro-white marriages in the District of Columbia." Catholic University of America. (unpublished)

Hoffman, F. C. (1896) Race Traits and Tendencies of the American Negro. New York: Macmillan.

Hunt, C. L. and R. W. Collier (1957) "Intermarriage and cultural change: a study of Philippine-American Marriages." Social Forces 35 (March): 223–230.

Kennedy, R. J. R. (1952) "Single or triple melting pot? Intermarriage trends in New Haven, 1870–1950." Amer. J. of Sociology 58:56–69.

______. (1944) "Single or triple melting pot? Intermarriage trends in New Haven. 1870–1940." Amer. J. of Sociology 49: 331–339.

Kornacker, M. (1971) "Cultural significance of intermarriage: a comparative approach." Inter. J. of Sociology of the Family I (May): 147–156.

Larason, C. [ed.] (1965) Marriage Across the Color Line. Chicago: Johnson Publishing.

Lazar, R. J. (1971) "Toward a theory of intermarriage." Inter. J. of Sociology of the Family I (May): 1–9.

Lehrman, S. R. (1967) "Psychopathology in mixed marriages." Psychoanalytic Q. 36 (January): 67–82.

Little, C. (1942) "Analytic reflections on mixed marriages." Psychoanalytic Rev. 29 (January): 20–25.

Lynn, A. Q. (1967) "Interracial marriages in Washington, D.C." J. of Negro Education 36 (Fall): 428–433.

______. (1956) "Some aspects of interracial marriage in Washington, D.C." J. of Negro Education 25 (Fall): 380–391.

______. (1953) "Interracial marriage in Washington, D.C., 1940–1947." Ph.D. dissertation, Catholic University of America. (unpublished)

______. (1950) "Interracial marriage: a study of fifteen negro-white marriages in New York City, and the metropolitan area." Catholic University of America. (unpublished)

McDowell, S. (1971) "Black-white intermarriage in the United States." Inter. J. of Sociology of the Family I (May): 49–58.

Massaquoi, H. (1965) "Would you want your daughter to marry one?" Ebony 20 (August): 82–90.

Mayer, A. J. and S. M. Smock (1960) "Negro-white intermarriage for Detroit, 1899–1957." Population Index 26 (July): 210–211.

Merton, R. K. (q94q) "Intermarriage and the social structure: fact and theory." Psychiatry 4 (August): 361–374.

Monahan, T. P. (1973) "Marriage across racial lines in Indiana." J. of Marriage and the Family 35 (November): 632–640.

______. (1971) "Interracial marriages in the United States: some data on upstate New York." Inter J. of Sociology and the Family I (March): 94–105.

______. (1970) "Are interracial marriages really less stable?" Social Forces 48: 461–473.

Moore, P. (1975) "Social status: judging people—it's the job that counts." Psychology Today 9 (July) 32, 84.

Osmundsen, J. A. (1965) "Doctor discusses 'mixed' marriage." *New York Times* (November 7): 73L.

Panunzio, C. (1942) "Intermarriage in Los Angeles, 1924–1933." Amer. J. of Sociology 47 (March): 690–701.

Pavela, T. H. (1964) "An exploratory study of negro-white intermarriage in Indiana." Marriage and Family Living 26 (May): 209–211.

Pittsburgh Courier (1958) "Who wants intermarriage? Most courier readers stand against interracial unions." (September 20): 6.

Powledge, F. (1963) "Negro-white marriages on rise here." *New York Times* (October 18); I. 18.

Rainwater, L. (1966) "Marital stability and patterns of status variables: a comment." J. of Marriage and the Family 27 (November): 442–445.

Reuter, E. B. (1934) Race and Culture Contacts. New York: McGraw-Hill.

______. (1931) Race Mixture: Studies in Intermarriage and Miscegenation. New York: McGraw-Hill.

______. (1918) The Mulatto in the United States. Boston: Badger Books.

Risdon, R. (1954) "A study of interracial marriages based on data for Los Angeles County," sociology and Social Research 39 (November–December): 92–95.

Roberts, R. E. T. (1956) "A comparative study of stratification and intermarriage in multiracial societies." Ph.D. dissertation, University of Chicago. (unpublished)

______. (1940) "Negro-white intermarriage: a study of social control." University of Chicago. (unpublished)

Rodman, H. (1965) "Technical note on two rates of mixed marriage." Amer. Soc. Rev. 30 (October):: 776–778.

Sampson, W. A. and P. H. Rossi (1975) "Race and family social standing." Amer. Soc. Rev. 40 (April): 201–214.

Sass, H. R. (1956) "Mixed schools and mixed blood." Atlantic Monthly 198 (November): 45–49.

Schermerhorn, R. A. (1966) "Marital stability and patterns of status variables: a comment." J. of Marriage and the Family 27 (November): 440–441.

Schnepp, G. J. and A. M. Yui (1955) "Cultural and marital adjustment of Japanese war-brides." Amer. J. of Sociology 61 (July): 48–50.

Schuyler, G. S. (1930) Racial Intermarriage in the United States. Girard, K. S.: Haldeman-Julius.
Shaffer, H. B. (1961) "Mixed marriage." Editorial Research Reports I (May 24): 381–397.
Smith, C. E. (1960) "Negro-white intermarriage in metropolitan New York: a qualitative case analysis." Ph.D. dissertation, Columbia University. (unpublished)
Staples, R. (1974) "The black family in evolutionary perspective." Black Scholar 5 (June): 2–9.
______. (1973) The Black Woman in America. Chicago: Nelson Hall Publishers.
Stern, C. (1940) Principles of Human Genetics. San Francisco: W. H. Freeman.
Stone, A. H. (1908) Studies in the American Race Problem. New York: Doubleday.
Stonequist, E. V. (1937) The Marginal Man. New York: Scribner's.
Strauss, A. L. (1954) "Strain and harmony in American-Japanese war-bride marriages." Marriage and Family Living 16 (May): 99–106.
Svalastoga, K. (1965) Social Differentiation. New York: David McKay.
Toynbee, A. J. (1934) A Study of History. London: Oxford Univ. Press.
Tumlin, M. M. (1967) Social Stratification: The Forms and Functions of Inequality. Englewood Cliffs, N.J.: Prentice-Hall.
Udry, J. R. (1967) "Marital instability by race and income based on 1960 census data." Amer. J. of Sociology 72 (May): 673–674.
______. (1966) "Marital instability by race, sex, education, and occupations using 1960 census data." Amer. J. of Sociology 72 (September): 203–309.
United States News and World Report (1967) "Now that mixed marriage is legal." 62 (June 26): 25.
______. (1964) "Intermarriage and the race problem as leading authorities see it." 55 (November 18): 84–93.
______. (1958) "What the South really fears about mixed schools." 45 (September 19) 76ff.
Warner, W. L. (1936) "American caste and class." Amer. J. of Sociology 42 (September): 234–237.
Washington, J. (1970) Marriage in Black and White. Boston: Beacon Press.
Wehmann, E. M. (1934) "A study of ten cases of white-negro intermarriage." Smith College. For abstract see "Abstracts of theses." Smith College Studies in Social Work 5 (December): 211. (unpublished)
Wilber, G. I., and R. J. Hagan (1974) "Alternative sets of occupation scores from the 1970 PUS." Public Data USE 2 (October): 40–44.
Wilkinson, D. Y. (1975) "Black Male/White female. New York: Schenkman.
Wirth, L. and H. Goldhamer (1944) "The hybrid and the problem of misconception," in O. Klineberg (ed.) Characteristics of the American Negro. New York: Harper & Row.

CHAPTER FIVE

Economic Issues

Cheryl Leggon explores the double-minority status of Black female professionals and finds technical criteria and race as predictors of on the job treatment. The author studied medical doctors, attorneys and holders of M.B.A. degrees. Most of the respondents indicated they experienced more discrimination on the basis of race than on the basis of sex. The author also pointed out the ease with which Black professional women cope with the dual demands of career and home. Leggon concludes that the Black professional woman does not gain benefits from her double-negative status.

Betty Collier and Louis Williams examine beliefs concerning differential economic statuses of Black males and Black females and find such beliefs to be invalid. Their findings indicate social scientists are both victims and offenders in perpetuating misconceptions about the differential status of Black men and women. They call for the construction of a black social science based on emancipatory theory and leading to liberatory praxis must begin with the reconstruction of social knowledge.

Finally, Delores Aldridge explores the relationships between occupational status, educational status and earnings as valid indicators of the position of Black females in the labor force. The occupations in which Black women participate are assessed in terms of the distribution of all women who work. Further, some special problems confronting Black working women are presented. Data suggests that while the trend of economic gains for Black working women is clear, they have yet to attain equality in the working world.

Black Female Professionals: Dilemmas and Contradictions of Status

Cheryl Bernadette Leggon

Everett Hughes, the author of one of the seminal essays on dilemmas and contradictions of status, argues that when

> *new kinds of people in established professional positions are assessed by others, that that assessment of their statuses and the role activity associated with them is likely to be made on the basis of both universally accented technical criteria and in terms of "auxiliary" characteristics carried over from such other social contexts as race and sex [Hughes, 1945:353].*

This, coupled with the fact that in contemporary American society, Blacks and women qualify as "new kinds of people in established professional positions,";[1] suggests that the case of elite Black professional women should certainly pose an interesting problem for investigation.

The expectations concerning the "auxiliary" characteristics are both created in and reinforced by what Blumer (1958) refers to as the "public arena," which includes public forums, "everyday talk," and the mass media—newspapers, magazines, radio, movies, and especially television.[2] People tend to hold a dual image of professionals: On the one hand, they associate with being a professional, a certain amount of technical skill (for example, specialized training or licensing); on the other hand, they associate certain auxiliary characteristics. For example, when one thinks of a physician, the image of a "Marcus Welby" type comes to mind: mature, competent, white, Anglo-Saxon, Protestant, and male. What happens when a potential client encounters a professional who does not fit the image? Hughes' study focused upon the dilemmas occasioned for an individual encountering a status-discrepant professional such as a Black physician or a female attorney. My study focuses upon the status-discrepant professional herself rather than on the client.

Hughes argues that when an individual encounters a status-discrepant professional, the outcome of that encounter depends upon the situation: whether or not it is defined as an emergency and/or whether or not another professional (presumably a non-status-discrepant professional) is available. If the situation is defined as an emergency or if the individual decides that "there is no other way," then she/he may feel forced to relate to the status-discrepant professional on a purely professional basis. Should the potential client not be forced to relate to the status-discrepant professional on a purely professional basis, what emerges is the fact (pointed out by Hughes) that there are "master status traits"; namely, that certain statuses tend to overpower any other characteristics which might run counter to them. For many, race and sex are master status traits; that is, when encountering a status-discrepant professional, the potential client encounters a Black or a woman first and a doctor or lawyer second. What emerges, then, is a status hierarchy with ascribed status (race, sex) on the top and achieved status (for example, professional) below.

According to my findings (and consonant with those of Hughes), not only is there a status hierarchy in which ascribed status is placed above achieved status, but within that top stratum of ascribed status the Black female professionals whom I interviewed perceive a hierarchy in which race usually ranks above sex. It is my contention that their double-ascribed minority statuses—Black and female—place Black professional women in what Epstein (1973a) has called "a double bind," in that they share in the economic discrimination patterns based on sex which prevail in American society in addition to those economic discrimination patterns imposed on all Blacks; the latter are enforced more strictly than the former. Further, this double bind and its effects are greater than the sum of its parts, the two minority-ascribed statuses of race and sex (Dumont and Wilson, 1957). The Black female professional is the product of the confluence of unique sociohistorical, economic, and psychological factors. Although statistics can yield an abundance of useful information, they cannot measure or even delineate the psychological and social psychological problems peculiar to the Black female professional. These problems are the focal point of my inquiry.

This study of elite Black professional women is more of an ethnographic field study than a verification study of explicit theoretical propositions. The theoretical framework resembles what Dumont and Wilson (1957) have called a theory sketch,

> *a more or less vague indication of the propositions and initial conditions considered as relevant, but needs 'filling out' to develop into a full-fledged theory. The theory sketch suggests the direction for further research required in the filling our process.*

Specifically, my pilot study[3] of elite Black professional women sought to determine

1. whether elite Black professional women perceived race discrimination as more salient than sex discrimination in their professional experiences, and to what extent, if any,

there is a cumulative effect from both racial and sexual discrimination in the professions; and

2. the extent to which the status-discrepant individual (i.e., the elite Black female professional) recognizes her status-discrepant position and the way(s) in which she attempts to cope with it.

Since there is a great deal of dissension as to which occupations should be included under the category "professions," I chose to examine three of those occupations that are consistently highly ranked on prestige-ranking scales such as that of Hodge and Rossi (see Blau, 1967)[4]: medical doctors, attorneys (who have graduated from law school and passed at least one bar examination), and women with Masters degrees in Business Administration (M.B.A.s).

The pilot study was conducted in the Chicago metropolitan area during the academic year 1974–1975. The Chicago metropolitan area is statistically interested in terms of Black professionals: Although Chicago has the largest number of Black attorneys of any American city (approximately 330 in 1975), the number of Black physicians has decreased 13.5 percent since 1961 (Blan and Duncan, 1967). This decrease is partially attributable to the increase in opportunities for Black physicians in the United States, particularly in the South and West. In 1974, Chicago had 212 Black doctors, of which 52.7 percent were over 50 years of age (McClory, 1975: 1). The membership roll of the Cook County Bar Association, the nation's oldest and largest local Black bar association, greatly facilitated the task of estimating and locating the universe of approximately 31 Black female attorneys; this task was somewhat more difficult for physicians because most lists contained only last names and first initials—perhaps because many people are wary of female doctors except in "traditionally female" specialties of obstetrics and pediatrics. At the same time my study was being conducted, another study of Black physicians in Chicago was being conducted by Comprehensive Research and Development, Inc., which independently estimated the number of Black female physicians in Chicago to be between 15 and 25; using the snowball technique, I obtained the names of 18. Of these, four were eliminated from my sample because they were foreign-born and raised,[5] and one was eliminated because she suffered a stroke and was unable to be interviewed. It was most difficult to assess the number of Black females with M.B.A.s in the Chicago area. Although I am confident that I located all of those who received M.B.A.s from the University of Chicago and who remained in the Chicago area, the Dean's office of the Graduate School of Business of the University of Chicago informed me that the school did not keep records by sex until 1971. The Dean's office of the Graduate School of Business of Northwestern University did not have records of its graduates broken down by race and sex. Therefore, from those names I did receive, I asked each for the name of any other Black female M.B.A. they knew. Excepting three who were impossible to locate and one who refused to be interviewed, the sample consisted of six M.B.A.s and one Certified Public Accountant (one of two in the Chicago area, and one of six Black female C.P.A.s in the county at that time). Names of doctors, attorneys, and M.B.A.s were obtained from the membership roll of the League of Black Women, an organization founded in 1972, whose membership includes women from all areas of life and a representative cross-section of professionals. Each woman contacted was asked to name three of four other women (either in her profession and/or others included in the study) whom she recommended the interviewer contact. This snowballing technique proved useful in locating those women not members of organizations and thereby enlarged the population from which the sample was drawn.

The final sample consisted of 12 Black female attorneys, six Black female doctors, and seven Black female M.B.A.s (including one C.P.A.). A matched sample was utilized: Respondents in each occupational category were divided into two groups on the basis of whether they entered their profession before or after 1965 (the year in which Title VII of the Civil Rights Act of 1964 went into effect); this sampling procedure allowed for the detection of age-specific trends across occupations. Due to the complex and sensitive areas probed and in order to reduce interviewer bias, I personally interviewed all of the subjects; this is consonant with basic interviewing techniques based upon the experience of survey research organizations such as the National Opinion Research Center, which finds that the best results are obtained when Blacks interview Blacks, whites interview whites, and females as opposed to males are the interviewers. My sole instrument of data collection was an interview schedule designed to elicit information that relates the research questions on the professions, women, and Blacks implicit in my review of the literature and theoretical sketch of relevant propositions. Over three-fourths of the respondents grew up in the central city of a metropolitan area in the continental United States with a population of more than two million; further, most of the respondents came from families of three or fewer children.

The professionals in my study in both law and medicine tended to be concentrated in specialties traditionally labeled "women's specialties": For law, these specialties are domestic relations (divorce, adoption); for medicine, obstetrics and pediatrics. In business, the traditionally "female preserve" is personnel; the evidence in my study was insufficient to indicate any discernible trend toward concentration because, as a result of being in training for their companies, many of the M.B.A.s were assigned to different departments on a rotating basis. Further, at the time of my study, it was not clear as to which area/division of the company they would ultimately be assigned.

Black female professionals share certain problems with professionals in general—obtaining degrees, meeting licensing requirements, meeting professional standards, and the like. In addition, they share concerns specific to Blacks—that is, the problems of racial discrimination in hiring and professional advancement.

Although Black female professionals share certain problems/issues specific to Blacks, this does not mean that Black women can be subsumed under the category "Black professionals." To do so would obscure crucial differences between Black male and Black female professionals:

1. From 1940 through 1960, Black male professionals were shown to be more widely distributed than Black female professionals among the professions; female profes-

sionals were highly concentrated in a few occupations such as teaching, and Black female professionals appeared to be the most highly concentrated of all sex-race categories [Glenn, 1963: 443–448].

2. Black females have a greater chance of entering profession designated as open to women than Black males have of entering profession designated as open to men [Glenn, 1963: 443–448].

Some sociologists attribute this phenomenon to the "farmer's daughter effect" (Block, 1969: 17–26). That is, like farm families, Black families choose to spend their limited resources to educate daughters rather than sons because, since girls tend to do better than boys in school,[6] they have a better chance of going on for further training, which improves their chances of getting good jobs and/or marrying well when they migrate to urban areas. In addition, given the limited financial resources of the family, the male children are often pressured to contribute to the family resources, which usually leads to their dropping out of school. Another explanation offered by Jackson (1973) seems more plausible: This theoretical tendency among Black families to educate their daughters at the expense of their sons[7] may be interpreted as an effort to keep Black women away from domestic work[8] which is and has been, in addition to being a position in which Black women could "learn the ropes" of white society, a position of sexual vulnerability (Epstein, 1973b:917).

Although Black professional women share certain problems specific to women, such as the problems of maternity leave and its ramifications for professional advancement, this does not mean that Black women can be subsumed under the category "female professionals," because by so doing crucial differences between Black and white professional women would be obscured. Epstein (1973b) argues that one of these differences is that "because these women are Black they are perhaps not perceived as women; . . . they may be viewed as sexual objects." Sociohistorical evidence indicates that this argument is invalid; indeed, Black women have been viewed legally as well as socially in the United States as *sex objects par excellence* (Hernton, 1965)! Rather than one negatively valued ascribed status (race) cancelling out the effect(s) of the other (sex), my evidence indicates that the two operate to the disadvantage of Black professional women. The very fact that most of the respondents were unable to distinguish between race and sex as the basis on which they were being discriminated against indicates that these status-discrepant professionals felt that *both* are operant. Therefore, it seems to me that the crucial differences between Black and white professional women are those of expectations and orientations:

1. A greater percentage of Black women than white women work after marriage and childbirth; Black women work more years of their lives than do their white counterparts, yet their earnings are lower and their unemployment rate greater (Lerner, 1978).[9]
2. Whereas for the majority of white middle- and upper-class women the decision to pursue a career is optional, Black women are raised with the expectation that whether or not they marry, whether or not they have children, they will work most of their

adult lives; "work to them, unlike to white women, is not a liberating goal, but rather an *imposed* lifelong necessity (Lerner, 1978).

These expectations are consonant with Epstein's (1973b: 923) generalization that "black women are more concerned with the economic rewards of work than are white women." Further, these orientations help to account for the fact that, as a group, Black career women feel less guilt than do their white counterparts about spending less time with their family due to the demands their careers place on their time.

During preliminary conversations with Black professional women, the older women tended more frequently than did the younger women to attribute any lack of advancement in their career to racial discrimination. Therefore, I expected that the older women as a group—those entering professions before 1965 (the year in which Title VII of the Civil Rights Act of 1964 went into effect)—would tend to attribute their perceived lack of professional advancement to racial discrimination; if they mentioned sexual discrimination, I expected that it would be subordinate to racial discrimination. As a whole, I expected the younger women to attribute problems of advancement to sexual discrimination;[10] if mentioned, racial discrimination would be secondary.

My findings indicate that the ability to distinguish discrimination based on race from discrimination based on sex is profession-specific; that is, women in business and law are in a better position than their counterparts in medicine to encounter prospective clients and learn why they do not become actual clients. As one older physician put it, "I know why those who come to me come, but I don't know why those who don't, don't." A young attorney related an anecdote revealing reasons for one potential client seeking counsel elsewhere:

> *A woman obtained my name from the American Bar Association and sent her husband to me. He knew that I was a woman, but when he arrived and I introduced myself, and he saw that I am Black, he said, "I knew you were a woman, but this is too much," and he turned and left.*

This anecdote supports Hughes' finding that there is a status hierarchy in which ascribed status supercedes achieved status; further, it supports my finding that within the ascribed status hierarchy, the status of race supercedes that of sex. Finally, this anecdote does not lend support to Epstein's (1973b: 914) hypothesis that perhaps "two statuses in combination create a new status (for example, the hyphenated status of Black-woman-lawyer) which may have no established 'price' because it is unique." Quite the contrary, it indicates that the "new" status combination does indeed have a price and a very high one: loss of a potential client. Thus, contrary to my initial expectation, most respondents—including more than half of the younger respondents—experienced more discrimination on the basis of race than on the basis of sex, although many respondents added that it is often difficult to distinguish between the two, as one young woman in business describes:

Although it's difficult to distinguish between the two, most days I think it's sexual because I white women experiencing the same things I am . . . In the matter of salaries, you can't tell whether it is racist or sexist.

This quote seems more applicable to business than to medicine and law because (1) discrimination on the basis of sex is probably still more widespread in business than in medicine and law, and (2) women in business see more potential clients than do their counterparts in medicine and, perhaps, law. This is due to the tendency for prospective consumers to "shop around" less for medical and legal expertise than for business expertise because, generally, by the time they recognize the need for the former, the problem situation already exists and time presses them for a solution. In other words, those using medical and legal services tend to use them in a remedial way (that is, to remedy an already existing situation), whereas consumers of business services tend to use them in a preventive way. That most of the younger respondents—including all of those in business—report that they have personally experienced discrimination more on the basis of race than of sex may be attributed to the fact that civil rights gains made in the 1960s are being checked or even reversed; attempts to retard this process are evident in the attribution of greater importance on the part of the respondents to civil rights for Black rather than for women.[11] On the other hand, many respondents may believe that civil rights for Blacks include civil rights for Black women.

My second hypothesis was that whichever form of discrimination they perceived to have most frequently experienced should dictate which of the two liberation movements, the Black or the women's, is most important to them in terms of a coping mechanism for their status-discrepant position. Therefore, if a respondent replied that she has experienced more discrimination on the basis of race than of sex, than the Black Liberation Movement should be more important to her. Further, since the Black Liberation Movement was followed by the Women's Liberation Movement was followed by the Women's Liberation Movement. I hypothesized that younger women would be more likely than older women to feel tension because the Black Liberation Movement and the Women's Liberation Movement, because for older women professional success was viewed as "a credit to the race" and hence consonant with the struggle for racial equality. One unintended consequence of Title VII of the Civil Rights Act of 1964 (which prohibits discrimination in employment based on race, color, religion, sex, and national origin; and which covers discrimination by employee unions and employment agencies) was that many people believed it gave a competitive advantage to Black females in that prospective employers could get "two minorities for the price of one." Hernton (1965) points out that while this may be true in the most liberal parts of the North (New York City, Washington, D.C., and Chicago—from which the respondents in my study are drawn), this does not occur as frequently in the South. For the younger women, then, professional success could be viewed as dissonant with the struggle for racial equality, especially if these women are seen as being (and see themselves as being) in direct competition with Black males.

Contrary to expectation, for the younger respondents the Black Liberation Movement is more important than the Women's Liberation Movement: That is not to say that Black professional women are less concerned about the problems they encounter because of their sex than those they encounter because of their race (even assuming that the two can be distinguished, which they often cannot), but that the Black Liberation Movement does a better job of addressing the latter than does the Women's Liberation Movement the former. As it is presently constituted for the most part, the Women's Liberation Movement addresses more problems of non-Black than Black women; in response to this, the National Black Feminist Organization (NBFO) was formed in New York City in 1972 and presently has chapters in many major metropolitan areas. Because it was relatively new at the time of my pilot study, man respondents were unaware of but expressed interest in the NBFO. Indeed, comparative research in the two feminist organizations—Black and white—would increase knowledge of the points of consensus and dissension between the ways in which Black and white professional women deal with the problems engendered by status inconsistency.

My third hypothesis concerns the ease with which Black women cope with the conflicting role demands of the professional and the "traditional female" roles. My findings support Epstein's claim that Black women experience less guilt than white women over the effects on their children of working. This claim is based on two considerations:

1. Since a greater percentage of Black women work after marriage and childbirth, having adult female members of the household working has been historically and continues to be a more usual experience for Blacks than for whites.
2. In contrast to the situation of her white counterpart, work for the Black woman is not an option, but a necessity if her family is to maintain its precarious middle-class status.

Therefore, rather than viewing her work as taking something away from her family, the Black professional women views her career as enabling her to make an even greater contribution to her family's stability and hence to its welfare. This is precisely because for Black women in general, work is obligatory rather than optional (as it is for their white counterparts). There is no social role toward which there is no ambivalence. Roles vary in the extent to which it is culturally and psychologically permissible to express ambivalence, to discuss or admit negative feelings toward them. Black women feel less ambivalence about working, precisely because they view their careers as consonant rather than dissonant with the maternal role: Their work contributes rather than detracts from the stability of their family. Consequently, I hypothesized that not only is it easier for Black women than for white women to cope with the demands of the role of professional and those of the "traditional female role," but that among Black women viewpoints of the "female" role along a "traditional-feminist" continuum would be divided along age lines: As a group, the older women would fall more toward the traditional end, while the younger women as a group would fall more toward the feminist end. While this held so far as agreement with the idea that women always have the "option" of being housewives (whether or not they work), most of the women—regardless of age—expressed at least a moderately feminist viewpoint.[12] This deviation from expectation was caused by older women in business and law expressing strongly feminist viewpoints.[13] This, in turn, is probably due to the fact that Black women in business and law would be expected to be more sensitive to discrimination against women and would be more likely to espouse less traditional viewpoints than would their counterparts in medicine. Thus, viewpoint of the female role (traditional or feminist) is a function of the age of the respondent and her profession.

Location of respondents according to viewpoint of the female role along the traditional-feminist continuum is necessary, but not sufficient to ascertain how individuals coped with the strain(s) engendered by their status-inconsistency. It was necessary to inquire (1) whether a respondent anticipated problems before marriage in combining marriage, and perhaps motherhood, with career; and (2) the extent to which their expectations affected the amount of strain perceived and the coping mechanisms adopted to deal with the strain. The responses vary with the respondent's age and profession, as discussed in the following sections.

(1) Age. The older Black professional women increased the compatibility or decreased the incompatibility of the role demands of professional and "traditional" female (wife and mother) by deciding a priori that marriage and family would take precedence over their career. Perhaps this type of adjustment was necessitated for this group as a whole by the strength of the societal expectations (prevalent during their youth) that a woman should marry and that the home is her primary responsibility whether or not she is working. However, the lag between the societal definition of women's role ("woman's place is in the home") and certain economic realities (for example, that realization of the American Dream—a house in the suburbs with a two-car garage—requires both husband and wife to work) affects Black women less than white women because societal standards concerning women (including standards of beauty) have been and continue to be based on white women. In addition, unlike whites, most Black women are raised with the expectation that whether they marry or not, they will be working most of their adult lives. I found evidence for the older women of the self-fulfilling prophecy: Those who decided before marriage that marriage would take precedence over career found that that expectation materialized. Further, many of these women attributed to this decision their perceived lack of professional progress (for example, "If I hadn't decided that my family would come first, I would be farther along in my career than I am now."). It is difficult to test the accuracy of this perception, although support of it is indicated by the following observations:

(a) Most of the older women in medicine were in private practice so that they could set their hours to coincide with family needs; they gave this as one of their most important reasons for going into private practice;
(b) Older physicians tended to be in general practice or obstetrics and gynecology rather than in areas characterized by longer training and less flexible hours (for example, surgery);

(c) Older attorneys stated the desirability of shorter and more flexible work hours and achieved this end by limiting themselves to cases that require the attorney to spend relatively little time in court (such as in adoption or divorce cases) as opposed to the more lucrative but time-consuming cases (such as criminal or anti-trust).

Because they are able to avail themselves of certain options easier than their older counterparts (for example, living with a mate without benefit of clergy, choosing not to have children), the younger respondents on the whole tend to feel the traditional expectations of marriage and motherhood to be less binding upon them. Nevertheless, that traditional expectations are still felt by today's young women is indicated by a young attorney who is married to an attorney:

> *Many women know that what they are doing is intellectually as important as what their husbands do, but they still feel guilty about not doing everything and keeping up the house. In the final analysis, it falls on the women's head if the house is messy.*

(2) Profession. Regardless of age, many respondents maintain that marriage can be combined easier with business and law than with medicine. Most physicians in my study—married and single—concur, and posit marriage to another physician as the best way for them to combine medicine with marriage: This enables their mate to understand, sympathize, and empathize with the demands medicine makes.

Whether or not they share the same profession, most respondents agree that the greater the personal and professional or occupational security of one's mate, the more able and willing he is to accept and encourage a professional wife, which in turn reduces the tension generated by the demands of profession, marriage, and family.

Taking as the dependent variable the strain(s) engendered by the confluence of the demands of the roles of professional and female, the strength of this strain is a function of the relative degree of commitment to each role: The more the commitment to each role, the greater the resulting strain. Commitment to the role of professional is determined by the amount of sunk costs involved (length of time in training, cost of training, and the like) and is profession-specific; commitment to the role of female—at least, as it has been traditionally defined—is more age-specific, in that current societal consensus on the definition of the female role is weakening and more options (for example, scientific and legal advances making birth control a more viable option) are open to the present generation. The independent variable, social support, can come from many sources: the family of procreation in terms of encouragement to continue (as well as to enter) a profession; spouse (which is a function of his own personal and professional security); relatives; outside help hired for household and/or child care tasks; and others with common experiences who will at least discuss common problems (so that these women know their problems result from larger structural constraints rather than from personal idiosyncracies) and who will articulate and seek solutions to common problems in long run and try to relieve the tensions generated by these problems in the short run.

The study of elite Black professional women affords an unusual opportunity to examine a variety of dilemmas and contradictions of status.

NOTES

1. The first Black female admitted to the bar in the United States was not admitted until 1897 (Lutie Lyttle in Topeka, Kansas); the first Black female to become a physician did so in 1864 (Rebecca Lee, Boston, Massachusetts). See Lerner (1973).
2. M. L. Ramsdell's study of 600 hours of eight soap operas in 1971–1972 found that 90 percent of the primary white male characters in one program were either doctors or lawyers Schrank, 1977).
3. Presently, I am in the process of conducting this study on a nationwide basis to ascertain the generalizability of these findings.
4. This is contrary to Epstein's argument (1973b) that two statuses in combination create a new status. For a detailed critique of this argument, see Leggon (1979).
5. The fact that my sample consisted solely of Black women born and raised in the United States, whereas Epstein's (1974) sample included Black women born and raised in the West Indies, accounts for the differences between her findings and mine. These differences are explored in detail in Leggon (1979).
6. Much of the sociological and social psychological literature on women documents this. For example, see Komarovsky (1945, 1950).
7. Jackson (1973) maintains that there appears to be no evidence supporting the systematic preference of Black parents to educate their daughters at the expense of their sons' education or their sons at the presence of their daughters'.
8. Of all the sex-race categories, Black women are most highly concentrated in the category of domestic service.
9. According to Axel (1977), the percentage of total population 16 years of age and over in the labor force is as follows:

Labor Force Participation Rates by Age, Sex, and Race

FEMALE	1950	1960	1965	1970	1975
White	n.a.[a]	36.0	37.7	42.0	45.4
Black, other	n.a.	47.2	48.1	48.9	48.7

a. Means not available.
SOURCE: Axel (1977)

10. One reason for this expectation was the fact that since sexual discrimination had recently become at that time a ''fashionable'' topic of discussion in the public arenas (the mass media; the legislature, both state and national), public attention began to focus on, or at least to recognize, the phenomenon of sex discrimination, whereas

heretofore, discrimination in the United States usually referred to racial discrimination.

11. Respondents were asked, "Which do you feel is more important, civil rights for Blacks or for women?" Forty-four percent of the older women in law and medicine said civil rights for Blacks; 44 percent of the older women in law and medicine said that civil rights for Blacks is as important as civil rights for women; and 11 percent of the older women in law and medicine and 50 percent of the older women in business said that civil rights for women is more important than civil rights for Blacks. In contrast, 88 percent of the younger women in law and medicine and 40 percent of the younger women in business said that civil rights for Blacks is more important, while only 11 percent of the younger women in law and medicine said that civil rights for women was more important.
12. Respondents were asked: "What is your reaction to the following statement: 'Even if she has a career, a woman always has the option of being a housewife'?" Response categories were strongly agree, agree somewhat, somewhat disagree, disagree strongly, and neutral.
13. Respondents were asked to indicate the extent to which their own views approximate the "feminist" or "traditional" viewpoint. The "feminist viewpoint" stresses greater equality and similarity in the roles of men and women than now exist, with greater participation of women in leadership positions in politics, the professions, and business. The "traditional viewpoint" stresses the differences between the roles of men and women, in which women's lives center on home and family and their job participation is in such fields as teaching, social work, nursing, and secretarial service.

REFERENCES

Axel, H. [ed.] (1977) A Guide to Consumer Markets (1977/1978. New York: The Conference Board, Inc.

Blau, P. and O. D. Duncan (1967) The American Occupational Structure. New York: John Wiley.

Blumer, H. (1958). "Race prejudice as a sense of group position." Pacific Sociological Review (Spring): 3–7.

Block, W. E.(1969) "Farmer's daughter effect: the case of the Negro female professional." Phylon 30: 17–26.

Degler, C. N. (1964) "Revolution without ideology: the changing place of women in America." Daedalus 93:658–670.

Dumont, R. G. and W. J. Wilson (1957) "Aspects of concept formation, explication and theory construction in sociology." American Sociological Review 32: 985–995.

Edwards, G. F. (1959) The Negro Professional. New York: Free Press.

Epstein, C. F. (1973a) "Black and female: the double whammy." Psychology Today (August): 57–61, 89.

__________ (1973b) "Positive effects of the multiple negative: explaining the success of Black professional women." American Journal of Sociology (January): 913–935.

Ginzberg, E. (1966) Life Styles of Educated Women. New York: Columbia University Press.

Glenn, N. D. (1963) "Some changes in the relative status of American non-whites: 1940–1960." Phylon 24: 443–448.

Goffman, E. (1959) The Presentation of Self in Everyday Life. Garden City, NY: Doubleday.

Gurin, P. and E. Epps (1966) "Some characteristics of students from poverty backgrounds attending predominantly Negro colleges in the Deep South." Journal of Negro Education 35: 336–350.

Hernton, C. C. (1965) Sex and Racism in America. New York: Grove Press.

Hughes, E. C. (1945) "Dilemmas and contradictions of status." American Journal of Sociology 50: 353–357.

Jackson, J. J. (1973) "Black women in racist society," in C. Willie (ed.) Racism and Mental Health, Pittsburgh: University of Pittsburgh Press.

Komarovsky, M. (1945) "Cultural contradictions and sex roles." American Journal of Sociology 52: 184–189.

________ (1950) "The functional analysis of sex roles." American Sociological Review 15: 508–516.

Leggon, C. B. (1979) "Some negative effects of the multiple negative." Chicago Circle: University of Illinois, (unpublished)

Lerner, G. [ed.] (1973) Black Women in White America: A Documentary History. New York: Random House.

McClory, R. J. (1975) "Fewer Black doctors in Chicago: foreign physicians practice in inner city with some bad side effects." The Chicago Reporter 4: 1.

Rossi, A. S. (n.d.) "The roots of ambivalence in American women." Chicago: National Opinion Research Center Study #483, 34 pp.

Schrank, J. (1977) Snap, Crackle and Popular Taste: The Illusion of Free Choice in America. New York: Delta Publishing.

Staples, R. E. (1973) The Black Woman in America: Sex, Marriage and the Family, Chicago: Nelson-Hall.

The Economic Status of the Black Male: A Myth Exploded

Betty J. Collier • Louis Williams

Reality is not directly available to inquiry. This is indeed no less true in the physical sciences as in the social sciences. Yet, particularly in the social sciences, reality becomes the documented product of our perceptions. As such, reality can be viewed as the consensually validated intersection of logic, axiology, and epistemology. Thus, even when existing evidence is contradictory, beliefs may continue to influence how we perceive certain phenomena. When such beliefs are further corroborated by erroneous facts, the sustained perpetuation of a distorted perception of reality is all but inescapable. This has been especially true relative to conceptions of the differential economic status of black males and females. In particular is the belief that slavery and oppression so structured the economic basis of black existence that the black man could not find work, making it necessary for the black woman to assume the economic responsibility for the black family (Moynihan, 1965).

This notion of black male economic inferiority has achieved such legitimacy that it is used axiomatically to explain the economic status of the black family. (See Rose, 1980; McAdoo, 1981a, 1981b). For instance, Lerner (1973), in *Black Women in White America: A Documentary History,* noted:

> *The black woman is liberated in her own mind, because she has taken on the responsibility for the black family and she works. Black women had to get into the labor force, because black men didn't have jobs [p. 586].*

Robert Staples (1973), in the *Black Woman in America,* integrated this assumption into his analysis:

Although the Black man could not find work, the Black woman returned to her familiar job, working in the white man's kitchen. She scrubbed, cooked, and cared for another woman's children and home in addition to her own. It was supposedly her ability to obtain this kind of work that gave the black woman the advantage over the unemployed black man [p. 18]

The assumption of the relative disadvantage of the black male has penetrated black literature and folklore as well. Martha Reeves and the Vandellas summarized an attitude when in 1967 they sang, "He's shiftless and he's lazy, he's about to drive me crazy, honeychile."

A careful examination of the assumption under consideration reveals that it is a conclusion based on several presuppositions. The first of these is the premise that absolutely more black females work than black males. Such a premise itself implies either that black men have extremely high levels of unemployment relative to black women or that black men have dropped out of the labor force. A second premise is a belief that even when black men work, their earnings are not only absolutely lower relative to white men but also absolutely lower relative to black women and white women. A subset of this premise is the notion that a greater percentage of black women hold professional and technical positions and that black women have more education than black men, a belief implicit in an assertion by Whitney Young (1964):

Historically, in the matriarchal Negro society mothers made sure that if one of their children had a chance for higher education, the daughter was the one to pursue it [p. 25].

A third premise is that white employment opportunities have been closed to black males, employment as a domestic has always been open to black females.

Another presupposition often included in this reasoning is the belief that a majority of black families are headed by a woman, thus creating a structure that places economic responsibility for the support of the family on the female. This assumption is supported by the belief that black male/female unions are (1) disrupted by extremely high rates of divorce and separation and (2) prevented by there being a "shortage" of available black men due to variables such as early death rates, imprisonment, and homosexuality (Jackson, 1978; McAdoo, 1981a, 1981b).

Although each of the suppositions mentioned can be subjected to various degrees of refutation (Collier, Arrington and Williams, 1980), they continue to be accepted and disseminated as truth by both black and white researchers and scholars. Central in this dissemination link are students, for they are the passive consumers of the knowledge produced by researchers. Therefore, our aim in this study is to examine the validity of these assumptions about the economic status of black males against existing evidence and to compare this evidence with the degree to which university students accept these assumptions. In doing so, we expect to show that many of these assumptions about black males persist as fact, even though they can be shown to be invalid by documented evidence. Finally, we wish to examine the theoretical implications of this persistent discontinuum between perception and reality. First, however, some attention will be given to the sociological process by which beliefs achieve the status of "facts," thereby deterministically intruding into individual and group behavior.

THE SOCIAL CONSTRUCTION OF "FACT"

Since Kant, we have understood that all inquiry is "theory-laden." Thus reality is not *directly* available to inquiry. This is no less true in the physical sciences as in the social sciences. Indeed, modern physical theory adopts a purely pragmatic stance as to whether reality has an *essential* physical structure independent of measurements. Even ignoring the theory-ladenness of "facts" are never *logical* impositions ascribable to irrefutable internal connections. Thus, ultimately, we are driven to the understanding that just as ideas must be situated within facts, so are facts situated within ideas, and *both* are constituents of reality as apprehended.

In saying this we bypass the interiority-exteriority, subjectivity-objectivity debate about reality that has plagued black scholarship since the 1970s. More simply, we recognize inquiry as an essentially *human* enterprise. As such, all inquiry—be it into man or into nature—is socially mediated, and the "realities" so constructed are *socially* constructed.

The process by which facts are produced is a complex one. A confluence of spatial-temporal-quality relationships at apprehension is produced as a situated fact of existence. Through conscious acts of the inquirer this fact is inscribed in the public record as a constituent of "primary" sources available to other researchers. Although the "fact" as final product for consumption by researchers may initially have been accompanied by an account and critique of the methodology of its production, it is the fact which achieves the status of "truth." It becomes a factual ingredient which combines with other factual ingredients in the hands of researchers to become new "knowledge" about social reality. Some facts even transcend their status as mere facts and become lodged in the public consciousness as elements of folklore. At each stop the fact gains in its power to facilitate the maintenance of the status quo in existing social relations by becoming the lenses through which individuals perceive reality and organize behavior.

Within societies characterized by oppression,,the system-serving power elites who control the "factories" which produce the various documents recording facts for the public record also control their dissemination and the uses to which such "facts" might be put. Thus, facts are not only socially produced but are ideologically saturated with the context of that production. *Ultimately, reality itself is appropriated to the terms of the dominant system, and whole universes of critical discourse collapse under the weight of "facts."* We note an advanced stage of this process in contemporary American society where certain questions are no longer asked (even by black social analysts) in that the facts speak so loudly for themselves. The myths that have developed surrounding the economic status of the black male exemplify this process.

THE ECONOMIC STATUS OF THE BLACK MALE: KNOWLEDGE RECONSTRUCTED

As mentioned earlier, a major conceptual package has been socially produced and "bought" by the American population relative to the economic status of the black male. Although each of the suppositions mentioned are generally accepted as truth, existing evidence does not support them. The fact is that more black men than black women participate in the labor force in an absolute and relative sense. That is, not only does a greater percentage of black men participate in the labor force, but there are absolutely more black men working and/or looking for work than black women (U.S. Department of Labor, 1980: 22–23, Table A3). In 1980, 73.9% of black men were either working or looking for work as compared with only 55% of black women (Manpower Report of the President, 1974: 253, 256–257). If one examines the labor force participation rates of black men relative to black women in earlier periods, the difference is even greater. In 1954, for example, 85.2% of black men participated in the labor force compared to 46.1% of black women. If the 1954 sample is narrowed from all black men to black men in the age bracket 25–34 in comparison to black women in this age bracket, the difference in levels of participation is even greater.

These statistics could be challenged on several counts. The most common charge is that government statistics on unemployment do not accurately reflect true rates of joblessness, since many of the hardcore unemployed drop out of the labor market. Unemployment data are also criticized on the basis that they do not take into account underemployment, as well as on the basis of other problems of data collection and analysis. The assertion herein is that while such criticisms are valid, such factors do not alter the relative differential in the data between black males and black females. Thus, the statistics presented depict a more or less accurate portrait of relative differences in labor force participation and employment between the black male and female in contemporary American society.

If, then, such statistics are accurate, why are assertions such as the one below found both in academic literature as well as casual conversation?

"In the labor market blacks receive low wages, are concentrated in low-skill menial occupations, have high unemployment rates, high turnover rates, and low labor force participation rates for males (though high participation of females)." Statements which use the terms "high" and "low" are innately comparative. The comparisons being made are between the labor force participation of black males relative to white males and black females relative to white females. This distinction is rarely made (even by academicians), and it is precisely the failure to underscore the fact that such conclusions are based on comparisons within the same-sex groupings that has contributed to the distortion. Even when one compares the labor force participation rate of black males with that of white males, however, the difference is slight. In 1954, the labor force participation rate of black males was 0.4% lower than for white males (Myers, 1978). Today it is only 6.2 percentage points lower (U.S. Department of Labor, 1980). The notion of the "high" labor force participation of black females can be attributed to the fact that in 1954, 46.1% of black females either worked or looked for work as compared with 33.3% of white females (Manpower

Report of the President, 1974). Today the differential is 3.7% (U.S. Department of Labor, 1980). Because there are absolutely fewer black women than white women, absolutely more white women than black women worked in 1954 and work today.

An examination of the supporting premises mentioned reveal that these, too, for the most part are either statistically distorted truths or false in their entirety. It is true, for example, that black males have median earnings which are 41% less than white males (U.S. Bureau of the Census, 1979a: 4). The earnings of black males, however, have been historically higher than that of black females. In 1948, black males earned 64% more than black females (1979a: 4). Today they earn some 50% more (p. 4).[1] Again, it is true that black women in 1978 had 0.9 more years of education than black males (U.S. Bureau of the Census, 1979b: 20). It is not correct that black females hold a larger share of professional jobs than black males. Only 5.4% of all female professionals are black, white 8.7% of all male professionals are black. Furthermore, as late as 1977, more than one-third of black females still worked as service workers (U.S. Bureau of the Census, 1979a: 188).

It is true that until World War II, a major source of employment of black women was as domestics. This source of work was nevertheless a limited market. A brief glance at income distribution in American society reveals that inequalities in the distribution of income rendered the proportion of more than black men—82.6% of black women compared to 50% of black men.

Although the survey instrument focused on beliefs about the economic status of the black male, social psychological questions were also asked. Almost 83% of the sample believed that there is a ''crisis'' between black men and black women. The differential pattern of beliefs between males and females continued. Fully 95.2% of males believed a crisis currently exists compared to 79.1% of females. Although more than half of black families are headed by a couple, 83.8% of respondents believed that most black families are headed by a female. The pattern reversed itself, with a slightly greater percentage of females than males holding this belief. Simultaneously, a slightly larger number of males than females believed that black women do not ''respect'' black women because of their low earning capacity. The figures were 70% and 64.7%, respectively. An overwhelming 91% of the sample believed that there exists twice as many black females as black males. Again, 95% of the males believed this to be true compared with 88.7% of the females.

Survey results, then, document two phenomena. First, there exists within the system of black education socially distorted knowledge of the socioeconomic status of black males relative to black females. Second, the results indicate that there exists a slight difference in the acceptance of these myths by black males and females. Black males believed existing myths slightly more than black females.

IMPLICATIONS AND CONCLUSIONS

Sparingly, words are echoed which say it does not matter what is believed so long as proper conduct is followed. Psychology, as a science of behavior, supports the assertion that behavior is a direct consequence of convictions and beliefs as well as experiences. Our findings indicate that social scientists are both victims and offenders in perpetuating misconceptions about the differential status of black men and women. More important, however, the role of scholars in the perpetuation of this documented gap between perception and reality demonstrates that researchers and educators must become even more vigilant in their efforts to resist intellectual imperialism by the larger society. The construction of a black social science based on emancipatory theory and leading to liberatory praxis must begin with the reconstruction of social knowledge. The comments herein are reflective of this emerging trend.

NOTE

1. Moreover, in 87% of two-earner black families, the husband's earnings far exceed the wife's. See Hill (1971).

REFERENCES

Collier-Arrington, B. J. and L. Williams (1980) "The myth of economic superiority of the black female." Urban League Rev. 5, 1:66–70.

Hill, R. B. (1971) The Strengths of Black Families. New York: National Urban League.

Jackson, J. (1978) "But where are the men?" in R. Staples (ed.) The Black Family: Essays and Studies. Belmont, CA: Wadsworth.

_______ (1971) "But where are the men?" The Black Scholar (December): 30–41.

Lerner, G. (1973) Black Women in White America: A Documentary History. New York: Vintage.

Manpower Report of the President (1974) Civilian Labor Force Participation by Sex and Color, 1954 and 1973. Washington, DC: Government Printing Office.

McAdoo, H. P. (1981a) Black Families. Beverly Hills, CA: Sage.

_______ (1981b) "Upward mobility and parenting in middle-income black families." J. of Black Psychology 8, 1:1–22.

Moynihan, D. P. (1965) The Negro Family: The Case for National Action. Office of Policy Planning and Research, U.S. Department of Labor, Washington, DC: Government Printing Office.

Myers, S. J. (1978) "Economic modeling of the black community." Western J. of Black Studies, 2, 2:95.

Rose, L.R. (ed.) (1980) The Black Woman. Beverly Hills, CA: Sage.

Staples, R. (1973) The Black Woman in America. Chicago: Nelson Hall.

Black Women in the Economic Marketplace: A Battle Unfinished

Delores Aldridge*

A continuing issue facing the nation is the equal employment opportunities of women and minorities. While there can be no denying that some progress has been made, the plight of black women remains particularly acute. Much of the data presented in this work was taken from massive data categorized as nonwhite. However, since blacks constitute between 92.5 and 95.0 percent of the nonwhites in the United States, it is reasonably safe to assume that data pertaining to nonwhites overwhelmingly obtains for blacks. Note, however, the West Indians, Chinese and Japanese are included in much of the nonwhite data, and they are more likely to be in the higher educational and occupational brackets (Epstein 1973, Moynihan 1971). Thus, gains made by black women may not be as great as they appear. Census data reveal that black women hold the least enviable position on the economic ladder, and industry has a marked absence of black women in the professional, technical and managerial levels. This void has been met by the clamor of black women in recent years over their status in America as many demonstrate their profound dissatisfaction over the nature of their relationships to the American economy.

This response might well be expected in view of the fact that employment status and occupation, more than other factors (more than income, education or family background, for example) contribute to the general social status of an individual (Blau and Duncan 1967). In the labor force, the occupation's position in the hierarchy is an important index to the status of the occupant, generally in society (Ferriss 1973). However, one is forced to question whether this is true where black people are concerned. For example, to be black in White America in and of itself constitutes one status irrespective of the individual's occupation, income or education. To be a professor implies a different kind of status. To be a black professor implies still quite a different status, and to be a black female professor, suggests yet another status. This latter 'status' might apply to both the larger white society and to values in the more immediate black culture.

It is common to hear utterances of how, indeed, black women have all the advantages going for them in terms of obtaining jobs of significant status and climbing the ladder once they are in an already high status job. Moreover, it is not unusual for black women to be told in all areas of employment: "You have come a long way, baby." Such avowals precipitated this study, for I question seriously whether black women have won the battle.

This paper, therefore, examines the participation of black women in the labor force in relation to occupational status, educational attainment and earnings to assess to what extent they have "made it" in the world of work. Though black women are the focus of the presentation, the occupations in which they participate are analyzed in terms of the distribution of all women who work. Further, some special problems facing black women in society accorded by the occupations in which they work, are evaluated in relation to their position in the total U.S. Population.

LABOR FORCE PARTICIPATION

Black women have gained much more access to higher paying positions than they used to have, but they still have a long way to go before achieving full equality within the economic market in the choice of jobs, opportunities for advancement and other matters related to employment and compensation. Much of this discrepancy can be attributed to direct discrimination. However, it is also the result of more subtle and complex factors growing out of cultural patterns that have been characteristic of most societies through the centuries. In either case, because the possibilities open to black women in general are restricted, they too often are not allowed to contribute a full measure of earnings to their families or to maximize their talents.

In 1971, there were 4.1 million black women in the labor force, or, nearly 50 percent of all black women (43 percent of all white women) who were workers. Numerically, however, the number was much smaller than for white women. Black women accounted for nearly 11 percent of all women 16 years of age and over in the population, but about 13 percent of all women workers. And although the overall rate of labor force participation was higher for black than white women, among teenagers the situation was reversed. The difference in labor force participation between black and white women was greater among those in the age group 25 to 34 years—59 and 44 percent respectively (U.S. Women's Bureau 1972).

THE HISTORICAL PERSPECTIVE

Black women have long been accustomed to working outside the home. They worked as domestics, beauticians, school teachers, librarians, social workers, nurses, secretaries, government employees and much less frequently as doctors and lawyers. To marry was not to become fully employed as a housewife as was the case for many white women. Black women were expected to continue to work because, in a society that measured a black worker's worth as less than that of whites, it was necessary that both partners be employed to make ends meet. This made the black woman an anomaly in a country where, until recently, the idealized female role was solely that of homebound wife and mother (Dewitt 1974).

The choice of staying at home or entering the labor force was never a real one for most black women. The causal factor underlying their entrance into the labor force in the past—necessity—continues to exist. However, there have been several developments which have made paid work outside the home an increasingly profitable venture. Other factors are: (1) The increased rate of industrial production, particularly since World War II, which has created a greater demand for labor. The gross private domestic product increased at an annual average rate of 2.2 percent during 1955–60, but stepped up to an annual average rate of 4.8 percent during 1960–65; (2) The Civil Rights Movement and legislation on fair employment practices which was exacerbated by black aggression of the 1960's; (3) The educational attainment of black women has been increasing, thereby improving their employability; (4) Black women have to a large extent always been dependent upon themselves (by choice or necessity) and are becoming even more so, as evidenced by (a) an increase in the portion of single black women, (b) a slight increase since 1960 in the percent of families and households with black female heads (Ferriss 1973, Jackson 1971).

THE WORKING BLACK WOMAN TODAY

Although the decisions of individual women to work outside the home are undoubtedly based on many different factors, the economic factors seem to be of overriding importance. The necessity to support oneself or others is one obvious reason but, surprisingly, black adult single women and women who have been separated from husbands or widowed are less likely to be in the labor force than are those black women with husbands (U.S. Women's Bureau 1972).

The increase in earnings opportunities, which proved to be such a powerful factor influencing the secular growth of women's participation in the labor force, is a similarly powerful factor influencing the pattern of women's participation at any given time. Thus, education and other training which affect the amount a woman can earn are strongly related to women's work patterns. The importance of education is such that, whether a woman is single, married or separated, the more education she has, the more likely she is to work (U.S. Women's Bureau 1973:95).

Although the probability that a black woman will work seems to vary with education and presence of children in much the same way as it does for all women, there is one very striking difference: the labor force participation of black women is higher. Marked differences are observed when the comparison of labor force participation is confined to married women living with their husbands. In March 1971, about 53 percent of black wives were in the labor force compared to 40 percent of white wives. However, it should be remembered there that numerically there are fewer black wives than white wives. One important reason why this difference in percentages between white and black working wives prevails may be that the earnings of black wives are closer to their husbands' than is the case among white married couples. In 1971, black married women who worked year-round, full time earned 73 percent as much as black married men who worked year-round, full time. Among whites the percentage was only 51 percent. Behind these relationships is that fact that black men earn considerably less than white men, while black women's earnings are much closer to white women's earnings (U.S. Women's Bureau 1073:96).

OCCUPATIONAL STATUS AND BLACK WOMEN

As mentioned earlier, one of the most important indices of social status is the occupational position one holds, but this has been obscured with respect to blacks who have a singularly constricting status—race. Their status of race tends to dilute whatever other indicators of status are used in measuring their social positions. Clearly, the occupational patterns of black women have witnessed some change over the past three decades. Slowly they are coming into line with the white work force; but the battle is far from over. The most dramatic and important movement has been away from agriculture. In Table 1, the percentage of black and white women are compared in ten major occupational categories for 1910, 1940, 1950, 1960 and 1970. The data indicate that in 1910, over 85 percent of black women were employed as agricultural laborers or domestics as contrasted with about 25 percent white women in the same occupation.

Between 1910 and 1940, the occupational progress of black women was extremely slight. Although the proportion of black women employed as agricultural laborers declined by nearly three-fourths, apparently many of them moved out of agriculture positions into domestic service as the proportion engaged in the latter showed an increase exceeding 50 percent between 1910 and 1940. Such a move was but a horizontal one, for both occupations were equally low in terms of remunerations. White women made significant gains during the same time span. The proportion of white women employed as clerical and sales personnel nearly doubled, reaching one-third of the white female labor force. In addition, the already small proportion engaged in domestics showed a decrease of nearly 40 percent in contrast to the increase among black women.

The decade of the 1940's was more favorable for black women in terms of occupational gains than was the period of 1910–1940. The proportion of black women employed in clerical and sales positions quadrupled, but even so was at only one-twentieth of th total black female labor force. The proportion employed as semi-skilled operatives in manufacturing rose two and one-half times, while the percentage engaged in domestic work declined by 30 percent.

From 1950 to 1970, the occupational distribution of black women continued to change marked by appreciable gains. By 1970, there were proportionately nearly four times as many black women employed as clerical and sales workers as in 1950. The percentage of black professional women doubled, while the relative number of domestics declined by more than 50 percent. Nevertheless the number in this category is still small as compared to

Table 1. Occupational Status of Women 14 Years of Age and Over by Race for 1910, 1940, 1950, 1960 and 1970

Occupational Category	1910		1940		1950		1960		1970	
	Black	White	Black	White	Black	White	Black	White	Black	White
Professional and Technical	1.5	11.6	4.3	14.7	5.3	13.3	7.7	14.1	10.0	15.5
Managers Officials and Proprietors except Farm	.2	1.5	.7	4.3	1.3	4.7	1.1	4.2	1.4	4.7
Clerical and Sales	.3	17.5	1.3	32.8	5.4	39.3	9.8	43.2	21.4	43.4
Craftsmen and Foremen	2.0	8.2	.2	1.1	.7	1.7	.7	1.4	.8	1.1
Operatives	1.4	21.2	6.2	20.3	15.2	21.5	14.3	17.6	16.8	14.5
Non-Farm Laborers	.9	1.5	.8	.9	1.6	.7	1.2	.5	.9	.4
Private Household Workers	38.5	17.2	59.9	10.9	42.0	4.3	38.1	4.4	19.5	3.7
Service Workers except Private Household	3.2	9.2	11.1	12.7	19.1	11.6	23.0	13.1	28.5	15.1
Farmers and Farm Managers	4.0	3.1	3.0	1.1	1.7	.6	.6	.5	.2	.3
Farm Laborers and Foremen	48.0	9.0	12.9	1.2	7.7	2.3	3.5	1.0	.3	1.3

Source: Data for 1910 from U.S. Bureau of the Census, 1940 Census of Population, *Comparative Occupation Statistics for the United States 1870–1940,* Table 15, pp. 166–172. Data for 1940 from U.S. Bureau of the Census, 1940 Census of Population, Volume III, *The Labor Force,* Table 52, pp. 87–88. Data for 1950 from U.S. Bureau of the Census, 1950 Census of Population, *Occupational Characteristics,* Table 3, pp. 29–37, Washington, D.C., 1953. Data for 1960 from U.S. Bureau of the Census, 1960 Census of Population, *Occupational Characteristics,* Table 3, pp. 11–21, Washington, D.C., 1963. Data for 1970 from U.S. Bureau of the Census, *Social and Economic Characteristics of the Population in Metropolitan and Nonmetropolitan Areas: 1970 and 1960 Current Population Reports.* U.S. Government Printing Office: Washington, D.C., 1971 and U.S. Bureau of the Census, *The Social and Economic Status of the Black Population in the United States, 1972.* Current Population Reports, Series P-23, No. 46. Washington, D.C.: Government Printing Office.

white women and white men. Black women are not primarily in white collar occupations as is the case for white women. Too many black women (19.5 percent) are still cleaning white women's houses. Much of whatever gains made can be attributed to the relatively high level of economic activity in the postwar period, the militant civil rights efforts and subsequent government legislation in the sixties. Additionally, considerable educational gains for black women permitted them to take advantage of available opportunities. However, with the increasing numbers of black females attending colleges and universities, one would expect a more dramatic increase in the percentage of those employed in professional and technical occupations than has been the case.

EDUCATION AND OCCUPATION

It is significant to look at education, even though it has not been accompanied by the increases in top level occupations as it might have been. Like the pattern for whites over 25, black women currently in the labor force have had more median years of schooling than black men, and more of them have been high school graduates. Furthermore, although black men in college now exceed black women, more black women over 25 are college graduates than are men in this age group (Epstein 1973). This fact does not hold for white women, where the case has been that of white men obtaining the college degrees.

While the general measure of high school education is significant in relation to the work force, there is little question that higher education is an important determinant of the participation of women in more lucrative employment (Blitz 1974:34). Thus, the educational gains made by black women in part account for their growing access to better positions in the labor market. Epstein (1973) makes this point with respect to black women and professional jobs. However, the gains with respect to white women have not been that dramatic. In 1940, nearly four times as many white women had graduated from college as black women. By 1970, black women had closed the gap to 35 percent, as reflected in Table 2.

Table 2. Level of Education for Black and White Women in the Labor Force, 1940–70

	Black	White	Black	White	Black	White
1940	7.0	11.7	23.8	4.1	2.0	7.4
1952	8.1	12.1	22.4	2.9	3.6	8.3
1957	9.6	12.2	15.7	2.4	4.3	8.4
1959	9.4	12.2	12.2	2.2	4.6	8.5
1962	10.5	12.0	9.8	2.1	6.7	10.0
1965	11.1	12.3	6.7	1.7	7.8	10.3
1968	11.7	12.4	5.9	1.3	7.8	10.9
1970	12.1	12.5	4.5	1.1	8.1	11.1

Source: Data for 1940 from U.S. Bureau of the census, 1940 Census of Population, *Volume on Education.* Table 17, pp. 75–81, Table 13, pp. 82–85, Washington, D.C., U.S. Government Printing Office, 1943. data for 1952–70 from U.S. Department of Labor, *Manpower Report of the President,* 1971. Washington, D.C., U.S. Government Printing Office, 1971.

In 1970, an interesting phenomenon surfaced. Black women with relatively high levels of education earned more than white women with comparable levels of education, as seen in Table 3. How is this to be explained? In terms of more fulltime, full-year employment for black than white women? According to the 1960 Census of Population among professional women (mainly occupations requiring some college, and usually college graduation), a higher proportion of whites, 39 percent, worked a full year as compared to about 37 percent for black women. Further in 1970, 40 percent of all white women worked fulltime, the same proportion as for black women (U.S. Bureau of the Census 1971). Perhaps the explanation is to be found in the fact that 54 percent of all black female professional workers were employed as teachers, as compared to only 39 percent for white female professional workers. And, teaching is a profession in which seniority is directly related to earnings. Data indicate that occupational mobility rates for black women who

Table 3. Income of Black and White Women 25 Years and Over by Years of Education for 1950, 1960, and 1970

Years of Education	1950 Black	1950 White	1950 Percent Black/ White	1960 Black	1960 White	1960 Percent Black/ White	1970 Black	1970 White	1970 Percent Black/ White
0–7	$ 490	$ 710	69	$ 732	$1090	67	$1290	$1440	90
8	734	925	80	970	1180	82	1605	1815	88
9–11	807	1110	73	1196	1680	71	2393	2388	100
12	1093	1590	69	1732	2220	78	3491	3380	103
13–15	1247	1680	74	2166	2420	90	4558	3616	126
16 or More	2103	2320	91	3740	3770	99	7744	5995	129

Source: Data from 1950 from U.S. Bureau of the Census, 1950 Census of Population, *Volume on Education,* Table 12, pp. 108–127, Washington, D.C., U.S. Government Printing Office, 1953. Data for 1960 from U.S. Bureau of the Census, 1960 Census of Population, *Educational Attainment,* Table 7, pp. 112–135, Washington,D.C.: U.S. Government Printing Office, 1963. Data for 1970 from U.S. Department of Commerce Current Population Reports, Consumer Income Series, P-60, No. 80, *Income in 1970 of Persons and Families in the United States,* Washington, D.C., U.S. Government Printing Office, 1971, Table 49, p. 109.

graduated from college are only 40 percent that of white women (Saben 1967). Accordingly, more blacks likely remain with one employer and thus earn higher incomes due to seniority relative to white women.

Indicative of the data in Table 3 is that the ratio of black to white earnings has increased for all levels of education from 1950–1970, and that as one moves up the educational ladder, the ratio of black to white income rises. While this suggests that there is less racial discrimination along economic lines against relatively well-educated black women than poorly-educated black women, it may raise another question. Is the decreasing discrimination toward black women reflective of continued or increasing discrimination of black men? Or, is, in fact, discrimination on the way out with respect to all race-sex groups?

EARNINGS IN THE LABOR FORCE

One of the most direct indicators of economic status is annual income. The low position of black women in the occupation hierarchy is indicated by their low median income in comparison with men and white women. The discrepancies between the earnings of black women and those of white women and men persist. However, the gap has been narrowing (U.S. Bureau of the Census 1969). In 1939, the median wage and salary income of black women was $246, abut one-third that of white women, and by 1959 it wa still only half as much (U.S. Department of Commerce 1971:129). But in the decade of the 1960's, considerable improvement in the economic status of black women took place. Thus, in 1970, the median wage or salary income of fully employed black women was $3,285 or about 85 percent as much as that of white women and 71 percent as much as that of black men (U.S. Women's Bureau 1972:9). Much of the gains are perhaps directly related to the increasing education of black women. Civil Rights Acts of the 1960's and a relatively healthy labor market up to 1970–71.

The yearly earnings statistics indicate that from 1939–58 the income of black men and women increased at the same rate, but that during the 1960's the income of black women climbed much faster than the income of black men. Accordingly, while black women earned only 39 percent as much as black men in1959, the earnings of the former increased to 71 percent of the earnings of the latter in 1970.

In 1970, as at every point in American history, black women earned less than white women (with the exception of the highly educated) who, in turn, made less than white or black men. This economic distribution is constant for every category of worker, including professionals, with the sole exception of domestic workers. Of course, that can be attributed to scarcity of any other race-sex group in this work category. These wage differentials, although illustrating the situation of black women, forces an appraisal of black men and their predicament vis-à-vis white men.

RACE-SEX DIFFERENTIALS IN EARNINGS

Looking at the income comparison of white and black men, the statistics are less favorable. From 1945 to 1966, black men earned about 60 percent of the income of white men. Since 1966, black male earnings have increased somewhat faster than the earnings of white males. However, in 1970 black men earned an average of $5,485 from wages and salaries, still one-third less than the $8,254 received by white males (U.S. Department of Commerce 1971:129).

The slow growth in the earnings of black men cannot be accounted for by the lack of growth in their average educational attainment. In fact, from 1952–1970 the median years of education of black men in the labor force increased 3.9 years compared to a gain of 1.6 years for white men (U.S. Department of Labor 1971:244).

A plausible explanation is that employers have preferred to hire black women instead of men because women have always come with a cheaper salary tag. It is also believed in some quarters that a sense of the threat of black men as colleagues and thus intellectual equals has prevented white men from ''opening the door'' to the potential enemy (Epstein 1973). Moreover, the hiring of black females allows the firm to technically fill two quotas at the same time—sex and race—thus complying with the provisions contained in the 1964 Civil Rights Act regarding racial and sexual discrimination in hiring. Therefore, economically this is a smart move.

SOME SPECIAL PROBLEMS OF THE BLACK WORKING WOMAN

Although slowly bettering their lots in terms of better occupational positions, increased earnings and higher schooling, black women have some special problems vis-à-vis all other race-sex groups. They have steadily closed the economic gap in relation to white women, but then, white women comprise but another exploited group so that goals cannot be established with respect to them. It has been suggested that the problem is to close the gap between black women and white men—the possessors of the greatest economic status in the labor force. But if this is done, then black women and white men will be the oppressors. The real problem is to change the system so that it ceases to be racist, chauvinistic or capitalistic.

The issue of teaming up with white women in the Women's Revolution Movement is a debatable one. For white women are aiming to get a greater hold on the top level positions, never having paid any dues in the really low-status jobs. They are ready to come out of the home and take over executive suites while black women have long been in the economic marketplace in large proportions. According to Epstein (1973), black women have no real need to join white women in the struggle for professional jobs—jobs which command the greatest economic status. She states that black women constitute a larger proportion of the black professional community than women in the white professional world. Furthermore, black women are found in professions and occupations known to be difficult for white women to penetrate. The edge black women hold is attributed to the likelihood that they are more likely to be perceived as serious professionals and not as sexual objects or simply women out to get husbands.

While there is agreement that both white and black women need freedom from the white man since he is the "oppressor," there is also black consensus to let white women worry about their own sex hangups with white men (Hare and Hare 1970:180).

It is perhaps psychologically easier to deal with the problems concerning white men and women than those relating to the black male. Nevertheless, this is one problem that black women will have to resolve as they continue their battle for economic equality in the labor force.

> *Black men are generally recognized by black women to have been on the rise in recent years, but many women also feel that black men believe they have failed their roles and need to be "helped along" toward full manhood. The black woman anticipates that the rejection of the traditional female role would be psychologically threatening to the black male. She must encourage him and lay as much groundwork for black liberation as he will let her. It is necessary to be patient with black men whenever they engage in symbolic manliness. She must not dominate but merely assist strongly (Hare and Hare 1970:279).*

Some blacks share the view that successful black working women are competitors to black men or at least impediments to the progress of black men (Dewitt 1974:18). Proponents of this view feel that black women should stay in the background, while black men assume significant and primary positions, thus dispelling the image of a matriarchal black society. This suggestion is rooted in western standards and implies that there is only one alternative to the issue. This is a fallacy. Still others argue that black women are creative equals to black men, and they have a right, indeed, an obligation, to maximize their skills and abilities (Jackson 1973).

If one is to be guided by the data presented in this paper, it is apparent that black women have only gradually made appreciable gains and no doubt at great costs. Therefore, while they can and do empathize with black men, they are still members of the most exploited group of workers in the American labor force and would strike a negative blow for themselves and blacks in general were they not to use their skills and work experiences toward continued gains in the economic marketplace. They real issue is not who goes first but who goes at all toward the singular goal of liberation for black people. Black men and women must ever be moving forward for the good of all black people.

CONCLUSIONS

Black women have fought against formidable obstacles in the labor force. Undoubtedly they have not been unscathed by the limits set upon their entry and promotion through the ranks. They have made some gains even though they remain at the bottom of the economic ladder. They continue to be heavily concentrated in service and lower level occupations, but they are also increasing as a percent of the employees in professional occupations. As a percent of the total in each occupation they are increasing, especially among clerical workers and "other service" occupations, while proportionate increases in the more remunerative professional and technical occupations are at a much slower pace.

Much of the gains made by black women may be attributed to triple force: the Civil Rights Movement, educational attainments and a lively and expanding economic market in the last several decades. However, while trends are favorable the position of black women workers is still a precarious one. Black women, as a group, are still very vulnerable to economic changes, despite improvement during recent years in their educational attainment and occupational status. The need continues to exist for increased stress on providing equal employment and training opportunities for black women who cannot afford to get caught up in issues centering around being background figures in deference to black men in the world of work. Black women continue to be plagued by their sex and race with the line often being blurred as to which is the more damnable. They must continue to move ahead toward the singular goal of achieving economic parity with those at the top of the economic ladder—white men. The battle of black working women within our overall struggle for liberation is yet an unfinished one.

REFERENCES

Blau P. and Duncan, O. D. 1967. *The American Population Structure.* New York: John Wiley and Sons, Inc.

Blitz, R. C. 1974. "Women in the Professions, 1870–1970." *Monthly Labor Review* (May):34–39. Washington,D.C.: Department of Labor.

Dewitt, K. 1974. "Black Women in Business." *Black Enterprise* 5 (August): 14–19.

Epstein, C. 1973. "Positive Effects of the Multiple Negative: Explaining the Success of Black Professional Women."*American Journal of Sociology* 78(April): 912–935.

Ferriss, A. L. 1973. *Indicators of Trends in the Status of American Women.* New York: Russell Sage Foundation.

Hare N. and Hare, J. 1970. "Black Women 1970," Pp. 178–181 in Judith M. Bardwick (ed.). *Readings on the Psychology of Women.* New York: Harper and Row Publishers.
Jackson, J. J. 1973. "Are Black Women Creative Equals to Black Men?" *Essence* (November): 56–72. 1971 "But Where Are the Men?" *Black Scholar* (December): 30–41.
Moynihan, D. P. 1971. "Employment, Income, and the Ordeal of the Negro Family."*Essays and Studies.* Belmont, California: Wadsworth Publishing Co., Inc.
Sabern, S. 1967. "Occupational Mobility of Employed Workers." *Monthly Labor Review* 90(June): 2–15.
U.S. Bureau of the Census. 1973. *The Social and Economic Status of the Black Population in the United States, 1972.* Current Population Reports, Series P-23, No. 46, Washington, D.C.: U.S. Government Printing Office.
1972. *General Social and Economic Characteristics.* Final Report, D.C. C17-C1. U.S. Summary. Washington, D.C.: Government Printing Office 1-379.
1971. *Social and Economic Characteristics of the Population in Metropolitan and Nonmetropolitan Areas: 1970 and 1960.* Current Population Reports, Special Studies. Washington, D.C.: U.S. Government Printing Office.
1969. *The Social and Economic Status of Negroes in the United States,1969.* Washington, D.C.: U.S. Government Printing Office.
1963a. *Educational Attainment.* Table 7:112–135. Washington, D.C.: Government Printing Office.
1963b. *Occupational Characteristics.* Table 3:11–21. Washington, D.C.: U.S. Government Printing Office.
1953a. *Occupational Characteristics.* Table 3:20–37. Washington, D.C.: U.S. Government Printing Office.
1953b. U.S. Census of the Population. *Volume on Education.* Table 12:108–127. Washington, D.C.: U.S. Government Printing Office.
1943a. *Comparative Occupation Statistics for the United States 1870–1940.* Table 15:166–172. Washington, D.C.: U.S. Government Printing Office.
1943b. 1940 Census of the Population. *Volume on Education.* Table 13 and Table 17:75–85.
U.S. Department of Commerce. 1971. Income in 1970 of Families and Persons in the United States. Current Population Reports, Income Series P-60, No. 80. Table 49:109. Washington, D.C.: U.S. Government Printing Office.
U.S. Department Labor. 1971. Manpower Report of the U.S. President, 1971. Washington, D.C.: U.S. Government Printing Office.
1967. Negro Women in the Population and the Labor Force. Washington, D.C.: U.S. Government Printing Office.
U.S. National Center for Health Statistics. 1967. Suicide in the United States 1950–1964. Public Health Service Publication 1000, Series 20, No. 5. Washington, D.C.: U.S. Department of Health, Education and Welfare.
U.S. Women's Bureau. 1973. The Economic Role of Women. Reprinted from Economic Report of the President, 1973. Washington, D.C.: U.S. Department of Labor.
1972. Facts on Women Workers of Minority Races. Washington, D.C.: U.S. Department of Labor.
1945. Negro Women War Workers. Bulletin 205. Washington, D.C.: U.S. Government Printing Office.

CHAPTER SIX

Religious Issues

James Cone provides a backdrop for understanding the relationship of Black theology, Black churches, and Black women to feminism in different historical periods. He cautions Black male ministers and theologians about responsibilities they have in the church that affect how women are received and what opportunities are made available to them for the fullest development of their potential for service to god in the church and in society. He ends with suggestions for Black men and Black women of the church to work more effectively toward the development of each other.

Jacquelyn Grant's work is unique in its data-based focus upon the subsidiary role played by Black women in the Black church. What is ironical is the non-recognition among scholars of the new Black theology to recognize sexism as a viable topic to be confronted. She, like Cone, is particularly adept at shedding new light on the relationship of Black men and women in the church and the challenge that Black theology faces.

Black Theology, Black Churches, and Black Women

James Cone

O how careful ought we to be, lest through our bylaws of church government and discipline we bring into disrepute even the word of life. For as unseemly as it may appear nowadays for a woman to preach, it should be remembered that nothing is impossible with God. And why should it be thought impossible, heterodox, or improper for a woman to preach, seeing the Savior died for the women as well as the man?

Reverend Jarena Lee, 1836[1]

We'll have our rights. See if we don't. And you can't stop us from them. See if you can.

Sojourner Truth, 1853[2]

To be a woman, black, and active in religious institutions in the American scene is to labor under triple jeopardy.

Theressa Hoover[3]

If theology, like the church, has no word for Black women, its conception of liberation is inauthentic.

Jacquelyn Grant[4]

Although black male theologians and church leaders have progressive and often revolutionary ideas regarding the equality of blacks in American society, they do not have similar ideas regarding the equality of women in the black church and community. Why is it that many black men cannot see the analogy between racism and sexism, especially in view of the fact that so many black women in the church and in society have expressed clearly their experience of oppression? What is it that blinds black men to the truth regarding the suffering of their sisters? What is it that makes black churchmen insensitive to the pain of women suffering that we have inflicted on them?

Of course many black men, like whites in relation to racism, would deny that they are sexist. But an emphatic denial of being prejudiced against black women is no proof that black men are free of sexism: those who are not the victims of a particular form of oppression are seldom capable of developing criteria to test whether it has been eliminated. The persons best capable of evaluating sexism in the black community and church are black women who are feminists and thus engaged in the struggle to eliminate it from our community. Black churchmen today need not be surprised by militant female voices: black church women have been speaking out for a long time.

NINETEENTH-CENTURY FEMINISM IN THE BLACK CHURCH

Black feminism was developed in the context of the aboitionist movement and the rise of white feminism in the second half of the nineteenth century. It is especially important for black men to note that Frederick Douglass, the great abolitionist, was also an outspoken advocate of women's rights.[5] He was one of the first to see the connection between the freedom of African slaves and the liberation of women. That was why he attended the first women's rights convention, in Seneca Falls, New York, in 1848. Without his unqualified support, the controversial resolution of that convention on women's suffrage would not have been approved.

Nineteenth century black women did not remain silent on the issue of women's rights. Like white women who became acutely aware of sexism during their involvement in the abolitionist movement, black women also developed a similar consciousness. Sojourner Truth was one of their most outstanding advocates. A former slave, she attended several women's rights conventions, giving her support to the cause. She is best known for her famous "Ain't I a Woman?" speech, delivered at the women's convention in 1851 in Akron, Ohio. One clergyman, who spoke at the convention, told women "to beware of selling their birthright of consideration and deference for a mess of equality pottage. What man," he asked, "would help a political or business rival into a carriage, or lift her over a ditch?"[6] To which Sojourner replied:

> *That man over there says that women needs to be helped into carriage, and lifted over ditches, and to have the best place everywhere. Nobody ever helps me into carriages, or over mudpuddles, or gives me any best place! And ain't I a woman? Look at me! Look at my arm! I have ploughed, and planted, and gathered into barns, and no man could head me! And ain't I a woman? I could work as much and eat as much as a man—when I could get it—and bear the lash as well! And ain't I a woman? I have borne thirteen children and seen them most all sold off to slavery, and when I cried out with my mother's grief, none but Jesus heard me! And ain't I a woman?*[7]

Another preacher in the same convention had claimed superior rights and privileges for men on the grounds of the manhood of Christ. "If God had desired the equality of women," he said, "he would have given some token of his will through the birth, life, and death of the Savior."[8] To which Sojourner responded:

> *"That little man in black there, he says women can't have as much rights as men, because Christ wasn't a woman!" Then she paused, with her burning eyes focused on the minister who had made the comment: "Where did your Christ come from?"She repeated her question, "Where did your Christ come from?" Then she answered her own question, her voice ringing like an organ with all the stops pulled: "From God and a woman! Man had nothing to do with him."*[9]

Sojourner concluded her speech with the observation that "if the first woman God ever made was strong enough to turn the world upside down all alone, these women together ought to be able to turn it back, and get it right side up again! And now they are asking to do it, the men better let them."[10]

When there was debate about black men receiving the right to vote but not women, Sojourner shared the sentiment of other women's rights activists who strongly objected, seeing it as a bonding of white and black men against women of both colors:

> *There is a great stir about colored men getting their rights, but not a word about colored women; and if colored men get theirs, and not colored women theirs, you see the colored men will be the masters over the women, and it will be just as bad as before. So I am for keeping the thing going while the things are stirring; because if we wait till it is still, it will take a great while to get it going again."*

Sojourner Truth was not the only nineteenth-century black woman to stand up for women's rights. Harriet Tubman was called the "Moses" of her people because of her leading more than three hundred slaves to freedom. She also attended several women's suffrage conventions and became involved in the National Federation of Afro-American Women. Ida B. Wells-Barnett, a journalist and graduate of Rust College, is best known for her solitary campaign against lynching and her involvement in the work of black club women. Mary Church Terrell, a leading club woman, organized the National Association of Colored Women (1897) and was elected its first president. She was also a charter member of the NAACP (1909), a suffragist and close friend of Susan B. Anthony and Jane Addams, Francis Ellen Watkins Harper, also a club woman and feminist, was a founder and vice president of the National Association of Colored Women.

It is important to note that black women, unlike black men and white women, could not choose between the issues of sexism and racism: they were victims of both. Black feminists today call it double jeopardy. White feminists and abolitionists parted ways at the 1869 meeting of the Equal Rights Association, because of the latters' support of the Fourteenth and Fifteenth Amendments, which excluded franchise for women. White feminists could afford to ignore racism, just as black men could sexism. But black women fought for both rights.[12]

Black women *in the church* had an additional burden, which led Theressa Hoover to call it triple jeopardy.[13] Although black churches agreed with Sojourner Truth, Harriett

Tubman, Ida Wells, and other black women regarding the abolition of slavery, lynching, and other forms of white racism, they rejected their views on women's rights.

Black church attitudes toward women ministers were similar to those of white denominations. In the AME Church, a progressive denomination in comparison with some other independent black churches, women were not permitted ordination in the nineteenth century. They were permitted only to exhort and preach without a license. Largely because of their insistence that they were called by God to preach the gospel, the offices of stewardess and deaconess were created in 1868 and 1900, respectively. Although some AME ministers licensed women to preach, the denomination did not make it official until 1884 and limited their preaching to the subordinate office of "evangelist."

Bishop Henry McNeal Turner was publicly reprimanded for ordaining a woman to preach. Later the 1888 General Conference made its position clear:

> *Whereas Bishop H. M. Turner has seen fit to ordain a woman to the order of a deacon; and whereas said act is contrary to the usage of our church, and without precedent in any other body of Christians in the known world; and as it cannot be proved by the scriptures that a woman has ever been ordained to the order of the ministry; therefore be it enacted, that the bishops of the African Methodist Episcopal Church be and hereby [are] forbidden to ordain a woman to the order of deacon or elder in our church.*[14]

Despite the limitations placed on black women ministers, several distinguished themselves. Jarena Lee, the first female preacher in the AME Church, was one of the most prominent. Born in 1783, she recorded the story of her conversion and call to preach in *The Life and Religious Experience of Jarena Lee.* When she told Richard Allen about her call to preach, his reply was: "As to women preaching, . . . our discipline knew nothing at all about it—that it did not call for women preachers."[15] But Jarena Lee asked: "If the man may preach, because the Savior died for him, why not the woman, seeing he died for her also? Is he not a whole Savior, instead of a half one, as those who hold it wrong for a woman to preach would seem to make it appear?"[16] Because of her persistence, Allen accepted her as a woman preacher even though he did not ordain her. In one year she traveled over two thousand miles and delivered 178 sermons.

There were other black women of the nineteenth century whose call to the ministry outweighed the rules defined by the black male clergy. When asked "by what authority" she "spoke against slavery" and whether she had been ordained, a woman named Elizabeth replied that although she had not been "commissioned of men's hands, if the Lord had ordained me, I needed nothing better."[17] As black male ministers continued to reject them outright or forced upon them "the extra burden of proving their call," black women found ways to respond to God's call to preach the gospel.

It can be concluded that black churches were similar to white churches in their attitudes toward women during the nineteenth century. The same was true of the black community as a whole at that time.

BLACK FEMINISM IN THE CIVIL RIGHTS AND BLACK POWER ERA

The recent struggle of black women in the churches has drawn not only upon nineteenth-century sources but upon the feminist outcry of the 1960s and '70s. The language used to name women's oppression, as suggested in such terms as "patriarchy," "misogyny," and "sexism," was developed first by women in the white community. White women initially created the language of contemporary radical feminism in response to women's subordination in the SNCC and later in reaction to a much more oppressive subordination in radical left white male groups, such as the Students for a Democratic Society (SDS).[18]

For black women, however, white feminism was not always adequate or appropriate, partly because feminism was sometimes racist and partly because patriarchy had distinctive characteristics in the struggle for racial freedom. Women seldom received the credit they deserved for contributions to the freedom movement of the late 1950s and '60s. They sometimes served as symbols for a brief time, as in the case of Rosa Parks, but seldom did men acknowledge their role in any substantive decision-making process.

Most persons do not know that Ella Baker served as the first executive director of the SCLC and that she was responsible for the founding of the SNCC in the spring of 1960.[19] Many do not know of Anna A. Hedgeman and the role she played in putting race on the agenda of the NCC.[20] Seldom mentioned are the contributions of Fannie Lou Hamer in Mississippi,[21] Daisy Bates in the 1957 crisis at Little Rock Central High School,[22] Ruby Doris Robinson and Diana Nash Bevel in the SNCC.[23] Only men—Martin Luther King, Jr., Malcolm X, Andrea Young, Stokely Carmichael, James Forman, and others like them—are given major recognition for their achievements in the black freedom struggle. The invisibility of black women in the freedom movement and the hostility of black men toward women's equality helped drive black women to form their own feminist organizations.

A more blatant display of black patriarchy in the struggle for black power was the inordinate emphasis on violence and masculine assertiveness, the stress on black women's passivity and weakness, and the glorification of the pimp and the black male's sexual exploits in such movies as Melvin Van Peeble's *Sweet Sweetback's Baadasssss Song* (1971) and his Broadway play *Ain't Supposed to Die a Natural Death* (1973). In his book *Soul on Ice* (1968), Eldridge Cleaver thematized rape as a political act, and other black male so-called revolutionaries followed suit. Most of the plays, novels, and movies that were created by black men during the civil rights and black power revolution of the 1960s accented patriarchal values similar to those in white society.

For many black men, freedom meant the assertion of their manhood, which they identified as violence against the black man with guns, rape of the white woman, and unlimited physical and mental brutality against the black woman. Inasmuch as black women were the most accessible and least capable of defending themselves, black men often made black women victims of displaced anger, doing to their sisters what they really wanted to do to white society.

No one was more influential in defining the black consciousness movement than Amiri Baraka, formerly called LeRoi Jones, by his writings and speeches, and in the organizations he headed. But, as is the case of many other radical black men, Baraka's sexism created contradictions in his nationalist philosophy. On one occasion he was asked whether a militant black man could have a white woman companion, and he replied:

> *Jim Brown put it pretty straight and this is really quite true. He says that there are black men and white men, then there are women. So you can indeed be going through a black militant thing and have yourself a woman. The fact that she happens to be black or white is no longer impressive to anybody, but a man who gets himself a woman is what's impressive. The battle is really between white men and black men. Whether we like to admit it, that is the battlefield at this time.*[24]

Sexism, like racism, encourages violence as a way to subjugate the other. Baraka dramatized his nationalist view in his play *Madheart.* In one scene, the black male protagonist of the play demonstrates his power to use force to subdue the black woman who is urging him to leave the white woman and come to her:

BLACK MAN: I'll get you back. If I need to.

WOMAN (*laughs*): You need to baby . . . just look around you. You better get me back, if you know what's good for you . . . you better.

BLACK MAN (*looking around at her squarely, he advances*): I better? . . . (*a soft laugh*) Yes. Now is where we always are . . . that now. . . . (*He wheels and suddenly slaps her crosswise, back and forth across the face.*).

WOMAN: Wha??? What . . . oh love . . . please . . . don't hit me. (*He hits her, slaps her again.*)

BLACK MAN: I want you woman, as a woman. Go down. (*He slaps her again.*) Go down, submit, submit . . . to love . . . and to man, now, forever.

WOMAN (*weeping, turning her head from side to side*): Please don't hit me . . . please. . . . (*She bends.*) The years are so long, without you, man, I've waited . . . waited for you. . . .

BLACK MAN: And I've waited.

WOMAN: I've seen you humbled, black man, seen you crawl for dogs and devils.

BLACK MAN: And I've seen you raped by savages and beasts, and bear bleach-shit of children of apes.

WOMAN: You permitted it . . . you could . . . do nothing.

BLACK MAN: But now I can. (*He slaps her . . . drags her to him, kissing her deeply on the lips.*) That shit is ended, woman, you with me, and the world is mine.[25]

At first black women were reluctant to speak the language of feminism, because they did not want to detract from the importance of the struggle of the black community against white racism. Furthermore, they wanted to give black men a chance to "stand up like men" in the presence of white men in order to protect and to provide for the black family.

This was also partly due to reaction to the myth of black female matriarchy and partly as a response to black male proclamations of assumed and justified leadership.

In an *Ebony* article, "The Black Woman and Women's Lib," Helen H. King suggested that many black women in the civil rights and black power movements accepted their place behind black men and were proud to see them stand up and demand liberalization for the black community.

"We should stand behind our men, not against them," said a black woman opponent of the women's liberation movement.[26] Another is quoted as saying: "This movement won't be any different from the woman suffrage thing. White women won the right to vote way back then, but black people, including black women, didn't win this right until more than a hundred years later!"[27] Still another black woman opponent characterized the women's movement as "just a bunch of bored white women with nothing to do—they're just trying to attract attention away from the black liberation movement."[28]

Prominent black women joined the chorus denouncing the women's movement as a white and middle-class phenomenon, and thus unrelated to the black struggle for freedom. Nikki Giovanni said:

> *I think that it's a moot issue. Just another freedom of white people to find out what black people are doing or to control what we are doing. . . . They [white women] want "equality" to deal with black women because they've certainly dealt with black men. They're so upset about black women not coming in because they're ultimately trying to control us. There aren't any other reasons why they could be upset. Black women consider their first reality to be black, and given that reality we know from birth that we are going to be oppressed—man, woman, or eunuch!*[29]

The well-known poet Gwendolyn Brooks echoed the same theme:

> *Black women, like all women, certainly want, and are entitled to, equal pay and privileges. But black women have a second "twoness." Today's black men, at last flamingly assertive and proud, need their black women beside them, not organizing against them.*[30]

Although there were a few exceptions,[31] most black women of the early 1970s remained apart from and critical of the women's movement. But when black revolutionaries began "to talk black and sleep white," black women began to question the nature of black men's commitment to the black freedom struggle and to reevaluate their place *behind* the black man. Black women started to realize that to be liberated, from both white racism and male domination, they would have to do the job themselves.

Of course, just as many blacks submitted to racism, many black women accepted the sexist role defined by so-called revolutionary black men. Some black women were willing to walk two steps behind their men and remain silent and passive. Black women wanted to be taken care of by "strong" black men, as white men had supposedly done for white women. Therefore black women were slow to complain about black male brutality.

Because black men knew that black women were deeply committed to the racial struggle, they did not even take seriously black women's concern for sexual oppression. They merely laughed, treating the hurt and pain of our sisters as a joke. When asked about the role of women in the movement, Stokely Carmichael is reported to have said, "The only position for women in SNCC is prone."[32]

Because we were so insensitive, we left black women with no choice but to declare publicly that sexism does exist in the black community and, like racism, it must be eliminated. One of the earlier texts on black feminism is entitled *The Black Woman* (1970), an anthology edited by Toni Cade.[33] But it was not until Ntozake Shange's play *For Colored Girls* . . . (1976)[34] and Michele Wallace's book *Black Macho and the Myth of the Superwoman* (1979)[35] that the idea of a black feminism became widely discussed in the black community..[36]

Although the black church has seldom been willing to accept new ideas that were not directly related to the elimination of white racism, the enormous impact of Shange's play and Wallace's book make it impossible for many black women in the church and seminary to avoid the issue of black patriarchy. One does not have to agree with the perspectives of Shange or Wallace in order to know that black women are oppressed by black men, and especially in the church by male ministers.

BLACK THEOLOGY AND BLACK WOMEN

Just as the struggles of the 1960 and '70s reinforced sexism in the black community generally, sexism in the church particularly seemed more blatant in those years. Black clergymen became bold advocates of women's inferiority, emphasizing their supposed lack of intelligence, natural weakness, and passivity. As some white male ministers began to retreat in the face of the emerging power of the women's movement in the seminary and church, black clergymen laughed at white men's inability to keep women in their place. At the same time they mimicked white antifeminist conservatives by preaching about the value of the American family in which wives are subordinate to their husbands. This was the sanctimonious—supposedly biblical—version of the male revolutionary's demand that black women stand behind their men.

Such attitudes limit women's roles in the church. Women are expected to sing in the choir, serve on the usher and stewardess boards, participate in the missionary society, cook in the kitchen, teach children in the Sunday School, and serve in all those positions that men regard as "women's work." But unlike men, women are not encouraged to enter the ministry. Women are tolerated when they insist that God has called them to preach the word. Indeed a woman's calling is often questioned until her talent and faith remove skeptics' doubts. A man's call is never questioned until a lack of faith or talent or moral integrity create skepticism among the community of believers. A man may live the most immoral life imaginable, be "converted," and still be accepted by the church for service in God's ministry. But an immoral woman who "gets" religion and then receives the call would hardly be given a similar opportunity for service in the church.

In some black churches women are still excluded entirely from the ordained ministry.[37] But even in churches that do ordain women, female ministers do not have the same opportunities as men for the exercise of their ministry. For instance, there is, to my knowledge, only one women presiding elder, but no bishops, general officers, college presidents, or pastors of major churches in the AME Church.[38] When women push through the male-oriented pattern of expectations and *insist* that God has called them to preach, men often tell them to become evangelists, a ministry with no institutional authority. If women should insist on being pastors, they are usually urged to become assistants to male pastors. If they insist on being the head pastor, the bishop usually appoints them to small churches that men do not want. In other black denominations, the offices may have different names but the results are the same: men say to women, ''This far and no farther.''

Turning to theology, it is clear from earlier chapters that black theology arose out of the black church and in response to the black power movement. It is shameful but scarcely surprising that black theology learned the patriarchal bad habits of its progenitors. Only one woman, Dr. Anna Hedgeman, author and staff member of the NCC commission on religion and race, wa asked to sign the NCBC ''Black Power Statement'' of 1966.[39] The NCBC has not been a public advocate of equality for women in the ministry. During my involvement in most of its early history, the issue of women in the ministry was seldom discussed, because the NCBC was controlled by black male theologians and ministers. When the issue was raised most men either laughed or assigned it a low priority in the struggle for black freedom. A woman has served in the position of secretary to the executive director and the board of directors. A few women have even served on the board.

The very name NCBC, with the last letter representing Church—men, indicated clearly the reactionary perspective of black male ministers regarding women's equality in church and society. According to the reports of some black women, the NCBC male leadership, despite repeated appeals, remained adamant in its refusal to replace the word ''Churchmen'' with ''Christians,'' insisting that the word ''men'' is generic and not sexist. Only in late 1982 did the NCBC soften its views on the matter and change its name to National Conference of Black Christians.[40]

At first, there were only a few black women theologians who began to criticize black male theology. They included Pauli Murray,[41] an Episcopal priest and lawyer, and Theressa Hoover, an executive of the Board of Global Ministries of the United Methodist Church.[42] But they were the exceptions, and black male theologians and ministers either ignored them or laughed at their arguments. The situation changed, however, in the mid-1970s.

I remember the first time that black men and women at Union Theological Seminary came together to discuss women in the ministry. Because I had been ''converted'' to women's equality in society, church, and the doing of theology, and because I had just read a paper addressing that theme at Garrett Evangelical Seminary in Evanston (October 1986), Jacquelyn Grant, then a graduate student at Union and now a professor of theology at the Interdenominational Theological Center, asked me to present the same paper to black men and women at Union.

When I now read that October 1976 paper, I am embarrassed by how mildly and carefully I approached the theme of women's equality in the church. It was anything but radical, somewhat analogous to a southern white liberal reflecting on racism. But black male seminarians, almost without exception, were greatly disturbed by my paper. If my paper can be compared to that of a southern white liberal, the reactions of many black male seminarians were similar to those of most reactionary southern white racists. They quoted the bible to justify that women should not be ordained, and some even insisted that they should not even be in the pulpit. I was shocked, as were my black colleagues, Professors James Forbes and James Washington. But black women seminarians were not surprised. They were even aware of the attitudes that kept them subordinate in the church, as well as invisible in black theology.

From like encounters, repeated and multiplied countless times, black women saw the need for a black feminist theology. In this project they have had the ambiguous models of black male theology and white feminist theology. Beginning with Mary Daly's *The Church and the Second Sex* (1968),[43] feminist theology was further developed in the prolific writings of Rosemary Ruether, Letty Russell, Beverly Harrison, Sheila Collins, Judith Plaskow, Carol Christ, and many others.[44] Most black women either ignored these writings or criticized them as irrelevant to black women and the black church. However, as black feminist theology emerges, black women are affirming in varying degrees the value of their white sisters' work.

The invisibility of black women in both black and feminist theologies is striking. The most that both theologies do is to mention in passing the names of Sojourner Truth, Harriet Tubman, and perhaps Rosa Parks. But for neither is black women's experience a part of the structure and substance of the theology itself. Black women's experience is merely added to theologies whose style and content are determined by other experiences. That is why Jarena Lee, Maria Stewart, Frances Ellen Watkins Harper, Ida Wells-Barnett, and Anna Julia Cooper are seldom mentioned in either black male or white feminist theology.

Only black women can do black feminist theology: their experience is truly theirs. Therefore, even if white feminists were not so racist and black males were not so sexist, there would still be a need for black feminist theology. The need arises from the uniqueness of black women's experience. If theology arises out of the attempt to reconcile faith with life, and if black women have an experience of faith in God that is not exhausted by white women or black men, then there is a need to articulate the faith of black women so that the universal church can learn from their experience with God. Black women, by giving an account of their faith in worship and living out their faith in the world, create the context for authentic theological reflection.

Among the black women seminarians and professors who have begun to develop a black feminist theology are Jacquelyn Grant, Pauli Murray, Katie Cannon, Delores Williams, Kelly Brown, and Cherl Gilkes. Although black women's experience is related to some aspects of both women and blacks generally, their experience is not exhausted by either group. Black women have begun to feel the need to articulate the uniqueness of their experience *theologically.*

Black feminist theologians in the U.S.A. have been aided by theological reflection arising from the struggles of other minority women in the U.S.A. and women in Africa, Asia, and Latin America. When black women theologians and ministers encountered Third World women in the WCC and other ecumenical settings, they realized that they were not the only women in an oppressed community concerned about women's equality.[45] Meeting Third World women and reading their writings on women's liberation helped black women to recognize the need for the development of a black feminist theology.[46]

Black women may have been reluctant to join in a coalition with white women, but they are less reluctant to express their solidarity with African and other non-European women. The WCC, EATWOT, and other ecumenical organizations have provided many an occasion for dialogues between African-American and Third World women in the church.

A WORD TO BLACK MALE MINISTERS AND THEOLOGIANS

As a male theologian, I am in no position to say what the content and form of a black feminist theology should be. I can only support its development and be instructed by the Black women who assume the responsibility to create it. However, I should like to offer some thoughts to black male theologians and ministers whose attitudes range from indifference to mild support of the development of women's fullest potential as human beings in the church and community. There are responsibilities that we have in the church that affect how women are received and what opportunities are made available to them for the fullest development of their potential for service to God in the church and in society.

It is important for black men to realize that women's liberation is a viable issue.[47] We must recognize it and help others in the church to treat it seriously. It is not a joke. To get others to accept it as an issue that deserves serious consideration and discussion is the first step. As ministers in the church, how we treat the issue will affect the attitudes of others in our pastoral care. I realize that many women give the appearance of accepting the place set aside for them by men as is still true of many blacks in relation to whites. But just as whites were responsible for creating the societal structures that aided black self-hate, so black men are responsible for creating a similar situation among black women in the church. Saying that women like their place is no different from saying that blacks like theirs.

It is also important that we learn how to listen to women tell their stories of pain and struggle. The art of listening is not easy, especially for oppressors whose very position of power inhibits them from hearing and understanding anything that contradicts their values.

When we try to understand something of the depth of sexism and how it functions in black churches and community, it is helpful to think of racism in American society and white churches. Although racism and sexism are different in many respects, they share many similarities. If black men deny this connection between sexism and racism, it is unlikely that they will recognize the depth of the problem of sexism.

To aid our comprehension of the complexity of the issue, it is necessary to read as much as possible about the history of sexism and women's struggles, especially in the Third World and particularly in the black community and its churches in the U.S.A. Just as blacks become impatient with whites who do not take the time and discipline to inform themselves about the history of their brutality against them and their struggle against that brutality, black women will have a similar feeling regarding our failure to study their history.

Black women are beginning to develop their own leadership styles. Black men should support them. But it is already clear that the leadership roles and styles of black women will be quite different from those that have been defined for them by black male ministers and theologians. Just as blacks and other oppressed groups develop styles in ministry that are different from those of oppressor whites, so the experience of women provide ways of doing ministry that will be quite different from the patriarchal and authoritarian leadership of men. It is our responsibility as men to be open to new styles of ministry and to help our congregations to be open to them. This will involve the necessity of being critical of our brothers who are opposed to women's taking leadership positions in the church and in society. We should be prepared to lose some "friends" as we work for change in the patriarchal structures in black churches and seek to create ones that are humane and just.

Black male ministers should also insist on affirmative action for black women in churches and in the community. The goal should be to have at least as many black women in positions of responsibility in churches and in community organizations as will reflect their percentage of the overall population. We can never achieve this goal without a plan of action for its accomplishment. Blacks have used this approach vis-à-vis racism; it seems logical to apply it to the situation of black women in our churches and communities. The principle of affirmative action should be applied to all positions, including those of bishop, pastor, general officer, steward, and deacon.

Finally, it is very important for black male ministers to support black women in their attempt to discover role models of the past. In my reading and discussions with black women, they often speak of the lack of role models—both past and present. What is needed therefore is for black women (and also black men) to discover their sisters of the past and to find community with those of the present so they can share experiences with each other and thereby be encouraged to keep fighting for recognition and justice in the church. Through a discovery of their sisters and mothers of the past and the creation of community in the present, self-confidence can be enhanced and the struggle for liberation strengthened.

In addition to the suggestions mentioned above, there are many other things that black men and women can do—both together and separately. My suggestions are intended only to engender serious discussion on the role of black women in the church and in society. I firmly believe that the black church cannot regain its Christian integrity unless it is willing to face head-on the evil of patriarchy and seek to eliminate it.

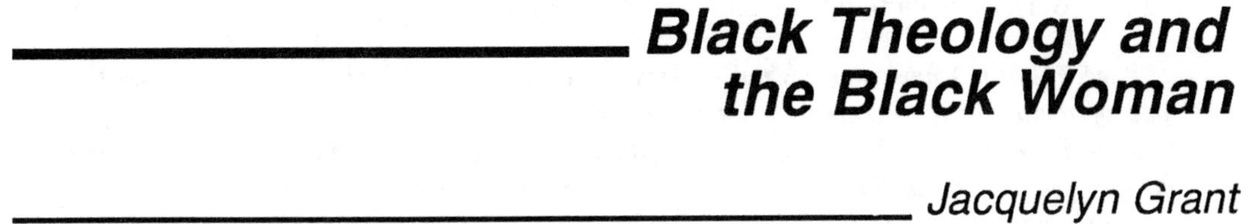

Black Theology and the Black Woman

Jacquelyn Grant

Liberation theologies have arisen out of the contexts of the liberation struggles of Black Americans, Latin Americans, American women, Black South Africans and Asians. These theologies represent a departure from traditional Christian theology. As a collective critique, liberation theologies raise serious questions about the normative use of Scripture, tradition and experience in Christian theology. Liberation theologians assert that the reigning theologies of the West have been used to legitimate the established order. Those to whom the church has entrusted the task of interpreting the meaning of God's activity in the world have been too content to represent the ruling classes. For this reason, say the liberation theologians, theology has generally not spoken to those who are oppressed by the political establishment.

Ironically, the criticism that liberation theology makes against classical theology has been turned against liberation theology itself. Just as most European and American theologians have acquiesced with the oppression of the West, for which they have been taken to task by liberation theologians, some liberation theologians have acquiesced in one or more oppressive aspects of the liberation struggle itself. Where racism is rejected, sexism has been embraced. Where classicism is called into question, racism and sexism have been tolerated. And where sexism is repudiated racism and classicism are often ignored.

Although there is a certain validity to the argument that any one analysis—race, class or sex—is not sufficiently universal to embrace the needs of all oppressed peoples, these particular analyses, nonetheless, have all been well presented and are crucial for a comprehensive and authentic liberation theology. In order for liberation theology to be faithful to itself it must hear the critique coming to it from the perspective of the Black woman—perhaps the most oppressed of all the oppressed.

I am concerned in this essay with how the experience of the Black woman calls into question certain assumptions in Liberation Theology in general, and Black Theology in particular. In the Latin American context this has already been done by women such as Beatriz Melano Couch and Consuelo Urquiza. A few Latin American theologians have begun to respond. Beatriz Couch, for example, accepts the starting point of Latin American theologians, but criticizes them for their exclusivism with respect to race and sex. She says:

> *. . . we in Latin America stress the importance of the starting point, the praxis, and the use of social science to analyze our political, historical situation. In this I am in full agreement with my male colleagues . . . with one qualitative difference. I stress the need to give importance to the different cultural forms that express oppression; to the ideology that divides people not only according to class, but to race and sex. Racism and sexism are oppressive ideologies which deserve a specific treatment in the theology of liberation.*[1]

More recently, Consuelo Urquiza called for the unification of Hispanic-American women in struggling against their oppression in the church and society. In commenting on the contradiction in the Pauline Epistles which undergird the oppression of the Hispanic-American woman, Urquiza said: "At the present time all Christians will agree with Paul in the first part of [Galatians 3:28] about freedom and slavery that there should not be slaves. . . . However, the next part of this verse . . . has been ignored and the equality between man and woman is not accepted. They would rather skip that line and go to the epistle to Timothy [2:9–15]."[2] Women theologians of Latin background are beginning to do theology and to sensitize other women to the necessity of participating in decisions which affect their lives and the life of their communities. Latin American theology will gain from these inputs which women are making to the theological process.

Third World and Black women[3] in the United States will soon collaborate in an attack on another aspect of Liberation Theology—Feminist Theology. Black and Third World women have begun to articulate their differences and similarities with the Feminist Movement, which is dominated by White American women who until now have been the chief authors of Feminist Theology. It is my contention that the theological perspectives of Black and Third World women should reflect these differences and similarities with Feminist Theology. It is my purpose, however, to look critically at Black Theology as a Black woman in an effort to determine how adequate is its conception of liberation for the total Black community. Pauli Murray and Theressa Hoover have in their own ways challenged Black Theology. Because their articles appear in this section (Documents 39 and 37), it is unnecessary for me to explain their point of view. They have spoken for themselves.

I want to begin with the question: "Where are Black women in Black Theology?" They are, in fact, invisible in Black Theology and we need to know why this is the case. Because the Black church experience and Black experience in general are important sources for doing Black Theology, we need to look at the Black woman in relation to both in order to understand the way Black Theology has applied its conception of liberation. Finally, in view of the status of the Black woman vis-à-vis Black Theology, the Black Church and the Black experience, a challenge needs to be presented to Black Theology. This is how I propose to discuss this important question.

THE INVISIBILITY OF BLACK WOMEN IN BLACK THEOLOGY

In examining Black Theology it is necessary to make one of two assumptions: *(1)* either Black women have no place in the enterprise, or *(2)* Black men are capable of speaking for us. Both of these assumptions are false and need to be discarded. They arise out of a male-dominated culture which restricts women to certain areas of the society. In such a culture, men are given the warrant to speak for women on all matters of significance. It is no accident that all of the recognized Black theologians are men. This is what might be expected given the status and power accorded the discipline of theology. Professional theology is done by whose who are highly trained. It requires, moreover, mastery of that power most accepted in the definition of manhood, the power or ability to "reason." This is supposedly what opens the door to participation in logical, philosophical debates and discussions presupposing rigorous intellectual training, for most of history, outside the "women's sphere." Whereas the nature of men has been defined in terms of reason and the intellect, that of women has to do with intuition and emotionalism. Women were limited to matters related to the home while men carried out the more important work, involving use of the rational faculties.[4] These distinctions were not as clear in the slave community.[5] Slaves and women were thought to share the characteristics of emotionality and irrationality. As we move further away from the slave culture, however, a dualism between Black men and women increasingly emerges. This means that Black males have gradually increased their power and participation in the male-dominated society, while Black females have continued to endure the stereotypes and oppressions of an earlier period.

When sexual dualism has finally run its course in the Black community (and I believe that it has), it will not be difficult to see why Black woman are invisible in Black Theology. Just as White women formerly had no place in White Theology—except as the receptors of White men's theological interpretations—Black women have had no place in the development of Black Theology. By self-appointment, or by the sinecure of a male-dominated society. Black men have deemed it proper to speak for the entire Black community, male and female.

In a sense, Black men's acceptance of the patriarchal model is logical and to be expected. Black male slaves were unable to reap the benefits of patriarchy. Before emancipation they were not given the opportunity to serve as protector and provider for Black women and children, as White men were able to do for their women and children. Much of what was considered "manhood" had to do with how well one could perform these functions. It seems only natural that the post-emancipation Black men would view as primary importance the reclaiming of their property—their women and their children. Moreover, it is natural that Black men would claim their "natural" right to the "man's world." But it should be emphasized that this is logical and natural only if one has accepted without question the terms and values of patriarchy—the concept of male control and supremacy.

Black men must ask themselves a difficult question. How can a White society characterized by Black enslavement, colonialism, and imperialism provide the normative conception of women for Black society? How can the sphere of the woman, as defined by White men, be free from the evils and oppressions that are found in the White society? The important point is that in matters relative to the relationship between the sexes, Black men have accepted without question the patriarchal structures of the White society as normative for the Black community. How can a Black minister preach in a way which advocates St. Paul's dictum concerning women while ignoring or repudiating his dictum concerning slaves? Many Black women are enraged as they listen to "liberated" Black men speak about the "place of women" in words and phrases similar to those of the very White oppressors they condemn.

Black women have been invisible in theology because theological scholarship has not been a part of the woman's sphere. The first of the above two assumptions results, therefore, from the historical orientation of the dominant culture. The second follows from the first. If women have no place in theology it becomes the natural prerogative of men to monopolize theological concerns, including those relating specifically to women. Inasmuch as Black men have accepted the sexual dualisms of the dominant culture they presume to speak for Black women.

Before finally dismissing the two assumptions a pertinent question should be raised. Does the absence of Black women in the circles producing Black Theology necessarily mean that the resultant theology cannot be in the best interest of Black women? The answer is obvious. Feminist theologians during the past few years have shown how theology done by men in male-dominated cultures has served to undergird patriarchal structures in society.[6] If Black men have accepted those structures, is there any reason to believe that the theology written by Black men would be any more liberating of Black women than White Theology was for White women? It would seem that in view of the oppression that Black people have suffered Black men would be particularly sensitive to the oppression of others.[7]

James Cone has stated that the task of Black Theology "is to analyze the nature of the gospel of Jesus Christ in the light of oppressed Black people so they will see the gospel as inseparable from their humiliated condition, bestowing on them the necessary power to break the chains of oppression. This means that it is a theology of and for the Black community, seeking to interpret the religious dimensions of the forces of liberation in that community."[8] What are the forces of liberation in the Black community and the Black Church? Are they to be exclusively defined by the struggle against racism? My answer to that question is No. There are oppressive realities in the Black community which are related to, but independent of, the fact of racism. Sexism is one such reality. Black men seek to liberate themselves from racial stereotypes and the conditions of oppression without giving due attention to the stereotypes and oppressions against women which parallel those against Blacks. Blacks fight to be free of the stereotype that all Blacks are dirty and ugly, or that Black represents evil and darkness.[9] The slogan "Black is Beautiful" was a counterattack on these stereotypes. The parallel for women is the history of women as "unclean" especially during menstruation and after childbirth. Because the model of beauty in the White male-dominated society is the "long-haired blonde," with all that goes along with that mystique, Black women have an additional problem with the Western idea of "ugliness," particularly as they encounter Black men who have adopted this White model of beauty.

Similarly, the Christian teaching that woman is responsible for the fall of *mankind* and is, therefore, the source of evil has had a detrimental effect in the experience of Black women.

Like all oppressed peoples the self-image of Blacks has suffered damage. In addition they have not been in control of their own destiny. It is the goal of the Black liberation struggle to change radically the socioeconomic and political conditions of Black people by inculcating self-love, self-control, self-reliance, and political power. The concepts of self-love, self-control, self-reliance, and political participation certainly have broad significance for Black women, even though they were taught that, by virtue of their sex, they had to be completely dependent on *man;* yet while their historical situation reflected the need for dependence, the powerlessness of Black men made it necessary for them to seek those values for themselves.

Racism and sexism are interrelated just as all forms of oppression are interrelated. Sexism, however, has a reality and significance of its own because it represents that peculiar form of oppression suffered by Black women at the hands of Black men. It is important to examine this reality of sexism as it operated in both the Black community and the Black Church. We will consider first the Black Church and secondly the Black community to determine to what extent Black Theology has measured up to its defined task with respect to the liberation of Black women.[10]

THE BLACK CHURCH AND THE BLACK WOMAN

I can agree with Karl Barth as he describes the peculiar function of theology as the church's "subjecting herself to a self-test." She [the church] faces herself with the question of truth, i.e., she measures her action, her language about God, against her existence as a Church."[11]

On the one hand, Black Theology must continue to criticize classical theology and the White Church. But on the other hand, Black Theology must subject the Black Church to a "self-test." The task of the church according to James Cone is threefold: *()* "It proclaims the reality of divine liberation. . . . It is not possible to receive the good news of freedom and also keep it to ourselves; it must be told to the whole world. . . ." *(2)* "It actively shares in the liberation struggle." *(3)* It "is a visible manifestation that the gospel is a reality. . . . *(3)* It "is a visible manifestation that the gospel is a reality. . . . If it [the church] lives according to the old order (as it actually has), then no one will believe its message."[12] It is clear that Black Theology must ask whether or not the Black Church is faithful to this task. Moreover, the language of the Black Church about God must be consistent with its action.[13] These requirements of the church's faithfulness in the struggle for liberation have not been met as far as the issue of women is concerned.

If the liberation of women is not proclaimed, the church's proclamation cannot be about divine liberation. If the church does not share in the liberation struggle of Black women, its liberation struggle is not authentic. If women are oppressed, the church cannot possibly be "a visible manifestation that the gospel is a reality"—for the gospel cannot be real in that context. One can see the contradictions between the church's language or proclamation of liberation and its action by looking both at the status of Black women in the church as laity and Black women in the ordained ministry of the church.

It is often said that women are the "backbone" of the church. On the surface this may appear to be a compliment, especially when none considers the function of the backbone in the human anatomy. Theressa Hoover prefers to use the term "glue" to describe the function of women in the Black Church. In any case, the telling portion of the word backbone is "back."It has become apparent to me that most of the ministers who use this term have reference to location rather than function. What they really mean is that women are in the "background" and should be kept there. They are merely support workers. This is borne out by my observation that in many churches women are consistently given responsibilities in the kitchen, while men are elected or appointed to the important boards and leadership positions. While decisions and policies may be discussed in the kitchen, they are certainly not made there. Recently I conducted a study in one conference of the African Methodist Episcopal Church which indicated that women are accorded greater participation on the decision-making boards of smaller rather than larger churches.[14] This political maneuver helps to keep women "in their place" in the denomination as well as in the local congregations. The conspiracy to keep women relegated to the background is also aided by the continuous psychological and political strategizing that keeps women from realizing their own potential power in the church. Not only are they rewarded for performance in "backbone" or supportive positions, but they are penalized for trying to move from the backbone of the head position—the leadership of the church. It is by considering the distinction between prescribed support positions and the policy-making, leadership positions that the oppression of Black women in the Black Church can be seen more clearly.

For the most part, men have monopolized the ministry as a profession. The ministry of women as fully ordained clergypersons has always been controversial. The Black church fathers were unable to see the injustices of their own practices, even when they paralleled the injustices in the White Church against which they rebelled.

In the early nineteenth century, the Rev. Richard Allen perceived that it was unjust for Blacks, free and slaves, to be relegated to the balcony and restricted to a special time to pray and kneel at the communion table; for this he should be praised. Yet because of his acceptance of the patriarchal system Allen was unable to see the injustice in relegating women to one area of the church—the pews—by withholding ordination from women as he did in the case of Mrs. Jarena Lee.[15] Lee recorded Allen's response when she informed him of her call to "go preach the Gospel":

> *He replied by asking in what sphere I wished to move in? I said, among the Methodists. He then replied, that a Mrs. Cook, a Methodist lady, had also some time before requested the same privilege; who it was believed, had done much good in the way of* exhortation, *and* holding prayer meetings; *and who had been permitted to do so by the* verbal license *of the preacher in charge at the time. But as to women preaching, he said that our Discipline knew nothing at all about it—that* it did not call *for women preachers.*[16]

Because of this response Jarena Lee's preaching ministry was delayed for eight years. She was not unaware of the sexist injustice in Allen's response.

> *Oh how careful ought we be,lest through our by-laws of church government and discipline, we bring into disrepute even the word of life. For as unseemly as it may appear nowadays for a women to preach, it should be remembered that nothing is impossible with God. And why should it be thought impossible, heterodox, or improper for a woman to preach, seeing the Saviour died for the woman as well as the man?*[17]

Another "colored minister of the gospel," Elizabeth, was greatly troubled over her call to preach, or more accurately, over the response of men to her call to preach. She said:

> *I often felt that I was unfit to assemble with the congregation with whom I had gathered. . . . I felt that I was despised on account of this gracious calling, and was looked upon as a speckled bird by the ministers to whom I looked for instruction . . . some [of the ministers] would cry out, "you are an enthusiast," and others said, "the Discipline did not allow of any such division of work."*[18]

Sometime later when questioned about her authority to preach against slavery and her ordination status, she responded that she preached "not by the commission of men's hands: if the Lord had ordained me, I needed nothing better."[19] With this commitment to God rather than to a male-dominated church structure she led a fruitful ministry.

Mrs. Amanda Berry Smith, like Mrs. Jarena Lee, had to conduct her ministry outside the structure of the A.M.E. Church. Smith described herself as a "plain Christian woman" with "no money" and "no prominence."[20] But she was intrigued with the idea of attending the General Conference of 1872 in Nashville, Tennessee. Her inquiry into the cost of going to Nashville brought the following comments from some of the A.M.E. brethren:

> *"I tell you, Sister, it will cost money to go down there; and if you ain't got plenty of it, it's no use to go"; . . . another said:*
> *"What does she want to go for?"*
> *"Woman preacher; they want to be ordained," was they reply.*
> *"I mean to fight that thing," said the other.*
> *"Yes, indeed, so will I," said another.*[21]

The oppression of women in the ministry took many forms. In addition to not being granted ordination, the authenticity of "the call" of women was frequently put to the test. Lee, Elizabeth, and Smith spoke of the many souls they had brought to Christ through their preaching and singing in local Black congregations, as well as in White and mixed congregations. It was not until Bishop Richard Allen heard Jarena Lee preach that he was convinced that she was of the Spirit. He, however, still refused to ordain her. The "brethren," including some bishops of the 1872 General Conference of the A.M.E. Church were convinced that Amanda Berry Smith was blessed with the Spirit of God after hearing her sing at a session held at Fisk University. Smith tells us that ". . . the Spirit of the Lord seemed to fall on all the people. The preachers got happy. . . ." This experience brought invitations for her to preach at several churches, but it did not bring an appointment to a local congregation as pastor or the right of ordination. She summed up the experience in this way: ". . . after that many of my brethren believed in me, especially as the question of ordination of women never was mooted in the Conference."[22]

Several Black denominations have since begun to ordain women.[23] But this matter of women preachers having the extra burden of proving their call to an extent not required of men still prevails in the Black Church today. A study in which I participated at Union Theological Seminary in New York City bears this out. Interviews with Black ministers of different denominations revealed that their prejudices against women, and especially women in the ministry, resulted in unfair expectations and unjust treatment of women ministers whom they encountered.[24]

It is the unfair expectations placed upon women and blatant discrimination that keeps them "in the pew" and "out of the pulpit." This matter of keeping women in the pew has been carried to ridiculous extremes. At the 1971 Annual Convocation of the National Conference of Black Churchmen,[25] held at the Liberty Baptist Church in Chicago, I was slightly amused when, as I approached the pulpit to place my cassette tape recorder near the speaker, Walter Fauntroy, as several brothers had already done, I was stopped by a man who informed me that I could not enter the pulpit area. When I asked why not, he directed me to the pastor who told me that women were not permitted in the pulpit, but that he would have a man place the recorder there for me. Although I could not believe that explanation a serious one, I agreed to have a man place it on the pulpit for me and returned to my seat in the sanctuary for the continuation of the convocation. The seriousness of the pastor's statement became clear to me later at that meeting when Mary Jane Patterson, a Presbyterian Church executive, was refused the right to speak from the pulpit.[26] This was clearly a case of sex discrimination in a Black church—keeping women "in the pew" and "out of the pulpit."

As far as the issue of women is concerned it is obvious that the Black Church described by C. Eric Lincoln has not fared much better than the Negro Church of E. Franklin Frazier.[27] The failure of the Black Church and Black Theology to proclaim explicitly the liberation of Black women indicates that they cannot claim to be agents of divine liberation. If the theology, like the church, has no word for Black women, its conception of liberation is inauthentic.

THE BLACK EXPERIENCE AND THE BLACK WOMAN

For the most part, Black church*men* have not dealt with the oppression of Black women in either the Black Church or the Black community. Frederick Douglass was one notable exception in the 19th century. His active advocacy for women's rights was a demonstration against the contradiction between preaching "justice for all" and practicing the continued oppression of women. He, therefore, "dared not claim a right [for himself' which he would not concede to women.''[28] These words describe the convictions of a man who was active both in the church and in the larger Black community. This is significant because there is usually a direct relationship between what goes on in the Black Church and the Black secular community.

The status of Black women in the community parallels that of Black women in the church. Black Theology considers the Black experience to be the context out of which its questions about God and human existence are formulated. This is assumed to be the context in which God's revelation is received and interpreted. Only from the perspective of the poor and the oppressed can theology be adequately done. Arising out of the Black Power Movement of the 1960s, Black Theology purports to take seriously the experience of the larger community's struggle for liberation. But if this is, indeed, the case, Black Theology must function in the secular community in the same way as it should function in the church community. It must serve as a ''self-test'' to see whether the rhetoric or proclamation of the Black community's struggle for liberation is consistent with its practices. How does the ''self-test'' principle operate among the poor and the oppressed? Certainly Black Theology has spoken to some of the forms of oppression which exist within the community of the oppressed. Many of the injustices it has attacked are the same as those which gave rise to the prophets of the Old Testament. But the fact that Black Theology does not include sexism specifically as one of those injustices is all too evident. It suggests that the theologians do not understand sexism to be one of the oppressive realities of the Black community. Silence on this specific issue can only mean conformity with the status quo. The most prominent Black theologian, James Cone, has recently broken this silence.

> *The Black church, like all other churches, is a male-dominated church. The difficulty that Black male ministers have in supporting the equality of women in the church and society stems partly from the lack of a clear liberation-criterion rooted in the gospel and in the present struggles of oppressed peoples. . . . It is truly amazing that many black male ministers, young and old, can hear the message of liberation in the gospel when related to racism but remain deaf to a similar message in the context of sexism. . . .*[29]

It is difficult to understand how Black men manage to exclude the liberation of Black women from their interpretation of the liberating gospel. Any correct analysis of the poor and oppressed would reveal some interesting and inescapable facts about the situation of women within oppressed groups. Without succumbing to the long and fruitless debate of ''who is more oppressed than whom?'' I want to make some pointed suggestions to Black male theologians.

It would not be very difficult to argue that since Black women are the poorest of the poor, the most oppressed of the oppressed, their experience provides a more fruitful context for doing Black Theology. The research of Jacquelyne Jackson attests to the extreme deprivation of Black women. Jackson supports her claim with statistical data that ''in comparison with black males and white males and females, black women yet constitute the most disadvantaged group in the US, as evidenced especially by their largely unenviable educational, occupational, employment and income levels, and availability of marital partners."[30] In other words, in spite of the "quite insignificant" educational advantage that Black women have over Black men, they have "had the greatest access to the worst jobs at the lowest earnings."[31] It is important to emphasize this fact in order to elevate to its rightful level of concern the condition of Black women, not only in the world at large, but in the Black community and the Black Church. It is my contention that if Black Theology speaks of the Black community as if the special problems of Black women do not exist, it is no different from the White Theology it claims to reject precisely because of its inability to take account of the existence of Black people in its theological formulations.

It is instructive to note that the experience of Black women working in the Black Power movement further accented the problem of the oppression of women in the Black community. Because of their invisibility in the leadership of the movement they, like women of the church, provided the "support" segment of the movement. They filled the streets when numbers were needed for demonstrations. They stuffed the envelopes in the offices and performed other menial tasks. Kathleen Cleaver, in a *Black Scholar* interview, revealed some of the problems in the movement which caused her to become involved in women's liberation issues. While underscoring the crucial role played by women as Black Power activists, Kathleen Cleaver, nonetheless, acknowledged the presence of sex discrimination.

> *I viewed myself as assisting everything that was done. . . . The form of assistance that women give in political movements to men is just as crucial as the leadership that men give to those movements. And this is something that is never recognized and never dealt with.* Because women are always relegated to assistance *and this is where I became interested in the liberation of women. Conflicts, constant conflicts came up, conflicts that would rise as a result of the fact that I was married to a member of the Central Committee and I was also an officer in the Party. Things that I would have suggested myself would be implemented. But if I suggested them the suggestion might be rejected. If they were suggested by a man the suggestion would be implemented.*
>
> *It seemed throughout the history of my working with the Party, I always had to struggle with this. The suggestion itself was never viewed objectively.* The fact that the suggestion came from a women gave it some lesser value. *And it seemed that it had something to do with the egos of the men involved. I know that the first demonstration that we had at the courthouse for Huey Newton I was very instrumental in organizing; the first time we went out on the soundtracks, I was on the soundtracks; the first leaflet we put out, I wrote; the first demonstration, I made up the pamphlets. And the members of that demonstration for the most part were women. I've noticed that throughout my dealings in the black movement in the United States, that the* most anxious, the most eager, the most active, the most quick to understand the problem and quick to move are women.[32]

Cleaver exposed the fact that even when leadership was given to women, sexism lurked in the wings. As executive secretary of the Student Nonviolent Coordinating Committee (SNCC), Ruby Doris Robinson was described as the "heart beat of SNCC." Yet there were "the constant conflicts, the constant struggles that she was subjected to because she was a woman."[33]

Notwithstanding all the evidence to the contrary, some might want to argue that the central problem of Black women is related to their race and not their sex. Such an argument then presumes that the problem cannot be resolved apart from the Black struggle. I contend that as long as the Black struggle refuses to recognize and deal with its sexism, the idea that women will receive justice from that struggle alone will never work. It will not work because Black women will no long allow Black men to ignore their unique problems and needs in the name of some distorted view of the "liberation of the total community." I would bring to the minds of the proponents of this argument the words of President Sekou Toure as he wrote about the role of African women in the revolution. He said, "if African women cannot possibly conduct their struggle in isolation from the struggle that our people wage for African liberation, African freedom, conversely, is not effective unless it brings about the liberation of African women."[34] Black men who have an investment in the patriarchal structure of White America and who intend to do Christian theology have yet to realize that if Jesus is liberator of the oppressed, all of the oppressed must be liberated. Perhaps the proponents of the argument that the case of Black women must be subsumed under a larger cause should look to South African theologians Sabelo Ntwasa and Basil Moore. They affirm that "Black theology, as it struggles to formulate a theology of liberation relevant to South Africa, cannot afford to perpetuate any form of domination, not even male domination. If its liberation is not human enough to include the liberation of women, it will not be liberation."[35]

A CHALLENGE TO BLACK THEOLOGY

My central argument is this: Black Theology cannot continue to treat Black women as if they were invisible creatures who are on the outside looking into the Black experience, the Black Church, and the Black theological enterprise. It will have to deal with the community of believers in all aspects as integral parts of the whole community. Black Theology, therefore, must speak to the bishops who hide behind the statement "Women don't want women pastors." It must speak to the pastors who say, "My church isn't ready for women preachers yet." It must teach the seminarians who feel that "women have no place in the seminary." It must address the women in the church and community who are content and complacent with their oppression. It must challenge the educators who would reeducate the people on every issue except the issue of the dignity and equality of women.

Black women represent more than 50 percent of the Black community and more than 70 percent of the Black Church. How then can an authentic theology of liberation arise out of these communities without specifically addressing the liberation of the women in both places? Does the fact that certain questions are raised by Black women make them any less Black concerns? If, as I contend, the liberation of Black men and women is inseparable, then a radical split cannot be made between racism and sexism. Black women are oppressed by racism *and* sexism. It is therefore necessary that Black men and women be actively involved in combating both evils.

Only as Black women in greater numbers make their way from the background to the forefront will the true strength of the Black community be fully realized. There is already a heritage of strong Black women and men upon which a stronger nation can be built. There is a tradition which declares that God is at work in the experience of the Black woman. This tradition, in the context of the total Black experience, can provide data for the development of a wholistic Black theology. Such a theology will repudiate the God of classical theology who is presented as an absolute Patriarch, a deserting father who created Black men and women and then "walked out" in the face of responsibility. Such a theology will look at the meaning of the total Jesus Christ Event; it will consider not only how God through Jesus Christ is related to the oppressed men, but to women as well. Such a theology will "allow" God through the Holy Spirit to work through persons without regard to race, sex, or class. This theology will exercise its prophetic function, and serve as a "self-test" in a church characterized by the sins of racism, sexism, and other forms of oppression. Until Black women theologians are fully participating in the theological enterprise, it is important to keep Black male theologians and Black leaders cognizant of their dereliction. They must be made aware of the fact that Black women are needed not only as Christian educators, but as theologians and church leaders. It is only when Black women and men share jointly the leadership in theology and in the church and community that the Black nation will become strong and liberated. Only then will there be the possibility that Black Theology can become a theology of divine liberation.

One final word for those who argue that the issues of racism and sexism are too complicated and should not be confused. I agree that the issues should not be "confused." But the elimination of both racism and sexism is so crucial for the liberation of Black persons that we cannot shrink from facing them together. Sojourner Truth tells us why this is so. In 1867 she spoke out on the issue of suffrage and what she said at that time is still relevant to us as we deal with the liberation of Black women today.

> *I feel that if I have to answer for the deeds done in my body just as much as a man, I have a right to have just as much as a man. There is a great stir about colored men getting their rights, but not a word about the colored women; and if colored men get their rights, and not colored women theirs, you see the colored men will be masters over the women, and it will be just as bad as it was before. So I am for keeping the thing going while things are stirring; because if we wait till it is still, it will take a great while to get it going again. . . .*[36]

Black women have to keep the issue of sexism "going" in the Black community, in the Black Church, and in Black Theology until it has been eliminated. To do otherwise means that they will be pushed aside until eternity. Therefore, with Sojourner Truth, I'm for "keeping things going while things are stirring. . . ."

NOTES

1. Beatriz Melano Couch, remarks on the feminist panel of Theology in the Americas Conference in Detroit in August 1975, printed in *Theology in the Americas,* ed. Sergio Torres and John Eagleson (Maryknoll, N.Y.: Orbis Books, 1976), p. 375.
2. Consuelo Urquiza, ''A Message from a Hispanic-American Woman,'' *The Fifth Commission: A Monitor for Third World Concerns* IV (June–July 1978) insert. The Fifth Commission is a commission of the National Council of the Churches of Christ in the USA (NCC), 475 Riverside Drive, New York, N.Y.
3. I agree with the Fifth Commission that ''the Third World is not a geographical entity, but rather the world of oppressed peoples in their struggle for liberation.'' In this sense, Black women are included in the term ''Third World.'' However, in order to accent the peculiar identity, problems, and needs of Black women in the First World or the Third World contexts, I choose to make the distinction between Black and other Third World women.
4. For a discussion of sexual dualisms in our society, see Rosemary Ruether, *New Woman/New Earth* (New York: Seabury Press, 1975), chap. 1; and *Liberation Theology* (New York: Paulist Press,,1972), pp. 16ff. Also for a discussion of sexual (social) dualisms as related to the brain hemispheres, see Sheila Collins, *A Different Heaven and Earth* (Valley Forge: Judson Press, 1974), pp.169–170.
5. Angela Davis, ''Reflections on the Black Woman's Role in the Community of Slaves,'' *The Black Scholar,* vol. 4 no.3 (December 1971), pp. 3–15. I do take issue with Davis's point, however. The Black community may have experienced ''equality in inequality,'' but this was forced on them from the dominant or enslaving community. She does not deal with the inequality within the community itself.
6. See Sheila Collins, op. cit., Rosemary Ruether, op. cit., Letty Russell, *Human Liberation in the Feminist Perspective* (Philadelphia: Westminster Press, 1974); and Mary Daly, *Beyond God the Father* (Boston: Beacon Press, 1973).
7. Surely the factor of race would be absent, but one would have to do an in-depth analysis to determine the possible side effect on the status of Black women.
8. James Cone. *A Black Theology of Liberation* (Philadelphia: J. B. Lippincott, 1970), p. 23.
9. Eulalio Baltazar discusses color symbolism (white is good; black is evil) as a reflection of racism in the White Theology which perpetuates it. *The Dark Center: A Process Theology of Blackness* (New York: Paulist Press, 1973).
10. One may want to argue that Black Theology is not concerned with sexism but with racism. I will argue in this essay that such a theology could speak only half the truth, if truth at all.
11. Karl Barth, *Church Dogmatics,* vol. 1, part 1, p. 2.
12. Cone, op. cit., pp. 230–232.
13. James Cone and Albert Cleage do make this observation of the contemporary Black Church and its response to the struggles against racism. See Cleage, *The Black Messiah* (New York: Sheed and Ward, 1969), passim; and Cone, op. cit., passim.

14. A study that I conducted in the Philadelphia Conference of the African Methodist Episcopal Church, May 1976. It also included sporadic samplings of churches in other conferences in the First Episcopal District. As for example, a church of 1,660 members (600 men and 1,160 women) had a trustee board of 8 men and 1 woman and a steward board of 13 men and 6 women. A church of 100 members (35 men and 65 women) had a trustee board of 5 men and 4 women and a steward board of 5 men and 4 women.
15. Jarena Lee, *The Life and Religious Experience of Jenna Lee: A Colored Lady Giving an Account of Her Call to Preach the Gospel* (Philadelphia, 1836), printed in Dorothy Porter, ed., *Early Negro Writing 1760–1837* (Boston: Beacon Press, 1971), pp. 494–514.
16. Ibid., p. 503 (italics added). Carol George in *Segregated Sabbaths* (New York: Oxford University Press, 1973), presents a very positive picture of the relationship between Jarena Lee and Bishop Richard Allen. She feels that by the time Lee approached Allen, he had "modified his views on woman's rights" (p. 129). She contends that since Allen was free from the Methodist Church he was able to "determine his own policy" with respect to women under the auspices of the A.M.E. Church. It should be noted that Bishop Allen accepted the Rev. Jarena Lee as a woman preacher and not as an ordained preacher with full rights and privileges thereof. Even Carol George admitted that Lee traveled with Bishop Allen only "as an unofficial member of their delegation to conference sessions in New York and Baltimore," "to attend," not to participate in them. I agree that this does represent progress in Bishop Allen's view as compared to Lee's first approach; on the second approach, he was at least encouraging. Then he began "to promote her interests" (p. 129)—But he did not ordain her.
17. Ibid.
18. "Elizabeth: A Colored Minister of the Gospel," printed in Bert James Loewenberg and Ruth Bogin, ed., *Black Women in Nineteenth-Century American Life* (University Park, Pa.: The Pennsylvania State University Press, 1976), p. 132. The denomination of Elizabeth is not known to this writer. Her parents were Methodists, but she was separated from her parents at the age of eleven. However, the master from which she gained her freedom was Presbyterian. Her autobiography was published by the Philadelphia Quakers.
19. Ibid., p. 133.
20. Amanda Berry Smith, *An Autobiography: The Story of the Lord's Dealings with Mrs. Amanda Berry Smith, the Colored Evangelist* (Chicago, 1893); printed in Loewenberg and Bogin, op.cit., p. 157.
21. Ibid.
22. Ibid., p. 159.
23. The African Methodist Episcopal Church started ordaining women in 1948, according to the Rev. William P. Foley of Bridgestreet A.M.E. Church in Brooklyn, New York. The first ordained woman was Martha J. Keys.

The African Methodist Episcopal Zion Church ordained women as early as 1884. At that time, Mrs. Julia A. Foote was ordained Deacon in the New York Annual Conference. In 1894 Mrs. Mary J. Small was ordained Deacon and in 1898, she was ordained Elder. See David Henry Bradley, Sr., *A History of the A.M.E. Zion Church,* vol. (part) II, 1872–1968 (Nashville: The Parthenon Press, 1970), pp. 384, 393.

The Christian Methodist Episcopal Church enacted legislation to ordain women in the 1970 General Conference. Since then approximately 75 women have been ordained. See the Rev. N. Charles Thomas, general secretary of the C.M.E. Church and director of the Department of the Ministry, Memphis, Tennessee.

Many Baptist churches still do not ordain women. Some churches in the Pentecostal tradition do not ordain women. However, in some other Pentecostal churches, women are founders, pastors, elders, and bishops.

In the case of the A.M.E.Z. Church, where women were ordained as early as 1884, the important question would be, what happened to the women who were ordained? In addition, all of these churches (except for those which do give leadership to women) should answer the following questions: Have women been assigned to pastor ''class A'' churches? Have women been appointed as presiding elders? (There is currently one woman presiding elder in the A.M.E. Church.) Have women been elected to serve as bishop of any of these churches? Have women served as presidents of conventions?

24. Yolande Herron, Jacquelyn Grant, Gwendolyn Johnson, and Samuel Roberts, ''Black Women and the Field Education Experience at Union Theological Seminary: Problems and Prospects'' (New York: Union Theological Seminary, May 1978).
25. This organization continues to call itself the National Conference of Black Churchmen despite the protests of women members.
26. NCBC has since made the decision to examine the policies of its host institutions (churches) to avoid the reoccurrence of such incidents.
27. E. Franklin Frazier, *The Negro Church in America;* C. Eric Lincoln, *The Black Church Since Frazier* (New York: Schocken Books, 1974), passim.
28. Printed in Philip S. Foner, ed., *Frederick Douglass on Women's Rights* (Westport, Conn.: Greenwood Press), p. 51.
29. Cone,''Black Ecumenism and the Liberation Struggle,'' delivered at Yale University, February 16–17, 1978, and Quinn Chapel A.M.E. Church, May 22, 1978. In two other recent papers he has voiced concern on women's issues, relating them to the larger question of liberation. These papers are: ''New Roles in the Ministry: A Theological Appraisal'' and ''Black Theology and the Black Church:" Where Do We Go from Here?'' Both papers appear in this volume.
30. Jacquelyne Jackson, ''But Where Are the Men?'' *The Black Scholar,* op. cit., p. 30.
31. Ibid., p. 32.
32. Kathleen Cleaver was interviewed by Sister Julia Herve. Ibid., pp. 55–56.
33. Ibid., p. 55.

34. Sedkou Toure, "The Role of Women in the Revolution," *The Black Scholar,* vol. 6, no. 6 (March 1975), p. 32.
35. Sabelo Ntwasa and Basil Moore, "The Concept of God in Black Theology," in *The Challenge of Black Theology in South Africa,* ed. Basil Moore (Atlanta, Ga.: John Knox Press, 1974), pp. 25–26.
36. Sojourner Truth, "Keeping the Things Going While Things Are Stirring," printed in Miriam Schneir, ed., *Feminism: The Essential Historical Writings* (New York: Random House, 1972), pp. 129–130.

CHAPTER SEVEN

Psycho-Social Issues

Mwalimu David Burgest and Mary Goosby analyze games of love and power together with their effect upon Black male and Black female relationships. The authors limit their analysis and evaluation of the games to the specific behavior of the games rather than to a diagnosis of the underlying psychological dynamics. Burgest and Goosby hope the reader may be able to develop and increase self-awareness, self-insight, sensitivity, and human growth from the dynamics provided.

Clyde Franklin identifies two major sources for Black male and Black female conflict together with suggestions for reducing the conflict. The major sources of conflict are identified as (1) non-complementarily of sex role definitions internalized by Black males and Black females, and (2) structural barriers in the environments of Black males and Black females. The suggestions offered for attentuating the conflict include altering three social psychological phenomena: (1) Black male and Black female socialization experiences; (2) Black male and Black female role-playing strategies; and (3) Black male and Black female personal communication mechanisms.

La Francis Rodgers-Rose explores issues that confront black men and women as they interact in a dialectic process of creation and criticism. She, specifically, addresses some myths about Black men and women and properties of male-female relationships.

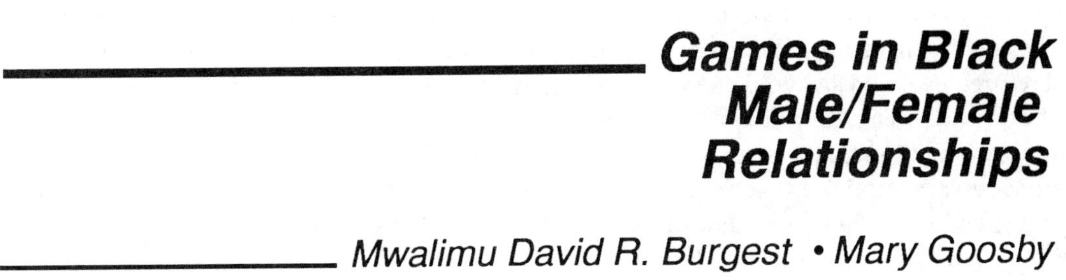

Games in Black Male/Female Relationships

Mwalimu David R. Burgest • Mary Goosby

As we analyze Black male/female relationships, we find that there are numerous negative interpersonal relationship games played that are destructive to sustaining a positive and healthy relationship. Most often, these "games people play" are responsible for the disintegration and disunity existing in Black male/female relationships. Eric Berne, in his book *Games People Play* (1964) defines games as a recurring set of transactions, often repetitions, superficially plausible, with a concealed motivation (conscious or unconscious) toward a hidden payoff. In a more colloquial term, he defines games as a series of moves with a snare or "gimmick." It is pertinent to emphasize that the games played may be conscious or unconscious. That is, individuals may not be consciously aware of the games they may be playing, and may be resistant to having those games brought to consciousness by the nonplayer. Unconscious games are probably the most destructive, in that the player is not aware of the unmet need being aroused, and those unconscious drives are brought into the relationship from early childhood relationships with parents and others.

The hidden payoff noted in the definition above may vary according to the psychological needs of the individual. For example, the hidden payoff may be a desire to attain oneupmanship, inflict pain, control another, seek favoritism, and so on. It is not suggested that all the games being enumerated in this article are unique to the Black male/female experience, for some of these games are generic to any male/female relationship in that the Black experience is part and parcel of the human experience. Nonetheless, the dynamics of all the games outlined in this article will elaborate on the characteristics unique to the Black experience.

Games in Black male/female interactions must be analyzed and understood from the perspective of prevailing negative myths, stereotypes, and assumptions that affect those relationships. The research and contributions of many scholars help to provide the theoretical and philosophical background necessary to comprehend components of Black male/female interaction from a game theory model. Robert Staples (1982) provides a social-scientific appraisal of the myths of Black male sexuality dispelling the negative stereotypes and myths that contribute to destructive games. According to Staples, Black males and females must recognize that they are both victims of racism and the racist myths; therefore, each must avoid actions that aid and abet these forces and contribute to a dialogue necessary to iron out the differences between Black men and women. Contributing to a breakdown in communication and interaction, there are a host of commonly held erroneous assumptions that Black women make about Black men (Burgest and Bowers, 1981a) and that Black men make about Black women (Burgest and Bowers, 1981b), in addition to the overall barriers developing genuine and authentic relations between Blacks (Burgest,1980).

The empirical research compiled on the thought, feelings, and aspirations of Black men (Gary, 1981) clearly calls for an evaluation of role definition in the Black male/female relationship. The exploration of games in the Black male/female interaction should help clarify inconsistencies in the definition of role. Moreover, the implication of racism, sexism, and women's liberation (Davis, 1981) cannot be ignored in the dynamics of Black male/female communications and interactions. Often, it is the Black American's assimilation and identification with the social value and social structure of the American society that contributes to the difficulty in interaction. As we review the makeup of games in the Black male/female relationship, it is apparent that racism and stereotypes play an important underlying part in prohibiting genuine communications.

The purpose of this article is to simply highlight, expose, and illuminate some of the games played in the Black male/female interaction. It is hoped that the reader may be able to develop and increase self-awareness, self-insight, sensitivity, and human growth from the dynamics provided. We will limit their analysis and evaluation of the games to the specific behavior of the games rather than a diagnosis of the underlying psychological dynamics. It is impossible to do otherwise without understanding the complete background and social histories of the individual(s) involved.

The few games chosen for this manuscript were selected on the basis of their common use and popularity in Black male/female interactions; yet some of them are among the more destructive and misunderstood games. These games are misunderstood in that they are not often taken as superficial, and for that reason those game are most destructive. By the same token, the popular and common use of the games provide them with legitimacy; nonetheless, it is those games that continue to foster disintegration and disunity in the Black male/female relationship. For organizational purposes only, these games are divided into games of love and games of power.

GAMES OF LOVE

If you love me you will . . . A general assumption in male/female relationships is that if you love me, you will . . . do this, that, or the other. In this instance, love is viewed as a mechanism used in the relationship to bargain, barter, and often manipulate situations and circumstances to one's advantage. The true test of *love* in this game is actualized both by the gratification one receives from having someone else do something for them against the other's will, as well as the fulfillment of the unmet need to control and manipulate.

The ultimate social and psychological dangers in this game rest in the manifestation of the "Russian roulette" syndrome, whereby one individual perpetually seeks a heightened reaffirmation of their notion of love: If you love me, you will jump off the building. Implicit in the minds of many is the belief that love is not love unless one's wishes and desires are totally submitted to by the other. Thus, this game makes love one-dimensional and one-directed by subjugating the feelings and desires of the other party. An adequate response to such a game being played is, "If you loved me, you wouldn't ask me that."

Second, the element of testing and bribing is inherent in this game. One party or both may engage in a process to try and measure "how much" love the other party is willing to submit to one's will. Therefore, if one's partner fails or refuses to acquiesce to the will of the other, an inventory is compiled for later use in the relationship to say "If you loved me, you would have."

One of the primary destructive features of such gamemanship is that individuals may consciously manipulate another person for their personal gratifications and needs under the rubric of love. The most dangerous element, however, rests with the individual's unawareness that such behavior is a game, he or she truly feels that the authenticity of love in the relationship is legitimized by such interaction.

Authentic and healthy love is not based on testing, manipulations, or bribes as depicted in the "If you love me, you will" game. Love must be based on the assumption of sharing, unity, and compromise, with the capacity for both to give and receive in the relationship. When one gives in the relationship, it should be devoid of persuasion or manipulation. By the same token, when one receives in the relationship, it should not be contaminated with an underlying element or manipulation or bribe. This is not to infer that partners should not please their spouses or mates by doing things to bring them joy or pleasure even though the giver may only be happy by pleasing the mate. Yet, those situations should not be forced by either partner under the rubric of "If you love me, you will."

If it weren't for you, I could . . . A common destructive element in relationships is for one partner to blame the other for blocking or prohibiting his or her goals, aspirations, and movement toward self-actualization and self-fulfillment. It is not uncommon to hear one partner boast about what he or she could have accomplished in life "if it weren't for" the other partner, or to boast about what he or she could have accomplished in life "if it weren't for the other party." The perceived obstacles are usually of a nature whereby one partner feels compelled to redirect his or her goals and aspirations to accommodate the other. In some extreme situations, one mate may oppose, reject, and fight the goals, plans, and aspirations of the other mate. Consequently, the mate under attack may decide to abolish his or her present aspirations in order to "keep peace" in the relationship. On the other hand, there is the situation where one mate may feel distressed and burdened by emotional conflicts in the relationship, and is unable to succeed in personal and professional endeavors to these conflicts.

There are probably an endless number of situations where the principles of "if it weren't for you" prevails. Inherent in this dynamics is a love-hate ambivalence whereby the individual who feels cheated and deprived questions the sacrifices he or she made based on the present rewards of the relationship. Nonetheless, the psychological payoff of the "if it weren't for you" game may provide a convenient scapegoat for the internal inadequacies and deficits felt about oneself. The game is to achieve the goal of soliciting sympathy for one's condition or indulging in self-pity. This is not to suggest that goals and plans are not sometimes altered or delayed due to authentic situations and circumstances in relationships. However, the search for fulfillment and actualization in life is a perpetual process requiring that one must psychologically transcend many obstacles and difficulties.

In the case of illness, death, and sickness, "if it weren't for you, I could . . ." game must be viewed from a different perspective than the obstacles in interpersonal relationships that one may perceive as destructive to goals. It is the dynamics of the latter that is being addressed here. The underlying problem in this kind of interaction and relationship is one of mutual goals-setting and priorities. One of the intentions of the hidden payoff is to provoke guilt and create a victim in the other party, rather than address insecurities and inadequacies in self.

The bottom line is that no individual can prevent another from attaining goals in life once the other individual has become aware that such games are being played. Therefore, the game "if it weren't for you, I could . . ." is inappropriate. Second, there is no need for one individual to feel guilty about his or her achievements and advancements as long as that individual is aware that he or she did not bribe or manipulate to get there. Again, the manipulation and bribe will not work as long as the other party becomes aware of the game.

Finally, success and happiness in a relationship is dependent on both parties becoming all each can become as individuals, and any subterfuge of this dynamics results in destructive unhappiness.

Why don't you make me happy? One of the greatest myths in an individual's relationships is that one can find another being who can "make me happy." It may be assumed that partners, mates, and spouses can work together for a fulfilled life and hope to move together as interdependent bodies. However, the realities are that individuals seek relationships in order to gain joy, happiness, and fulfillment. It is often misery, rather than love, that pulls individuals together in a relationship. The old adage that "misery loves company" is appropriate here, but few seem to recognize that "*love* loves company" also, and it is difficult for partners in relationship to determine if they come together out of love or misery. There are numerous accounts provided by individuals who say "I met my partner at a time when I was low and he brought me out of it."

As long as people believe the prevailing myth that someone else can make them happy, rather than look at enjoyment and happiness as internal and self-autonomous, the major obstacles to an effective successful relationship will be the need of one individual to be "made happy" by someone else.

On the other side of the coin, the "make me happy" syndrome and myth leaves individuals feelings as though they are responsible for making the other person happy. Yet, the sadness, loneliness, and despair that individuals face may not be related whatsoever to the relationship with the other partner. Many mates are unable to recognize the difference between the "unhappiness" caused by the relationship. Even if individuals recognized the difference, it may be assumed that there are those who would not acknowledge their unhappiness as being internal. Nonetheless, the premise of "Why don't you make me happy?" is not to be confused with loneliness and despair due to internal and individual conflict with self, but conflict in the relationship due to external unfulfilled needs.

In conclusion, the most destructive element in this game of "Why don't you make me happy?" rests with the fallacy that happiness is something that exists outside of oneself. There is a view that material things, commodities, and circumstances make one happy. For many people, happiness is like a butterfly. The more they chase after it, the more it eludes them; but the moment they sit patiently and get to know themselves, the butterfly comes and lands on their fingertip. Two happy people come together and create more happiness; otherwise misery will prevail.

You are not like the person I first met. The death of many relationships is caused by the "You are not like the person I first met" assumption. The irony of this attitude is that it is more than usual that the character and disposition of an individual that first attracts another person later destroys the relationship. In other words, the things that most attracted one individual to another become the very same things that may later drive away that individual.

People are usually attracted to someone else because the character of the other person fulfills some deficits the person may see in themself. Otherwise, there are persons who are attracted to another because the character they perceive is one that is found to be facilitative for their need. A woman may be attracted to a man because he is articulate, analytical, communicative, and intellectual. Those characteristics may be seen as the necessary qualities for conversation and dialogue, as well as the qualities for advancement in the career world. Yet, in the interpersonal relationship, those same qualities and characters may be used by the partner to persuade and coerce. When those qualities influence the interaction in the relationship, the other partner may feel helpless and distraught enough to say, "You are not like the person I first met."

It must be recognized that partners do outgrow each other and may grow in different directions as the relationship unfolds. This does happen. The fact of the matter is no two individuals are the same as they were when they were engaged in a relationship two, three, or four weeks, months, or years ago. The reality of the statement renders the game superficial.

The issues generally being spoken to in such a game is that one partner is feeling that the other is outgrowing him or her mentally, psychologically, socially, and spiritually the underlying assumption being that "my partner is growing 'away' from me." All individuals, like children, do not grow at the same speed or rate. "You are not the person I met'' should be counteracted with ''You might be right . . . but would you like to take the time to get to know me all over again?''

I am unhappy and I want you to be unhappy. It is an accepted fact that there are unhappy people in the world and their unhappiness is related to internal psychological causes that have little or nothing to do with other people. In other cases, unhappiness may be directly related to dynamics involving other people and circumstances, including problems in the relationship.

When unhappiness prevails in a relationship due to any of the above factors, the unhappy person often attempts to make the above person unhappy. It may be that one partner is functioning well in the area of unemployment, promotion, and social relations and the other partner feels jeopardized in those and other areas. The unhappy person does all that is within his or her power to dilute the happiness of the other partner. This may be manifested through degrading, minimizing, or placing obstacles in the path of the other partner. The overt behavior and options are plentiful, as is the destructiveness. The unhappy person may exaggerate his or her ''unhappiness'' as a means of soliciting increased sympathy and avoid participating in the happy moments of the other partner.

One of the inherent dangers in this game is that healthy partners tend to assume the burden and share in the ''unhappiness'' of their mates in spite of whether or not they are responsible. It is a revelation when the healthy partner liberates himself or herself. The unhealthy cycle is that the partner is not happy unless the other partner is unhappy. This is not to suggest that one person's happiness is dependent on the sadness of the other person, but that some people feels overshadowed by the prevailing joy of their partner. It is only through understanding the dynamics of these interactions that dialogue may develop to resolve the difficulties.

If you don't tell me you love me, you don't love me. There is a need for many partners to be reminded constantly that they are loved. They need to be told ''I love you'' by the other partner in the relationship; at the same time, there are individuals who find it difficult to verbalize their love to their partner or mate. A dilemma develops when a couple is composed of one individual who find it difficult to express love verbally and the other has a need to be constantly told ''I love you.'' For the partner who desires to hear repetitiously ''I love you,'' those words are necessary to consummate the affection that binds. There is usually no other action or need that may justify the affection and attitude of love except hearing the words ''I love you.'' Actions and deeds are not sufficient to justify love for the individual who needs always to hear ''I love you.'' There are those who feel that if you cannot say ''I love you,'' then there is no love in the relationship. On the other hand, there are individuals who are unable to verbalize the words ''I love you,'' for whatever reason. Many times, such inability is due to culture, childhood experiences, and family background, which has nothing to do with the feelings and strong emotions that may exist.

As for those individuals who are unable to say ''I love you'' because of a void feeling for love, the mere verbalization of ''I love you'' will be nothing more than the ''sound of a brass symbol,'' and thereby are not supported by action. Therefore, the emphasis of this game focuses on the individual who may demonstrate unspoken love in behavior, but never verbalizes "I love you."

Women, more than men, say "I like to hear you say it sometimes." Yet, there are men who either feel uncomfortable saying "I love you' or are just unable to do it. In mature and healthy relationships, the resolution to this game of "Tell me that you love me" can be resolved through the mutual respect for the sensitive emotions of others. This is true not only for one's deep-seated emotions regarding the verbalization of love, but includes other areas in which mutual distance may be needed.

GAMES OF POWER

I pay the cost to be the boss. In today's society many relationships are reduced to a basic economic one in which the transactions are as between partners in business, stockholders, and financial investors. The degree of decision making, collaboration, and feedback in the relationship is determined by the rank in salary. The greatest obstacle to this game is that "paying the cost to be the boss" is not limited to decision making; it is also related to the economic partnership existing in the social and sexual relationship. The underlying danger in the above game is the association of money, income, and salary with power and control. It is the view that if I bring more financially into this relationship than you, "What I say goes."

The hidden dimension of the "paying the cost" game often is the insecurities involving one's self-worth. Males and females in capitalist America tend to associate their self-worth, identity, and self-esteem with their economic and professional status in life. At the same time, power and prestige are associated with one's professional and economic status. Therefore, these artificial variables of self-concepts become intricately interwoven into the fabric of relationships, rather than the relationships being based on the element of human relations.

One must question the use and definition of "power" and "authority" in interpersonal relationships as an equation for such concepts in the economic and political world.

Don't you be here when I get back and don't you be gone. A major dilemma faced by partners in relationships is the double-bind and double-message in communications and actions. In other words, "You are damned if you do and damned if you don't." The underlying payoff is that the other partner is "doomed." Yet, such binds are never communicated so directly and the scapegoat is invariably put in a position to justify and prove his or her worthiness.

A partner may forget the spouse's birthday and try to compensate for it by getting something extra nice for the wedding anniversary. The spouse scolds the partner for forgetting the birthday and chastises him or her for the anniversary by saying "If you didn't get me anything for my birthday, you didn't have to get me anything for the anniversary." On the other hand, the spouse may get home late from work without calling and the partner may accuse him or her of cheating. Yet, when the spouse arrives home early and has the meal ready, the other partner accuses him or her of "operating out of guilt."

The creation of double-bind situations are very serious infringements in interpersonal social dynamics. The perpetrator is usually not aware of his or her behavior and the victim is unable to find contentment and enjoyment in the relationship. Usually, the victim's realization that the game is being played brings about a change. It is the responsibility of the victim to increase somehow the self-awareness of the perpetrator regarding actions in creating double-binds. If the situation of double-binding is severe, the resolution to this problem may require the intervention of a third party to facilitate a change, through counseling or other support groups.

I am dissatisfied, and don't you try to change it. It is a natural tendency for partners in relationships to try and cheer each other up in times of depression and despair irrespective of the causes of the melancholy. By the same token, it is natural that a partner's concern about the welfare of a dissatisfied mate will affect his or her spiritual state. Yet, it is difficult for many partners in interpersonal relationships to accept the realization that their mate may enjoy being dissatisfied and does not want it changed. It is a fact that there are people who are happy when they are complaining, and they seek to be dissatisfied. If you and your mate are out with others to enjoy a movie or theater, your mate will find reasons to be dissatisfied. He or she did not like the seats, the performance, or the length of the show. If you relocate to a different community for a job, your mate will find cause to be dissatisfied with the community. On vacation—and in most other areas of the mate's life—he or she will be dissatisfied and complaining.

The burden of dissatisfaction rests on the shoulders of a spouse or mate who continues to try and provide satisfying experiences and circumstances. When the mate meets the specification of the dissatisfied partner, there will be something else the mate will find dissatisfying.

One partner may be investing all the emotional energy into the relationship; however, the other partner may be interested in ownership of property, a professional career, or travel.As the motivated and inspired partner seeks advancement toward his or her goals, the other partner may proceed to sabotage the accomplishments. Yet, the game is inevitably self-destructive in that the motivated partner will not be satisfied with "staying there" with the other spouse, even if he or she were successful in reaching the goals.

The myth supporting the notion that "I don't want it' you can't have it" rests with the premise that when you help a spouse achieve goals, they will drop you for someone else. There are numerous examples cited about situations when the female worked and helped the male complete law or medical school, after which he terminated the relationship. It is this fear that supports the "stay here with me" or "I don't want it and I don't want you to have it" mentality. The "no-win dilemma' inherent in this game makes it so that the partner playing the game will lose what it was he or she did not want along with the individual he or she was trying to prevent from having it. Needless to say, the issue at hand is for those who play the game of "I don't want it and you can't have it" to resolve the contradiction inherent in the dilemma. If one chooses to withhold support or employ other tactics to cause the other person to remain with him or her, the relationship is bordering on conflict and termination. By the same token, the risks involved in losing a partner through preventing him or her from having what they want must be as great as the risk of supporting a partner and eliminating the "I don't want it, you can't have it (stay here with me)" game.

Getting even. This game occurs when one party, however incorrectly or correctly, perceives that he or she has been wronged by the other party. Therefore the party who feels that they have been wronged vows overtly or covertly to repeat the same or similar "wrongful" activity in an attempt to induce the same or similar pain in the other person.

In a military battle, it is easy to determine the extent of damage needed for "getting even," but in interpersonal relationships the investments and costs cannot be estimated. This is true mainly because of the different ethics,values, and principles that govern individual behavior; consequently, the personal cost that one party would have to pay in order to engage in activities similar to those of the other partner maybe too detrimental. On the other hand, "getting even" may be a mere justification for the need to engage in such activity desired in the first place.

This is not to suggest that the first inclination of a partner is to "strike back" at the other, once he or she perceived that they were wronged. The destructiveness of such a game may not be seen in the vicious cycle that is set up. A "pulling of the coat," or opening doors to communications could avoid a prolonged and serious relationship problem.

REFERENCES

Berne,E. (1964) Games People Play. New York: Grove.

Burgest, D. R. (1980) "Black awareness and authentic black-black relations," in M. Asante and A. Vandi (eds.) Contemporary Black Thought: Alternative Analysis in the Social and Behavioral Sciences. Beverly Hills, CA: Sage.

_______ and J.Bowers (1981a) "Erroneous assumptions black women make about black men." Black Male/Female Relationships 2, 5: 13–20.

_______ (1981b) "Erroneous assumptions black men make about black women." Black Male/Female Relationships 2, 6: 13–20.

Davis, A. Y. (1981) Women, Race and Class. New York: Random House.

Gary, L. E. (1981) Black Men. Beverly Hills, CA: Sage.

Staples, R. (1982) Black Masculinity: The Black Male's Role in Society. San Francisco: Black Scholar Press.

Black Male-Black Female Conflict: Individually Caused and Culturally Nurtured

Clyde W. Franklin II

Who is to blame? Currently, there is no dearth of attention directed to Black male-Black female relationships. Books, magazine articles, academic journal articles, public forums, radio programs, television shows, and everyday conversations have been devoted to Black male-Black female relationships for several years. Despite the fact that the topic has been discussed over the past several decades by some authors (e.g., Frazier, 1939; Drake and Clayton, 1945; Grier and Cobb, 1968), Wallace's *Black Macho and the Myth of the Superwoman* has been the point of departure for many contemporary discussions of the topic since its publication in 1979.

Actually, Wallace's analysis was not so different in content from other analyses of Black male-Black female relationships (e.g., Drake and Cayton's analysis of "lower-class life" in *Black Metropolis*). But Wallace's analysis was "timely." Coming so soon on the heels of the Black movement in the late 1960s and early 1970s, and at a time when many Black male-inspired gains for Blacks were disappearing rapidly, the book was explosive. Its theme, too, was provocative. Instead of repeating the rhetoric of the late 1960s and early 1970s that blamed conflictual relationships between Black men and Black women on White society, Wallace implied that the blame lay with Black males. In other words, the blame lay with those Black warriors who only recently had been perceived as the "saviors" of Black people in America. Wallace's lamenting theme is captured in a quote from her book: "While she stood by silently as he became a man, she assumed that he would finally glorify and dignify Black womanhood just as the White man has done for White women." Wallace goes on to say that this has not happened for Black women.

Wallace updates her attack on Black men in a later article entitled "A Black Feminist's Search for Sisterhood" (1982:9). Her theme, as before, is that Black men are just as oppressive of Black women as White men. She states:

> *Whenever I raised the question of a Black woman's humanity in conversations with a Black man, I got a similar reaction. Black men, at least the ones I knew, seemed totally confounded when it came to treating Black women like people. . . . I discovered my voice and when brothers talked to me, I talked back. This had its hazards. Almost got my eye blackened several times. My social life was like guerilla warfare. Here was the logic behind our grandmother's old saying, "A nigga man ain't shit."*

Wallace, however, is not alone in placing the blame on Black men for deteriorating relations between Black men and Black women. Allen (1938:62), in a recent edition of *Essence* magazine, states:

> *Black women have a tendency to be male-defined, subjugating their own needs for the good of that fragile male ego. . . . The major contradiction is that we Black women, in our hearts, have a tendency to believe Black men need more support and understanding than we do. We bought the Black Revolutionary line that a woman's place was three paces behind the man. We didn't stomp Stokeley when he made the statement that the only position for a woman in the movement was prone.*

Such attacks on Black men have been met with equally ferocious counterattacks by some Black authors (both Black men and Black women). A few months following the publication of Wallace's book, an entire issue of the *Black Scholar* was devoted to Black Male-Black Female relationships. Of the responses to Wallace by such scholars as Jones (1979), Karenga (1979), Staples (1979), and numerous others, Karenga's response is perhaps the most controversial and maybe the most volatile. Karenga launches a personal attack on Wallace suggesting that she is misguided and perhaps responding from personal hurt. Recognizing the complexity of Black male-Black female relationships, Karenga contends that much of it is due not to Black men but to the White power structure. Along similar lines, Moore (1980) has exhorted Black women to stop criticizing Black men and blame themselves for the disintegrating bonds between Black men and Black women.

Staples, in his response to Wallace and others who would place the blame on Black men for disruptive relationships between Black men and Black women, points out that while sexism within the Black culture may be an emerging problem, most Black men do not have the institutionalized power to oppress Black women. He believes that the Black male's "condition" in society is what bothers Black males. Staples devotes much attention to the institutional decimation of Black men and suggests that this is the reason for Black male-Black female conflict. Noting the high morality and suicide rates of Black men, the fact that half a million Black men are in prison, one-third of urban Black men are saddled with drug problems and that 25% to 30% do not have steady employment, Staples implied that Black male-Black female conflict may be related to *choice*. This means that a shortage of Black men may limit the choices that Black women have in selecting partners. As Braithwaite (1981) puts it, the insufficient supply of Black men places Black women at a disadvantage by giving Black men the upper hand. In a specific relationship, for example, if a Black woman fails to comply with the black man's wishes, the Black man has numerous other options, including not only other Black women but also women of other races.

In a more recent discussion of Black male-Black female relationships, Alvin Poussaint (1982:40) suggests that Black women "adopt a patient and creative approach in exploring and creating new dimensions of the Black male-Black female bond." Others, like Ronald Braithwaite, imply in their analyses of relationships with Black men and Black women that Black women's aggressiveness, thought to be a carryover from slavery, may be partly responsible for Black male-Black female conflict.

Succinctly, by and large, most Black male and Black female authors writing on the subject seem to agree that many Black male-Black female relationships today are destructive and potentially explosive. What they do not agree on, however, are the causes of the problems existing between Black men and Black women. As we have seen, some believe that Black men are the cause. Others contend that Black women contribute disproportionately to Black male-Black female conflict. Still others blame White racism solely, using basic assumptions that may be logically inadequate (see Franklin, 1980). Many specific reasons for the conflict often postulated include the notions that Black men are abusive toward Black women, that Black men are irresistibly attracted to White women (despite the fact that only approximately 120,000 Black men were married to White women in 1980), that too many Black men are homosexual, that Black women are too aggressive, that Black women don't support Black men—the list goes on. Few of these reasons, however, really explore the underlying cause of the conflict. Instead, they are descriptions of the conflict-behaviors that are indicators of the tension between Black men and Black women. But what is the cause of the behavior—the cause of the tension that so often disrupts harmony in Black male-Black female relationships?

Given the various approaches many Black authors have taken in analyzing Black male-Black female relationships, it is submitted that two major sources of Black male-Black female conflict can be identified: (1) the noncomplementary of sex-role definitions internalized by Black males and Black females; and (2) structural barriers in the environments of Black males and Black females. Each source is explored separately below.

SOURCES OF CONFLICT BETWEEN BLACK MEN AND BLACK WOMEN

Sex-Role Noncomplementarity among Black Males and Black Females

Much Black male-Black female conflict stems directly from incompatible role enactments by Black males and Black females. Incompatible role enactments by Black men and Black women occur because they internalize sex-role definitions that are noncomplementary. For example, a Black woman in a particular conflictual relationship with a Black male may feel that her Black man is supposed to assume a dominant role, but she also may be inclined to exhibit behaviors that are opposed to his dominance and her subordinance. In the same relationship, the Black man may pay lip service to assuming a dominant role but may behave ''passively'' with respect to some aspects of masculinity and in a dominant manner with respect to other aspects.

One reason for role conflict between Black men and Black women is that many contemporary Black women internalize two conflicting definitions of femininity, whereas many contemporary Black men internalize only a portion of the traditional definition of masculinity. Put simply, numerous Black women hold attitudes that are both highly masculine and highly feminine. On the other hand, their male courterparts develop traits that are highly consistent with certain aspects of society's definition of masculinity,but that are basically unrelated to other aspects of the definition. Thus, in a given relationship, one may find a Black woman who feels and behaves in ways that are both assertive and passive, dominant and subordinant, decisive and indecisive, and so on. Within that same relationship, a Black man may exhibit highly masculine behaviors, such as physical aggressiveness, sexual dominance, and even violence, but behave indifferently with respect to the masculine work ethic—assuming responsibility for family-related activities external to the home, being aggressive in the work place, and the like.

The reason these incongruent attitudes and behaviors exist among Black men and Black women is that they have received contradictory messages during early socialization. It is common for Black women to have received two messages: One message states, ''Because you will be a Black woman, it is imperative that you learn to take care of yourself because it is hard to find a Black man who will take care of you.'' A second message frequently received by young Black females that conflicts with the first message is ''your ultimate achievement will occur when you have snared a Black man who will take care of you.'' In discussing early socialization experiences with countless young Black women in recent years. I have found that most of them agree that these two messages were given them by socialization agents and agencies such as child caretakers, relatives, peer group members, the Black church, and the media.

When internalized, these two messages often produce a Black woman who seems to reject aspects of the traditional female sex role in America such as passivity, emotional and economic dependence, and female subordinance while accepting other aspects of the role such as expressiveness, warmth, and nurturance. This is precisely why Black women seem to be more androgynous than White women. Black women's androgyny, though, may be more a function of necessity than anything else. It may be related to the scarcity of Black men who assume traditional masculine roles in male-female relationships.

Whatever the reason for Black women's androgynous orientations, because of such orientations Black women oftentimes find themselves in conflictual relationships with Black men or in no stable relationships at all. The scenario generally can be described as follows. Many Black women in early adulthood usually begin a search for a Black Prince Charming. However, because of the dearth of Black men who can be or are willing to be Prince Charmings for Black women, Black women frequently soon give up the search for such a Black man. They give up the search, settle for less, and ''like'' what they settle for even less. This statement is important because many Black women's eventual choices are destined to become constant reminders that the "female independence" message received during the early socialization process is the correct message. But, because Black women also have to deal with the second socialization message, many come to feel that they have failed in their roles as women. In an effort to correct their mistakes, Black women often choose to enact the aspect of their androgynous role that is decidedly aggressive and/or independent. They may decide either to "go it alone" or to prod their Black men into becoming Prince Charmings. The first alternative for Black women often results in self-doubt, lowered self-esteem, and, generally, unhappiness and dissatisfaction. After all, society nurtures the "find a man" message far beyond early socialization. The second message, unfortunately, produces little more than the first message because Black women in such situations usually end up in conflictual relationships with Black men, who also have undergone a rather complicated socialization process. Let us explore briefly the conflicting messages numerous Black men receive during early socialization.

One can find generally that Black men, too, have received two conflicting messages during early socialization. One message received by young Black males is "to become a man means that you must become dominant, aggressive, decisive, responsible, and, in some instance, violent in social encounters with others." A second message received by young Black males that conflicts with the first is, "You are Black and you must not be too aggressive, too dominant, and so on, because the *man* will cut you down." Internalization of these two messages by some Black men (a substantial number) produces Black men who enact a portion of the traditional definition of masculinity but remain inactive with respect to other parts of traditional definitions of masculinity but remain inactive with respect to outer parts of traditional masculinity. Usually those aspects of traditional masculinity that can be enacted within the Black culture are the ones exhibited by these Black men. Other aspects of the sex role that require enactment external to the Black culture (e.g., aggressiveness in the work place) may be related to impassively by Black men. Unfortunately, these are aspects of the male sex role that must be enacted if a male is to be "productive" in American society.

Too many Black men fail to enact the more "productive" aspects of the male sex role. Instead, "being a man," for many Black males who internalize the mixed messages, becomes simply enacting sexual aggression, violence, sexism, and the like—all of which promote Black male-Black female conflict. In addition, contributing to the low visibility and low salience of "productive" masculine traits among Black men is the second socialization message, which provides a rationale for nonenactment of the role traits. Moreover, the "man will get you" message serves to attenuate Black men's motivations to enact more "positive" aspects of the traditional male sex role. We must keep in mind, however, that not all of the sources of Black male-Black female conflict are social-psychological. Some of the sources are structural, and in the next section these sources are discussed.

Structural Barriers Contributing to Black Male-Black Female Conflict

It is easy to place the blame for Black male-Black female conflict on "White Society." Several Black authors have used this explanatory approach in recent years (e.g., Anderson and Mealy, 1979). They have suggested that Black male-Black female conflict is a function of America's capitalistic orientation and White society's long-time subjugation of Black people. Certainly historical conditions are important to understand when discussing the status of Black people today. Often, however, too much emphasis is placed on the historical subjugation of Black people as the source of Black male-Black female conflict today. Implicit in such an emphasis is the notion that independent variables existing at some point in the distant past cause a multiplicity of negative behaviors between Black males and Black females that can be capsulized as Black male-Black female conflict. A careful analysis of the contemporary environments of Black men and women today will show, instead, that factors responsible, in part, for Black male-Black female conflict are inextricably interwoven in those environments. In other words, an approach to the analysis of conflict between Black men and Black women today must be ahistorical. Past conditions influence Black male-Black female relationships only in the sense that vestiges of these conditions exist currently and are identifiable.

Our society today undoubtedly remains structured in such a manner that the vast majority of Black men encounter insurmountable barriers to the attainment of a "masculine" status as defined by most Americans (Black and White Americans). Black men still largely are locked within the Black culture (which has relatively limited resources), unable to compete successfully for societal rewards—the attainment of which defines American males as "men." Unquestionably, Black men's powerlessness in society's basic institutions such as the government and the economy contributes greatly to the pathological states of many Black men. The high mortality and suicide rates of young Black men, the high incarceration rates of young Black men, the high incidence of drug addiction among Black men, and the high unemployment rate of Black men are all functions of societal barriers to Black male upward mobility. These barriers render millions of Black males socially impotent and/or socially dysfunctional. Moreover, as Staples has pointed out, such barriers also result in a scarcity of functional Black men, thereby limiting Black women's alternatives for mates.

While some may not be tempted to argue for a psychological explanation of Black male social impotence, it is suggested here than any such argument is misguided unless accompanied by a recognition of the role of cultural nurturance factors. Cultural nurturance factors such as the rigid castelike social stratum of Blacks in America foster and maintain Black men's social impotence. The result is powerless Black men primed for conflictual relationships with Black women. If Black men in our society were not "American," perhaps cultural nurturance of Black people's status in our society could not be translated into cultural nurturance of Black male-Black female conflict. That Black men are Americanized, however, is seen in the outcome of the Black movement of the last decade.

The Black movement of the late 1960s and early 1970s produced little structural change in America. To be sure, a few Black men (and even fewer Black women) achieved a measure of upward mobility; however, the vast majority did not reap gains from the Black movement. What did happen, though, was that Black people did get a glimpse of the rewards that can be achieved in America through violence and/or aggression. White society did bend when confronted by the Black movement, but it did not break. In addition, the few upward mobility doors that were ajar during the height of the movement were quickly slammed shut when the movement began to wane in the middle and late 1970s. Black men today find themselves in a position similar to the one Black men were in prior to the movement. The only difference this time around is that Black men are equipped with the psychological armor of aggression and violence as well as with a distorted perception of a target—Black women, the ones who "stood silently by."

Wallace's statement that Black women "stood silently by" must not be taken lightly. Black women did this; in addition, they further internalized American definitions of masculinity and femininity. Previously, Black women held modified definitions of masculinity and femininity because the society's definition did not fit their everyday experiences. During the Black movement they were exhorted by Black men to assume a sex role that was more in line with the traditional "feminine" role White women assumed in male-female relationships. Although this may have been a noble (verbal) effort on the part of Black men to place Black women on pedestals, it was shortsighted and doomed to fail. Failure was imminent because even during the peak of the Black movement, societal resistance to structural changes that would benefit Black people was strong. The strength of this resistance dictated that change in Black people's status in America could come about only through the united efforts of both Black men and Black women.

Unfortunately, the seeds of division between Black men and Black women were sown during the Black movement. Black men bought the Moynihan report (1965) that indirectly blamed Black women for Black people's underclass status in America. In doing so, Black men convinced themselves that they could be "men" only if they adopted the White male's sex role. An examination of this role reveals that it is characterized by numerous contradictions. The traditional White masculine role requires men to assume protective, condescending, and generally patriarchal stances with respect to women. It also requires, ironically, that men display dominant, aggressive, and often violent behaviors toward women. Just as important, though, is that White masculine role enactment can occur only when there is full participation in masculinist American culture. Because Black men continue to face barriers to full participation in American society, the latter requirement for White male sex-role assumption continues to be met by only a few Black men. The result has been that many Black men have adopted only a part of the culture's definition of masculinity because they are thwarted in their efforts to participate fully in society. Structural barriers to Black male sex-role adoption, then, have produced a Black male who is primed for a conflictual relationship with Black women. In the next section, an exploration is presented of some possible solutions to Black male-Black female conflict that arise from the interactive relationship between the noncomplementarity of sex-role internalization by Black men and Black women and structural barriers to Black men's advancement in American society.

TOWARD SOLVING BLACK MALE–BLACK FEMALE CONFLICT

Given that societal conditions are extremely resistant to rapid changes, the key to attenuating conflict between Black men and Black women lies in altering three social psychological phenomena: (1) Black male and Black female socialization experiences; (2) Black male and Black female role-playing strategies; and (3) Black male and Black female personal communication mechanisms. I first propose some alterations in Black male and Black female socialization experiences. . . .

Black female socialization must undergo change if Black men and Black women are to enjoy harmonious relationships. Those agents and agencies responsible for socializing young Black females must return to emphasizing a monolithic message in young Black female socialization. This message can stress warmth, caring, and nurturance, but it must stress simultaneously self-sufficiency, assertiveness, and responsibility. The latter portion of this message requires that young Black females must be cautioned against sexual freedom at relatively early ages—not necessarily for moral reasons, but because sexual freedom for Black women seems to operate against Black women's self-sufficiency, assertiveness, and responsibility. It is important to point out here, however, that this type of socialization message must be imparted without the accompanying castigation of Black men. To say "a nigger man ain't shit" informs any young Black female that at least one-half of herself "ain't shit." Without a doubt, this strategy teaches self-hate and sets the stage for future Black male-Black female conflict.

Young Black males, on the other hand,must be instructed in self-sufficiency, assertiveness, and responsibility without the accompanying warning opposed to these traits in Black males.. Such warnings serve only to provide rationales for future failures. To be sure, Black men do (and will) encounter barriers to upward mobility because they are black. But, as many Black men have shown, such barriers do not have to be insurmountable. Of course it is recognized that innumerable Black men have been victims of American racist policies, but some, too, have been victims because they perceived only that external factors hindered their upward mobility and did not focus on some internal barriers that may have thwarted their mobility. The former factors are emphasized much too often in the contradictory socialization messages received by most young Black males.

Along with the above messages, young Black males must learn that the strong bonds that they establish with their mothers can be extended to their relationships with other Black women. If Black men perceive their mothers to be symbols of strength and perseverance, they must also be taught that most other Black women acquire these same qualities and have done so for generations. It must become just as "cool," in places like urban Black barbershops, to speak of Black women's strength and dignity as it is now to hear of Black women's thighs, breasts, and hips.

On an issue closely related to the above, few persons reading this article can deny that Black men's attempts to enact the White male sex role in America are laughable. Black men are relatively powerless in this country, and their attempts at domination, aggression, and the like, while sacrificing humanity, are ludicrous. This becomes apparent when it is understood that usually the only people being dominated and aggressed against by Black men are Black women (and other Black men). Moreover, unlike White males, Black males receive no societal rewards for their efforts; instead, the result is Black male-Black female disharmony. Black men must avoid the tendency to emulate the nauseatingly traditional male sex role because their experiences clearly show that such a role is counterproductive for Black people. Because the Black man's experiences are different, his role-playing strategies must be different and made to be more complementary with Black females' altered role-playing strategies. The Black females' role-playing strategies, as we have seen, are androgynous, emphasizing neither the inferiority nor the superiority of male or female sex roles.

On a final note, it is important for Black people in our society to alter their personal communication mechanisms. Black men and Black women interact with each other in diverse ways and in diverse situations, ranging from intimate to impersonal. Perhaps the most important element of this diverse communication pattern is empathy. For Black people in recent years, this is precisely the element that has undergone unnecessary transformation. As Blacks in America have accepted increasingly White society's definition of male-female relationships, Black men and Black women have begun to interact with each other less in terms of empathy. While Black women have retained empathy in their male-female relationships to a greater degree than Black men have, Black men have become increasingly nonexpressive and nonempathic in their male-female relationships. Nearly 60% of Black women (approximately 25,000) in a recent *Essence* survey cited nonexpressiveness as a problem in male-female relationships; 56% also pointed out that Black male nonempathy was a problem (Edwards, 1982). It seems, then, that as Black males have attempted to become "men" in America they have shed some of the important qualities of humanity. Some Black women, too,who have embraced the feminist perspective also have discarded altruism. The result of both phenomena, for Black people as a whole, has been to divide Black men and Black women further. Further movement away from empathic understanding in Black male-Black female relationships by both Black men and Black women undoubtedly will be disastrous for Black people in America.

REFERENCES

Allen, B. 1983."The Price for Giving It Up." *Essence* (February):60–62, 118.

Anderson, S. E., and R. Mealy. 1979. "Who Organized the Crisis: A Historical Perspective." *Black Scholar* (May/June): 40–44.

Braithwaite, R. L. 1981. "Interpersonal Relations between Black Males and Black Females," In *Black Men,* L. E. Gary, ed. pp.83–97. Beverly Hills, Calif.: Sage.

Drake, S. C., and H. R. Cayton. 1945. *Black Metropolis.* New York: Harcourt.

Edwards, A. 1982. "Survey Results: How You're Feeling." *Essence* (December):73–76.

Franklin, C. W. II. 1980. "White Racism As a Cause of Black Male-Female Conflict: A Critique." *Western Journal of Black Studies* 4(1):42–49.

Frazier, E. F. 1939. *The Negro Family in the United States.* Chicago: University of Chicago Press.

Grier, W. H., and P. M. Cobb. 1968. *Black Rage.* New York: Basic Books.

Jones, T. 1979. "The Need to Go beyond Stereotypes." *Black Scholar* (May/June):48–49.

Karenga, M. R. 1979. "On Wallace's Myth: Wading through Troubled Waters." *Black Scholar* (May/June):36–39.

Moore, W. E. 1980. "Black Women, Stop Criticizing Black Men—Blame Yourselves." *Ebony* (December):128–130.

Moynihan, D. P. 1965. *The Negro Family: The Case for National Action.* Washington, D.C.: U.S. Department of Labor, Office of Planning and Research.

Poussaint, A. F. 1982."What Every Black Woman Should Know about Black Men." *Ebony* (August):36–40.

Staples, R. 1979. "The Myth of Black Macho: A Response to Angry Black Feminists." *Black Scholar* (March/April):24–32.

Wallace, M. 1979. *Black Macho and the Myth of the Superwoman.* New York: Dial.

1982. "A Black Feminist's Search for Sisterhood." In *All the Blacks Are Men, All the Women are White, but Some of Us are Brave,* G. T. Hull, et al., eds., pp. 5–8. Old Westbury, N.Y.: Feminist Press.

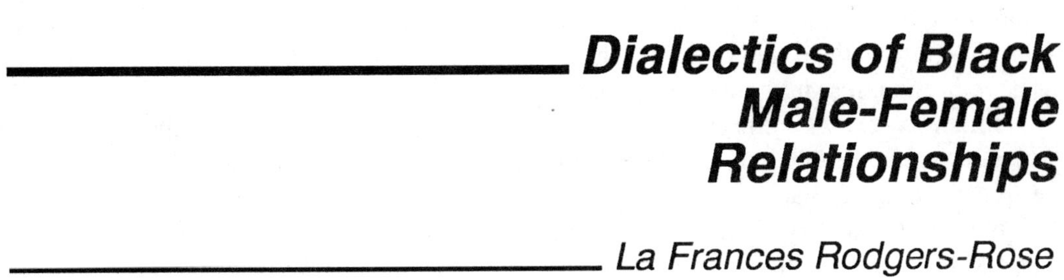

Dialectics of Black Male-Female Relationships

La Frances Rodgers-Rose

One of the most complex and pressing issues in the struggle for Black survival is centered in and grows out of the relationship between Black men and women. This relationship, in the final analysis, determines how they support each other as men and women and how they will raise their children.

The relationship between Black men and women does not take place in a vacuum. They act out their behavior in a society which has clearly defined role behavior. Men are supposed to be aggressive, women passive. With such a definition of role behavior, based on inequality rather than equality, the relationship between men and women cannot help but be tenuous. Moreover, any male-female relationship, there are the dialectics of creation and criticism which must take place in an environment of open discussion and sociability (Foote, 1953). This chapter will attempt to look at some of the issues that confront Black men and women as they interact in a process of criticism and creation. Specifically, I will discuss some myths about Black men and women and properties of male-female relationships.

MYTHS OF THE ROLES AND RELATIONSHIPS BETWEEN BLACK MEN AND WOMEN

If a situation is defined as real, then it is real in its consequences.

W. I. Thomas

Most of what we know about Black male-female relationships is a result of the biased research conducted by white social scientists. For example, we hear that in order for Black people to succeed, Black women must stand behind Black men—Black women must step back and let the Black man lead. The assumption, based on biased work of white researchers, is that Black women have led their men. But any objective look at Black history will show this has never been the case. Equality between Black men and women has been misrepresented as female dominance. What has happened is that some Black men and women have internalized the myths of white social scientists, and these definitions of situations have become real in their consequences.

Another myth that some Blacks have internalized is that the Black male is shiftless, that he does not want to work, that he would rather hang on the corner than look for a job. Objective reading of Black history shows the efforts that Black men have made to find jobs—jobs that paid very little and were demeaning in nature. Yet another myth in this country is that Black women earn more money than Black men, that Black women can get jobs when Black men cannot. U.S. Census Bureau data show that this is not true, nor has it ever been true. In fact, Black woman are the lowest paid group in the country: They make less money than white men and women and Black men (Ferris, 1971:141). Black women are, in general, the most unemployed and underemployed group. (1971:302–320) A related myth is that Black women are generally more educated than Black men, and historically this has been the case. However, today this is no longer as true (1971:23).

I am suggesting that a great deal of what is happening to Black men and women as the relate to one another is a consequence of definitions based on stereotypes of Blacks or biased research, and not from the reality systems of Black men and women. Before we can move toward defining Black male and female relationships, we must expose false definitions that grow out of thought systems which serve to divide and conquer Black people. To the extent that we are unaware of these false reality systems, we will believe them, define them as real, and, as W. I. Thomas suggested, they will become real in their consequences. For example, the Black woman is seen as having certain qualities and the Black man is seen as lacking these qualities. The Black woman is seen as needing little protecting either physically or mentally, while the Black man is seen as needing both physical and mental protection—he lacks the ability to survive in the outside world. The Black woman must protect him. Further, the Black woman is seen as a dominating matriarch: She emasculates the Black man and his character becomes "feminine" in nature. He does not know what to do unless he is told by the woman.

Growing out of this myth is the further notion that most Black households are headed by women, that the male is absent from the home, and that Black children do not have male models. The reality of the situation is that two-thirds of all Black households do have both male and female present. In some households, the male is not present to be counted by the census taker. He may be absent for strategic purposes—for example, a needy mother cannot get welfare if there is a man in the home; aid is given only to dependent children, not to struggling intact families. Moreover, white social scientists ignore the fact that Black women have boyfriends, fathers, brothers, and uncles who can and do serve as role models.

Finally, the Black man and woman are defined as being sexually aggressive. White mythology has asserted that both the Black male and female are anxious to have sexual relationships with whites. The female is defined as loose in her morals and out to sell her body to the highest bidder; she wants to establish meaningless relationships with white men at the expense of the Black man. Black men seek sexual relationships with white women. Again, when we unmask the myth, we find that less than two percent of all marriages in this country are between Black and white people. When Blacks are asked to rank the priority of things they want in this country, interracial marriage is ranked last, with economic and political equality ranked first.

As can be seen from the foregoing discussion, it is easy for Black people to internalize and use such false definitions of themselves. To the extent that an individual has internalized these definitions, his/her mode of interaction with the opposite sex will be affected. Therefore, when a relationship is not going well, the individual will resort to such negative definitions and interpretations as "Black women are too independent," "Black men are too possessive," "Black men's feelings are too easily hurt," "Black women are evil," "Black women argue too much," "Black men are weak," "Black men are castrated," and "Black women don't appreciate good treatment." Moreover, these negative definitions have already been supplied and are readily available to the actor. These ready-made definitions keep Black men and women from looking inward to what they contribute to the outcome of a particular relationship. One can easily blame the other. Such myths, then, have functioned to divide Black men and women, and they have served as rationalizations for the status quo. Myths keep the individuals focused on criticism rather than on the interplay between the critical and the creative aspects of any male-female relationship.

Properties of Dialectic Relationships Between Black Men and Women

Sociologists have in many cases failed to study the depth of interpersonal relationships between the groups of people they analyze. They have, instead, tended to study the surface areas—those aspects which can be easily defined, codified, and discussed. We know a great deal about financial and sexual aspects of marriage, but we know much less about what attracts one individual to another, what people are looking for in intimate relationships, and what qualities make for viable dialectic relationships. Likewise, we find that men and women are not socialized to look for nor can they articulate their needs in terms of qualities wanted. We are taught to pay more attention to the outward characteristics of a person: education, occupation, and income. Recently, sexual compatibility has been included in these characteristics. Thus, we find people in relationships not realizing what they want from that relationship.

QUALITIES IN MALE-FEMALE RELATIONSHIPS

This chapter is based on interviews of 49 Black women and 39 Black men. The data were collected in April and May 1975.[1] Each person was asked five questions: (1) What qualities do you want in a man/woman with whom you are having an intimate relationship? (2) What behavior/action would show the above qualities? (3) What qualities do you dislike/hate in a man/woman that would make you dissolve that relationship? (4) What behavior/action would show these negative qualities? (5) If you were dating steadily, how often would you like to see that person? The responses to each of these questions were recorded verbatim. Each response was then content analyzed. Background data on age, education, occupation, and marital status were also gathered. Table 1 shows the distribution of males and females by age groups on specific characteristics. As one can see from Table 1, there is a wide range and a similar age span for males and females. The educational level is above the national norm. Most are single or separated/divorced. Only 30 percent of the sample is presently married, and the professional category is overrepresented in the sample.

Table 1. Distribution of Males and Females by Age Group on Specific Status Characteristics

	Females		Males	
Characteristics	**Under 30 Years (N=24)**	**Over 30 Years (N=25)**	**Under 30 Years (N=22)**	**Over 30 Years (N=17)**
Mean Age	22.8	42.0	22.0	39.0
Mean Education	13.6	14.4	14.8	15.3
Dates/Week	4.0	2.2	3.4	3.4
Marital Status				
Single	16	1	16	5
Married	3	9	6	8
Separated	3	4	0	2
Divorced	1	7	0	2
Widowed	1	3	0	0
Occupation				
Professional	8	13	8	11
Clerical/Skilled	5	6	5	3
Unskilled	0	5	1	2
Student	7	0	5	1
Housewife	2	0	0	0

The following results were indicated for males and females. In the area of positive qualities, one may note from Table 2 that females under 30 years of age say that the qualities they most want in a man are understanding, honesty, and a person who is warm and gentle. These are the *global* qualities; that is, qualities showing the greatest frequencies. Only qualities mentioned by at least five persons are listed in the tables which follow; however, many other qualities were given. The aim of this study was to show those qualities that have some kind of consensus among age and sex groups. Other qualities mentioned by women under 30 years of age were intelligence, sense of humor, stability, and awareness of self. Table 2 for women over 30 indicates that the most outstanding desirable quality was honesty. This was the only global quality listed, while from women under 30, ınding had the same frequency. There is a greater consensus among n the positive qualities desired in a person with whom they are having ıip. For men under 30, the quality having the greatest frequency was independence—a characteristic which men traditionally do not like to see in women. Men over 30 show a global quality of good manners; for example, they mention "acts like a lady," "has good manner of speech," and "the way she carries herself in public." This quality, proper manners, indicates the more traditional way of viewing women. Also, in viewing Table 3, one may note that males over 30 list "character" traits of the individual rather than the "affective" qualities of the person.

When we turn to how these positive qualities are viewed in behavior, the picture changes. Here we find that women under 30 do not ask for a behavioral quality paralleling the qualities of understanding and honesty; rather, they say the person should be respectful and well-groomed. One must raise the following question: Is there an incongruency between stating that the most desired quality is understanding and stating that, behaviorally, one wants respect and a person who is well-groomed? One refers to effect—understanding—and the other talks about character traits—respectful. In general, males and females in this sample found it difficult to give behavioral/actions indicators than general qualities. And in several cases there were people who listed general qualities as behavior/action. It would seem that this is the area in which one needs to be able to identify the action that shows love. As Foote (1953) suggested, love is known by its works. It is an activity, a process. It is one thing to articulate qualities, but an entirely different thing to know that a certain behavior/action is love.

To summarize, for women over 30 years we find a consistency in the qualities wanted, "honesty," and the behavior indicated is "open communication." Women over 30 indicate affective behavioral qualities, while women under 30 consider character traits. For men in both age groups there is also a consistency of qualities and behavior. The males under 30 says they want a woman who is "calm"—cool in her behavior, one who is doing something to better herself, such as going to school or being employed. There are behavioral indicators of independence. Males over 30 say they want a woman who has "proper manners"; behaviorally, the global quality is "knowing when to listen," an indicator of proper manners.

In general, there seems to be a distinct difference among the four age groups on the qualities wanted in an intimate relationship. This is true particularly for the global qualities. However, in looking at the various qualities wanted, there is indeed overlap. But the significant point is the priority given the different qualities. It would seem that Black males and females differ among themselves and also within groups. In fact, a review of Tables 2 and 3 seems to suggest that females over 30 have more in common with males under 30, and that females under 30 have more in common with males over 30. A larger sample is needed before we can be sure of this possible relationship.

Table 2. Positive Qualities Wanted in a Male by Black Females

I. Black Females Under 30 (N = 24)

A. Global Qualities
1. Ideas
   - Aware of Self (6)
   - Black identity (6)
   - Independent (6)
2. Affectivity/Character
   - Understanding (14)
   - Honesty (14)
   - Warm/gentle (10)
3. Character I
   - Intelligent (8)
   - Sense of humor (8)
   - Positive self-concept (8)
   - Stable (8)
4. Character II
   - Nice looking (7)
   - Generous (7)

B. Behavioral Global Qualities
1. Ideas
   - Specific goals (7)
2. Character
   - Respectful (11)
   - Well-groomed (11)
3. Affective
   - Good lover (7)
   - Responds to my needs (7)
   - Encourages me (6)

II. Black Females Over 30 (N = 25)

A. Global Qualities
1. Affectivity
   - Understanding (9)
   - Aware of my needs (9)
   - Affectionate (8)
   - Aware of others (7)
2. Character I
   - Honesty (16)
3. Character II
   - Dependable (6)
   - Down-to-earth (7)
   - Handsome (5)
4. Character III
   - Intelligent (10)
   - Ambitious (11)

B. Behavioral Global Qualities
1. Affectivity
   - Sharing (6)
   - Kind to others (6)
2. Affectivity
   - Sexually compatible (6)
3. Affectivity
   - Open communication (15)
4. Affectivity
   - Takes me where he goes (10)
   - Gives self according to my needs (11)

Table 3. Positive Qualities Wanted in a Female by Black Males

I. Black Males Under 30 (N = 22)

A. Global Qualities
1. Affectivity
   - Loving/tender (13)
   - Understanding (10
   - Considerate (6)
   - Faithful (6)
2. Character I
   - Independent (17)
3. Character II
   - Honest (13)
   - Clean and neat (11)
   - Beautiful (7)
4. Character III
   - Strong self-concept (10)
   - Aware of self (8)
   - Intelligent (11)
5. Character IV
   - Open-minded (9)
   - Respectful of others (5)

B. Behavioral Global Qualities
   - Takes care of my needs (6)
   - Sexually compatible (6)
2. Character I
   - Manners (9)
   - Calm (10)
   - Going to school/employed (9)
3. Character II
   - Independent action (7)

II. Black Males over 30 (N = 17)

A. Global Qualities
1. Affectivity/Character
   - Understanding (8)
   - Honest (8)
   - Sensitive (7)
   - Tender and kind (7)
2. Character I
   - Proper manners (17)
3. Character II
   - Clean and neat (8)
   - Independent (8)
   - Intelligent (5)
4. Character III
   - Loyal (7)
   - Dependable (6)
   - Open and truthful (6)

B. Behavioral Global Qualities
1. Affectivity
   - Sexually compatible (4)
   - Kissing, holding, responding to me (4)
2. Character I
   - Knowing when to listen (9)
3. Character II
   - Active in sports (4)

When we turn to the negative qualities and behaviors disliked in a man/woman, we find that women were able to list more negative qualities disliked in males than vice versa. Whereas females have at least seven negative qualities, males only have four areas of negative qualities. Females under 30 say they dislike a male who dominates or who is selfish and dependent, while females over 30 say they dislike a male who is immature and dishonest. Here again we see a consistency in females over 30 in the things they like in a male ("honesty") and the things they dislike in a male ("dishonesty"). This consistency across positive and negative qualities is only true for this age and sex group. For males under 30, the qualities disliked—again, similar to females over 30—were dishonesty and a person who is unaffectionate. Males over 30 showed less of a consensus than any other age or sex group. The highest frequency for any quality disliked was listed by only five people. Here they list disrespectfulness, rigidity, irresponsibility, and dishonesty. Although listed as global qualities, these are not global in the same sense as other tables showing global qualities. Looking at the behavioral qualities disliked, we find that males over 30 and females under 30 both mention lying as the behavior most disliked. For women over 30, physical violence is most disliked, and for males under 30 it is a person who is unclean and one who cheats (runs around with other men).

It is interesting to note that in listing the qualities liked or the qualities disliked in intimate relationships the traditional variables that sociologists use in studying marriage and the family are not shown. That is, in the global qualities shown no one mentioned occupation, income, education, or sexual compatibility. But rather, qualities dealt more with the inner person—his/her character or the affective aspects of the person.

This preliminary study indicates that if we are to begin to understand the relationship between Black men and women, or for that matter women and men in general, we must move beyond the outer status of the person to the inner qualities of the person. When given an open-ended, unstructured question on the qualities liked and the qualities disliked in intimate relationships, this sample of Black men and women showed that they are concerned with qualities such as understanding, honesty, warmth, dress, respectability, open communication, sharing, independence, listening capability, dominance, selfishness, lying, unfaithfulness, immaturity, physical violence, lack of affection, and uncleanliness.

Research along this line will add to our knowledge of the relationship between Black men and women. Further, I feel that what is true for Black men and women will also be true for men and women in general. That is, people are concerned with intangible, hard-to-analyze qualities in a relationship rather than outward status variables. It remains to be seen whether Blacks and other racial groups will show the same diversity as this sample, or whether a larger, more random sample will produce the same results between Black males and females. I am presently pursuing the latter question of a larger, more random sample of Black men and women.

I have attempted to show in this brief research study that sociologists who have studied relationships between males and females have failed to study the qualities wanted in persons with whom intimate relations are established. Instead, they have studied the outward special characteristics of income, education, occupation, and sexual compatibility.

Table 4. Negative Qualities Disliked in Males by Black Females

I. Black Females Under 30 (N = 24)

A. Global Qualities
1. Character I
   - Dominant (14)
   - Selfish (14)
   - Dependent (12)
2. Character II
   - Unfaithful (8)
   - Possessive (8)
   - Dishonest (6)
3. Character III
   - Ignorant (7)
   - Immature (7)
4. Character IV
   - No patience (7)
   - No self-respect (5)

B. Behavioral Global Qualities
1. Affectivity
   - Sexually incompatible (5)
2. Character I
   - Lying (13)
3. Character II
   - Physical violence (9)
   - Stay-at-home (8)
   - Disrespectful (8)
   - Never show/late (8)
   - Lazy (7)
   - Loudmouth (5)
   - Drunken (5)

II. Black Females Over 30 (N = 25)

A. Global Qualities
1. Character I
   - Immature (11)
   - Dishonest (10)
2. Character II
   - No self-respect (6)
   - Dependent (5)
3. Character III
   - Ignorant (5)
   - Selfish (5)

B. Behavioral Global Qualities
1. Character I
   - Physically violent (13)
2. Character II
   - Drunken (9)
3. Character III
   - Other women (7)
4. Character IV
   - Verbal abuse (5)
   - Never show/late (5)
   - Gossipy (5)
   - Jealous (5)

Table 5. Negative Qualities Disliked in Females by Black Males

A. Global Qualities	B. Behavioral Global Qualities
I. Black Males Under 30 (N = 22)	
A. Global Qualities	B. Behavioral Global Qualities
1. Affectivity/Character	1. Character I
Unaffectionate (11)	Unclean (8)
Dishonest (11)	Cheats (8)
2. Character	2. Character II
Selfish (8)	Lying (6)
Irresponsible (8)	Disrespectful (5)
Poor outlook on life (8)	Nags (5)
II. Black Males Over 30 (N = 17)	
A. Global Qualities	B. Behavioral Global Qualities
1. Character	1. Character I
Disrespectful (5)	Lying (9)
Rigid (5)	
Irresponsible (5)	2. Character II
Dishonest (5)	Curses (6)
	Drunken (5)
	Unclean (5)

They have studied the first three properties of intimate relationships—conversation, monetary exchange, and sex—but they have paid little attention to the fourth property of the qualities wanted in a relationship. Further, we know very little about what men and women expect behaviorally from each other. A content analysis of 88 interviews with Black males and females show that they are concerned with inner qualities of the individual rather than outward qualities. Even the quality of sexual compatibility does not rank as high as the qualities of honesty, understanding, independence, and proper manners. Additional research along these lines would add to our limited knowledge of Black male-female relationships, and perhaps to male-female relationships in general. Further research in this area will begin to lead the way toward the kinds of variables that must be included in any study which seeks to understand the dialectics of male-female relationships. It is imperative that we begin to study the criticism and creativity in male-female relationships.

NOTES

1. A search and referral method was used to obtain the sample. The research initially made contact with a small number of Black men and women. They in turn were asked to refer the interviewer to another person.
2. Interviews ranged from 45 minutes to two hours.

REFERENCES

Alexander, T. and S. Sillen (1972) Racism and Psychiatry. New York: Brunner-Mazel.

Anderson, C. S. and J. Himes (1969) "Dating values and norms on a Negro college campus." Marriage and Family Living 21:227–229.

Bambara, T. C. (1972) "How Black women educate each other." Sexual Behavior 2: 12–13.

Beal, F. (1969) "Double jeopardy: to be Black and female." New Generations 5: 23–28.

Bernard, J. (1966a) "Marital stability and patterns of status variables." Journal of Marriage and the Family 28: 421–439.

________(1966b) Marriage and Family Among Negroes. Englewood Cliffs, NJ: Prentice-Hall.

Billingsley, A. (1966) Black Families in White America. Englewood Cliffs: NJ: Prentice-Hall.

________(1969) "Family functioning in the low-income Black community." Social Casework 50: 563–572.

Blood, R. and D. Wolfe (1960) Husbands and Wives: The Dynamics of Married Living. New York: Free Press.

Blumer, H. (1940) "The problem of the concept in social psychology." American Journal of Sociology 45: 707–719.

________ (1969) Symbolic Interactionism: Perspective and Method. Englewood Cliffs, NJ: Prentice-Hall.

Bond, J. and P. Berry (1974) "Is the Black male castrated?" in T. Cade (ed.) The Black Woman: An Anthology. New York: Signet.

Bradburn, N. (1969) "Working wives and marriage happiness." American Journal of Sociology 74: 392–407.

Burchinal, L. (1964) "The premarital dyad and love involvement," in H. T. Christensen (ed.) Handbook of Marriage and the Family. Chicago: Rand McNally.

Burgress, E. and P. Wallin (1953) Engagement and Marriage. Chicago: J. B. Lippincott.

Byrne, D. (1961) "Interpersonal attraction and attitude similarity." Journal of Abnormal and Social Psychology 62: 712–715.

Cooley, C. H. (1902) Human Nature and the Social Order. New York: Scribners.

Coser, R. L. [ed.] (1964) The Family: Its Structure and Functions. New York: St. Martin's Press.

Deutscher, I. (1973) What We Say/What We Do: Sentiments and Acts. Glenview, IL: Scott, Foresman.

Donnelly, M. (1963) "Towards a theory of courtship." Marriage and Family Living 25: 290–293.

Drake, S. C. and H. Cayton (1945) Black Metropolis. New York: Harcourt Brace Jovanovich.

DuBois, W. E. B. (1903) The Souls of Black Folks. Chicago: A. C. McClury.

Edwards, G. (1963) "Marriage and family life among Negroes." Journal of Negro Education 32: 451–465.

Farley, R. (1971) "Family stability: a comparison of trends between Blacks and whites." American Sociological Review 36: 1–17.

Foote, N. (1953) "Love." Psychiatry 16: 245–251.

Frazier, E. (1939) "The Negro Family in the United States. Chicago: University of Chicago Press.

Ferris, A. L. (1971) Indicators of Trends in the Status of American Women. New York: Russell Sage.

Geismar, L. (1962) "Measuring family disorganization." Marriage and Family Living 24: 51–56.

Glaser, B. and A. Strauss (1967) The Discovery of Grounded Theory. Chicago: AVC.

Glick, P. and A. Norton (1971) "Frequency, duration and probability of marriage and divorce." Journal of Marriage and the Family 33.
Goode, W. (1956) After Divorce. New York: Free Press.
________(1959) "The theoretical importance of love." American Sociological Review 24: 38–47.
Gorer, G. (1948) The American People: A Study in National Character. New York: W. W. Norton.
Gouldner, A. (1962) "Anti-minotaur: the myth of value free sociology." Social Problems 9: 199–213.
Habenstein, R. [ed.] (1970) Pathways to Data: Field Methods for Studying Ongoing Social Organizations. Chicago: AVC.
Hannerz, U. (1969) "The roots of Black manhood." Transaction: 6: 12–21.
Hare, N. (1964) "The frustrated masculinity of the Negro male." Negro Digest 14: 5–9.
Harper, R. (1958) "Honesty in courtship." The Humanist 18: 103–107.
Harris, A. O. (1974) "Dilemma of growing up Black and female." Journal of Social and Behavioral Sciences 20: 28–40.
Hernton, C. (1965) Sex and Racism. New York: Grove Press.
________(1974) Coming Together. New York: Random House.
Herr, D. (1958) "Dominance and the working wife." Social Forces 36: 341–347.
________(1963) "The measurement and bases of family power." Marriage and Family Living 25: 133–139.
Herskovitz, M. (1941) The Myth of the Negro Past. New York: Harper & Row.
Herzog, E. (1966) "Is there a "breakdown' of the Negro family?" Social Work 11:3–10.
Hewitt, L.(1958) "Student perceptions of traits desired in themselves as dating and marriage partners." Marriage and Family Living 20: 349–360.
Hill, R. (1945) "Campus norms in mate selection." Journal of Home Economics 37: 554–558.
Hill, R. (1972) The Strengths of Black Families. New York: National Urban League.
Hyman, H. and J. Reid (1969) "Black matriarch reconsidered: evidence from secondary analysis of sample survey." Public Opinion Quarterly 33: 346–354.
Jackson, J. (1971) "But where are the men?" The Black Scholar 2: 30–41.
________(1973) "Black women created equal to Black men." Essence (November): 56–72.
________ (1974) "Ordinary Black husbands: the truly hidden men." Journal of Social and Behavioral Sciences 20: 19–27.
Johnson, C. S. (1934) Shadow of the Plantation. Chicago: University of Chicago Press.
Ladner, J. (1972) Tomorrow's Tomorrow: The Black Woman. New York: Doubleday.
Kamii, C. and N. Radin (1967) "Class differences in the socialization practices of Negro mothers." Journal of Marriage and the Family 29: 302–310.
King, C. (1954) "The sex factor in marital adjustment." Marriage and Family Living 16: 237–240.
King, K. (1967) "A comparison of the Negro and white family power structure in low-income families." Child and Family 6: 65–74.
Lerner, G. (1972) Black Women in White America. New York: Pantheon.
Lewis, H. (1955) Blackways of Kent. Chapel Hill: University of North Carolina Press.
________(1965) "Child rearing among low-income families," L. Ferman et al. (eds.) Poverty in America. Ann Arbor: University of Michigan Press.
________(1967) "Culture, class, and family life among low-income urban Negroes," in A. Ross and H. Hill (eds.) Employment, Race and Poverty. New York: Harcourt Brace Jovanovich.
Liebow,E. (1967) Talley's Corner. Boston: Little, Brown.
Mack, D. (1971) "Where the Black matriarchy theorists went wrong." Psychology Today 4: 86–88.

Mannheim, K. (1936) Ideology and Utopia. New York: Harcourt Brace Jovanovich.

Maxwell, J. W. (1968) "Rural Negro father participation in family activities." Rural Sociology 33: 80–93.

Mead, G. H. (1934) Mind, Self and Society. Chicago: University of Chicago Press.

Miller, S. M. et al.(1965) "A critique of the non-deferred gratification pattern," in L. Ferman et al. (eds.) Poverty in America. Ann Arbor: University of Michigan Press.

Mills, C. W. (1940) "Methodological consequences of the sociology of knowledge." American Journal of Sociology 46: 316–330.

________(1959) The Sociological Imagination. New York: Oxford University Press.

Morgan, R. [ed.] (1970) Sisterhood is Powerful. New York: Vintage Books.

Moynihan, D. (1965) The Negro Family: The Call for National Action. Washington, DC: Department of Labor.

Myers, L. (1975) "Black women: selectivity among roles and reference groups in maintenance of self-esteem." Journal of Social and Behavioral Sciences 21: 39–47.

Nye, F. I. (1957) "Child adjustment in broken and in unhappy homes." Marriage and Family Living 19: 356–361.

Prescott,D. (1952) "The role of love in human development." Journal of Home Economics 44: 73–176.

Parker, S. and R. Kleiner (1966) "Characteristics of Negro mothers in single-headed households." Journal of Marriage and the Family 31: 500–506.

________(1969) "Social and psychological dimensions of the family role performance of the Negro male." Journal of Marriage and the Family 31: 500–506.

Prescott, D. (1952) "The role of love in human development." Journal of Home Economics 44: 73–176.

Rainwater, L. (1966) "Crucible of identity," in T. Parsons and K. Clark (eds.) The Negro American. Boston: Beacon.

Reid, I. (1972) Together Black Women. New York: Emerson Hall.

Reiss, I. (1960) Premarital Sexual Standards in America. New York: Free Press.

Scanzoni, J. (1971) The Black Family in Modern Society. Boston: Allyn & Bacon.

Schulz, D. (1969) Coming Up Black: Patterns of Ghetto Socialization. Englewood Cliffs, NJ: Prentice-Hall.

Staples, R. (1970a) "The myth of the Black matriarchy." The Black Scholar 1: 2–9.

________(1970b) "Educating the Black male at various class levels for marital roles."The Family Coordinator 30: 164–167.

________(1971) The Black Family: Essays and Studies. Belmont, CA: Wadsworth.

________(1972) "The sexuality of Black women." Sexual Behavior 2: 4–15.

________(1973) The Black Woman in America. Chicago: Nelson-Hall.

Stokes, G. (1968) "Black woman to Black man." Liberator 8: 17–19.

Sullivan, H. S. (1953) The Interpersonal Theory of Psychiatry. New York: W. W. Norton.